Preface Books

A series of scholarly and critical studies of major writers, intended for those needing modern and authoritative guidance through the characteristic difficulties of their work to reach an intelligent understanding and enjoyment of it.

General Editor: MAURICE HUSSEY

A Preface to Wordsworth	JOHN PURKIS
A Preface to Donne	JAMES WINNY
A Preface to Milton	LOIS POTTER
A Preface to Coleridge	ALLAN GRANT
A Preface to Jane Austen	CHRISTOPHER GILLIE
A Preface to Yeats	EDWARD MALINS
A Preface to Pope	I.R.F. GORDON
A Preface to Hardy	MERRYN WILLIAMS
A Preface to Dryden	DAVID WYKES
A Preface to Spenser	HELENA SHIRE
A Preface to James Joyce	SYDNEY BOLT
A Preface to Hopkins	GRAHAM STOREY
A Preface to Conrad	CEDRIC WATTS
A Preface to Lawrence	GĀMINI SALGADO
A Preface to Forster	CHRISTOPHER GILLIE

Titles in preparation:

A Preface to Auden	ALLAN RODWAY
A Preface to Dickens	ALLAN GRANT

A Preface to Forster

Christopher Gillie

Longman

LONGMAN GROUP LIMITED
Longman House
Burnt Mill, Harlow, Essex, CM20 2JE, England
and Associated companies throughout the world

Published in the United States of America
by Longman Inc. New York

© Longman Group Limited 1983

First published 1983

British Library Cataloguing in Publication Data
Gillie, Christopher
  A Preface to Forster.—(Preface books).
  1. Forster, E.M.—Criticism and interpretation
  I. Title   II. Series
  823′.912   PR6011.058Z/   81-12366

ISBN 0 582 35315 7 cased
     0 582 35314 9 paper

Set in Baskerville 169 10/11pt.

Printed in Hong Kong
by Astros Printing Ltd

197315

CHRISTOPHER GILLIE has taught English at Cambridge University for a considerable time, having been a lecturer at Trinity Hall until his recent retirement. He contributed the highly successful volume on Jane Austen to the Preface Books series in 1974 and has published the *Longman Companion to English Literature* (1972) and *Movements in English Literature 1900–1940* (Cambridge University Press, 1975).

Contents

LIST OF ILLUSTRATIONS   vii
ACKNOWLEDGEMENTS   viii
FOREWORD   ix
INTRODUCTION   xi

PART ONE : BACKGROUND AND ENVIRONMENT

Chronological table   2

1   *Ancestry: the Clapham Sect*   9

2   *Childhood*   14

3   *Education*   19
    The Apostles   21

4   *After Cambridge*   25
    Bloomsbury   26
    Other relationships   29
    Travels   33
    The sage   38

5   *Breaking the circles: the short stories*   40
    'The Story of a Panic'   40
    'The Road from Colonus'   43
    'The Eternal Moment'   44
    'The Machine Stops'   46

PART TWO : THE INTELLECTUAL SETTING

6   *The liberal tradition*   50
    Mill and Arnold   54
    Forster and Carpenter   62

7   *The art of the novel*   66
    Austen and Forster   67
    Narrative organisation   71
    Butler and Forster   73
    Meredith and Forster   75

8   *Essays and criticism*   82

PART THREE : THE NOVELS

9   *The sage and the artist:* Where Angels Fear to Tread   96
    The chief characters   97

Themes of the novel 106
Forster's techniques 108

10 *The personal and the social: explorations of mystery and muddle* 112
The Longest Journey 112
A Room with a View 116
Howards End 117
Maurice 126

11 *A Passage to India* 130
Whitman, Eliot and Forster's spiritual quest 134
'Mosque' 143
'Caves' 145
'Temples' 151
Passages from India 155

12 *The twentieth-century novelist* 158
Forster and D.H. Lawrence 158
Forster as twentieth-century novelist 164

PART FOUR : REFERENCE SECTION

Short biographies 172
Gazetteer 181
Bibliography 184

APPENDIX : Walt Whitman's *Passage to India* 187
INDEX 195

List of illustrations

frontispiece 'Rooksnest', Stevenage, home of E.M. Forster and his mother from 1883 to 1895. He used it as the basis for Howards End.

E.M. Forster's great-grandfather, Henry Thornton M.P. by
    John Hoppner (*c* 1814)   11
Forster's great-aunt, Marianne Thornton   15
Forster, aged 5, with his mother   17
George Moore (1873–1958)   23
Leonard Woolf (1880–1969) as an undergraduate at
    Cambridge, contemporary with Forster   28
At Lady Ottoline's, 1917–18. From left to right: Ottoline
    Morrell, Maria Nys, Lytton Strachey, Duncan Grant,
    Vanessa Bell   31
Goldsworthy Lowes Dickinson (1862–1932), Fellow of
    King's when Forster was undergraduate, and later one
    of his closest friends   35
Cover of the liberal 'Independent Review' including one of
    Forster's earliest contributions   52/3
John Stuart Mill (1806–1873) by G.F. Watts   56
Matthew Arnold (1822–1888)   60
Edward Carpenter by Roger Fry   65
George Meredith (1828–1909) by G.F. Watts   77
Thomas Hardy (1840–1928)   80
Roger Fry (1866–1934)   86
West Hackhurst, Abinger, Surrey, designed for Forster's
    aunt, Laura Forster, by his father. Forster inherited the
    lease in 1924, and lived there with his mother till her
    death in 1945.   93
San Gimignano, the basis for Monteriano   103
E.M. Forster, 1911, by Roger Fry   114
Forster in India, 1912–13   129
Forster with his friend Syed Ross Masood upon whom he
    based the character of Aziz   142
D.H. Lawrence (1885–1930) in 1923   161
Virginia Woolf (1882–1941) by her sister Vanessa Bell   166
Forster in old age in his bedroom at King's College,
    Cambridge   169

Acknowledgements

We are grateful to the following for permission to reproduce copyright material:

Edward Arnold (Publishers) Ltd and Harcourt Brace Jovanovich Inc for extracts from E.M. Forster's *Two Cheers for Democracy*, © 1951 by E.M. Forster; renewed 1979 by Donald Parry, *Aspects of the Novel* © 1927 by Harcourt Brace Jovanovich Inc; renewed 1955 by E.M. Forster, *A Passage to India* © 1924 by Harcourt Brace Jovanovich Inc; renewed 1952 by E.M. Forster and *Abinger Harvest*; Edward Arnold (Publishers) Ltd and Alfred A Knopf Inc for an extract from E.M. Forster's *A Room with a View*; Edward Arnold (Publishers) Ltd, Alfred A Knopf Inc and Curtis Brown Ltd for extracts from E.M. Forster's *Howards End* © 1921 by E.M. Forster and *Where Angels Fear to Tread* © 1920 by Alfred A Knopf Inc and renewed 1948 by Edward Morgan Forster; Faber and Faber Ltd and Random House Inc for Dedication to 'Journey to a War' from *Collected Shorter Poems* by W.H. Auden (American title 'To E.M. Forster' from *W.H. Auden: Collected Poems*, edited by Edward Mendelson) © 1945 by W.H. Auden; King's College, Cambridge and The Society of Authors as the literary representative of the E.M. Forster Estate for extracts from letters in P.N. Furbank's *E.M. Forster: A Life* Vols I and II; Sidgwick & Jackson Ltd for extracts from E.M. Forster's 'The Machine Stops' *Collected Shorter Stories* 1954, *The Celestial Omnibus* and *The Eternal Moment and Other Stories*.

We are grateful to the following for permission to reproduce photographs:

British Library, pages 52–53; Camera Press, page 169 (photo Cecil Beaton); Courtauld Institute of Art, University of London, pages 114 and 166 (private collections); King's College Library, Cambridge, pages ii, 15, 17, 35, 93 and 142; Mansell Collection, pages 80 and 103; National Portrait Gallery, pages 56, 60, 65, 77, 86 and 161 (courtesy executors of estate of Edmond X. Kapp); Mrs M.T. Parsons and Hogarth Press, page 28; Trinity College Library, Cambridge, page 23; Mrs Julian Vinogradoff, page 31; Mrs Wignall, page 11.

The painting *Jagannatha Temple* by a chitrakar of Puri, Orissa, 1920–30, is reproduced on the cover by permission of the British Library and India Office Library and Records.

Foreword

The long Indian summer of E.M. Forster spent at King's between 1945 and 1970 will be remembered by many who found access there to a great creative writer. It was indeed the most successful example in this country of the often satirised position of the 'artist in residence' at a university. Established artists such as Auden, Isherwood and Britten called; rather comically many literate Indians included him on their list of cultural monuments in England; but, more educationally important in the eyes of the College was the fact that undergraduates who had read his books found how open and unassuming yet how knowledgeable and wise he was in bridging the cultural gap between Edwardian and postwar England; and how prepared to talk.

Christopher Gillie, the author of the most successful volume on Jane Austen in the present series here very cogently develops the historical and critical patterns in the work of Forster, the Victorian sage and Edwardian novelist, the traditionalist who was also a literary experimenter in his time. Austen, especially on p. 67, features once more as the great forerunner whose handling of language with all its ironies and implications informs all her books and influences so much in his too: in Forster, we notice the wit and the dialogue but not the dancing. The explication of symbolic writing in his novels provides some of the most enlightening pages in Mr Gillie's critique, along with that type of spiritual ecology or cross-cultural moral patterning such as we find too in the pages of Henry James and D.H. Lawrence. Here is developed the character of the representative English and Italian people such as Forster places in his short stories and *Where Angels Fear to Tread*. Part Three of this *Preface* culminates in a profound discussion of that masterpiece of three cultures in which Forster 'excelled his apparent limits', *A Passage to India.*

This book, appearing virtually sixty years after that final volume, reminds us that, like Hardy, Forster abandoned novel-writing in mid-career and that neither of these has lost an appreciative readership with the years. Christopher Gillie's personal comprehensive account of his subject as both sage and artist will prove of great assistance to those beginning to study the work of one of the most satisfying novelists of the early years of the century and keen to clarify both the surface and the deeper currents in his art.

MAURICE HUSSEY General Editor

Introduction

'An extremely nice young man,' reported the sponsors of an extension lecture given by the young Forster, 'but perhaps not very intelligent.' Later, the novelist William Plomer wrote this description of him:

> Incurious fellow-passengers on a train, seeing him in a cheap cloth cap, and carrying the sort of little bag that might have been carried in 1890 by the man who came to wind the clocks, might have thought him a dim provincial of settled habits and taken no more notice of him. (*At Home*, 1958)

Plomer's point, of course, is not that Forster lacked distinction but that his distinction was elusive. Lytton Strachey also remarked on this elusiveness: he nicknamed him the 'taupe' (mole) because, explains Forster's biographer, 'he was drab-coloured and unobtrusive and came up in odd places and unexpected circles'. Still another and very different impression is implied by an acquaintance who remarked of him in middle age: 'Have you noticed how Morgan's friends drop their voices when they talk of him, as if he were Jesus Christ?'

Such impressions of Forster the man correspond to reactions to him as a writer. Some consider him overrated, and can see little in his work to justify his posthumous reputation; others consider him as indeed an important figure but an elusive one, who deliberately cultivated a humorous, casual-seeming style as a technique to avoid attracting attention to what is not truly important in order to evoke, eventually, what is. For others still he is a writer to be approached with reverence, as he was as a man in his lifetime. The last group included during his life figures who were not inclined to adopt reverential attitudes to anybody: J.R. Ackerley, for instance, literary editor of *The Listener* when that periodical was making its reputation, and Virginia Woolf, who wrote of him in her Diary:

> Morgan has the artist's mind; he says the simple things that clever people don't say; I find him the best of critics for that reason.

'The simple things that clever people don't say': the remark is applicable to Forster as a novelist, and so is the description of him as 'the best of critics', for it is as criticism of his age that Forster's fiction made its mark.

This reminds us that, in the words of a *New York Times* reviewer in 1979, his career showed a change in role 'from being a creator to a sage'. In the course of his long life (he was born in 1879 and died in 1970) he published five novels and wrote six, besides the short stories. Four of the five came out within six years, from 1905 to 1910; he then wrote *Maurice*, published after his death, and finally his masterpiece, *A Passage to India*, published in 1924. Thus it was less than a third of his lifespan that he gave to fiction. After 1924 he continued writing and his prestige continued to grow, but now he was essayist, biographer, librettist, broadcaster and literary critic. His achievements in these capacities had their own justification and they will not be ignored in this study. However, they not only derived most of their influence from the five published novels, but were fruit of that soil; accordingly, it is the novels that will be our main concern.

Is he, then, a 'major novelist'? He himself firmly denied it, but many of his admirers disagree with him. Their verdict, however, is not the only reason for studying him; a better one is that he was 'the great connecter' who made it his business, in his segmented society, to reawaken a sense of those relationships which prejudice and ignorance disposed its members to ignore or forget. Our own society, a hundred years from his birth, is different from that in which he grew up, but not so different as we are inclined to believe. For us, he is a 'connecter' in an additional sense: he shows us continuities between the nineteenth and the twentieth centuries better than any other novelist qualified to do so, conveying much that was best in the Victorian tradition without the Victorian defences and in a twentieth-century idiom.

Part One
Background and Environment

Chronological table

	FORSTER'S LIFE	BACKGROUND EVENTS
1879	Born at 6 Melcombe Place, Dorset Square, London NW1, only surviving child of Edward Morgan Forster, architect, and Lily, née Whichelo.	George Meredith: *The Egoist*.
1880	Death of his father from tuberculosis.	
1881		Henry James: *Portrait of a Lady*.
1882	Removal to Rooksnest, near Stevenage in Hertfordshire, original of the house in *Howards End*.	Virginia Stephen (later Woolf) born.
1884		Third Parliamentary Reform Act, granting universal male suffrage. Fabian Society founded.
1885		D.H. Lawrence born.
1886		Thomas Hardy: *The Mayor of Casterbridge*.
1887	Death of his great-aunt, Marianne Thornton: she bequeaths him £8000 in trust, the capital to be made over to him on his twenty-fifth birthday.	
1888		Suez Canal opened to ships of all nations.

1890	Preparatory school: Kent House, Eastbourne.	
1891		Thomas Hardy: *Tess of the D'Urbervilles*.
1893	Dayboy at Tonbridge School, the model for Sawston School in *The Longest Journey*. The Forsters leave Rooksnest to live at Dryhurst, Dry Hill Park Road, Tonbridge.	
1895		Thomas Hardy: *Jude the Obscure*.
1897	Enters King's College, Cambridge, where he studies Classics for three years and History for a fourth, obtaining a second in both. During his fourth year (1901) he is elected to the Apostles.	Joseph Conrad: *The Nigger of the Narcissus*.
1899		Outbreak of Boer War.
1900		Joseph Conrad: *Lord Jim*. Beginning of Labour Party.
1901	October: starts on a year's tour of Italy and Austria with his mother. Begins writing seriously with 'The Story of a Panic'.	Queen Victoria dies. Samuel Butler: *Erewhon Revisited* (sequel to *Erewhon*, 1872).
1902	Teaches Latin at a weekly class in the Working Men's College, Great Ormond Street, Bloomsbury, London. Cruise to Greece: 'The Road from Colonus'.	Peace of Vereeniging: end of Boer War.

1904	Begins contributing to the *Independent Review*; continues at the Working Men's College and lectures on Italian art and history for the Cambridge Local Lectures Board.	Joseph Conrad: *Nostromo*.
1905	Germany: tutors the children of Elizabeth, Countess von Arnim, at Nassenheide, Pomerania. *Where Angels Fear to Tread* published.	
1906	Tutors Syed Ross Masood in Latin; beginning of an important friendship.	Establishment of Liberal government of radical reform, supported by Labour.
1907	*The Longest Journey*.	Joseph Conrad: *The Secret Agent*.
1908	*A Room with a View*.	Arnold Bennett: *The Old Wives' Tale*.
1909		First cross-channel flight by Louis Blériot. George Meredith dies.
1910	*Howards End*: his first major success.	
1911	*The Celestial Omnibus*.	
1912	October: leaves for his first visit to India, where he stays with Masood and meets the Maharajahs of Chhaturpur and Dewas Senior. Begins *A Passage to India*.	
1913	Visits Edward Carpenter. Begins writing *Maurice*.	D.H. Lawrence: *Sons and Lovers*. Marcel Proust: first volume of *A la Recherche du temps perdu*.

1914	Becomes cataloguer at the National Gallery.	Outbreak of First World War.
1915	Begins working for the Red Cross in Alexandria; meets the Greek poet Cavafy of whose work he becomes the chief English exponent.	D.H. Lawrence: *The Rainbow*.
1916		Battle of the Somme. Easter Rebellion in Dublin. James Joyce: *A Portrait of the Artist as a Young Man*.
1917		October Revolution in Russia. T.S. Eliot: *Prufrock and other Observations*.
1918		Armistice. Lytton Strachey: *Eminent Victorians*.
1919	Returns to England. Finds publisher for *Alexandria: A History and a Guide*. Literary editor for two months on the *Daily Herald*.	J. Maynard Keynes: *The Economic Consequences of the Peace*.
1920		D.H. Lawrence: *Women in Love*.
1921	Second visit to India: private secretary to the Maharajah of Dewas Senior.	
1922	*Alexandria: A History and a Guide*.	T.S. Eliot: *The Waste Land*. James Joyce: *Ulysses*.
1923	*Pharos and Pharillon*: essays written during his wartime stay in Egypt.	

1924	*A Passage to India*: widely acclaimed.	
1925	Moves with his mother to West Hackhurst at Abinger Hammer, near Dorking. It had been designed by Forster's father for his aunt Laura who bequeaths him the lease.	Beginnings of Fascist state under Mussolini in Italy.
1926		General Strike in United Kingdom. T.E. Lawrence: *Seven Pillars of Wisdom*.
1927	Gives the Clark Lectures at Cambridge, published under the title *Aspects of the Novel*.	Virginia Woolf: *To the Lighthouse*.
1928	*The Eternal Moment*.	D.H. Lawrence: *Lady Chatterley's Lover*. Thomas Hardy (b. 1840) dies.
1929	Meets Bob Buckingham, a young policeman who becomes his closest friend.	
1930		D.H. Lawrence dies.
1931		Virginia Woolf: *The Waves*.
1933		Hitler becomes Chancellor of Germany.
1934	President of the National Council for Civil Liberties. Collaborates with the composer, Ralph Vaughan Williams, on the Abinger Pageant. *Goldsworthy Lowes Dickinson* published.	

1935		Christopher Isherwood: *Mr Norris Changes Trains*.
1936	*Abinger Harvest*.	Outbreak of Spanish Civil War (1936–9).
1938	Second collaboration with Vaughan Williams: the pageant *England's Pleasant Land*.	
1939		Outbreak of Second World War.
1941	Begins broadcasting to India.	Virginia Woolf dies.
1942	Again president of the National Council for Civil Liberties.	
1944	Presides at London PEN (Poets, Playwrights, Editors, Essayists and Novelists) Conference: tercentenary of Milton's *Areopagitica*.	
1945	Visits India for PEN. His mother dies. The lease of West Hackhurst expires and he is elected Honorary Fellow at King's College; moves to Cambridge.	Surrender of Germany. Atomic bombs on Hiroshima and Nagasaki.
1946		First General Assembly of UNO in London. Establishment of UNESCO (United Nations Educational, Scientific and Cultural Organisation).
1947	Visits United States, where he lectures on 'The Raison d'Etre of Criticism in the Arts' at Harvard.	Indian Independence Act.

1949	Second visit to USA: lectures on 'Art for Art's Sake' at Academy of Arts and Letters. Begins work on libretto of *Billy Budd*. Declines offer of knighthood.	
1951	*Two Cheers for Democracy*.	
1953	Made Companion of Honour. *Hill of Devi*.	
1956	*Marianne Thornton*.	Suez Crisis. Hungarian rising crushed by USSR.
1960		'Trial' of *Lady Chatterley's Lover*: found 'not guilty' of obscenity.
1969	Awarded Order of Merit.	
1970	7th June: dies in the home of Bob and May Buckingham.	
1971	Publication of *Maurice*.	
1972	Publication of *The Life to Come*.	

1 Ancestry: the Clapham Sect

Edward Morgan Forster was born on January 1, 1879, the only surviving child of an architect, who died the following year. His mother, Lily, had been a Whichelo. The Whichelos were a poor middle-class family with a tradition of artistic pursuits, but Forster's great-aunt on his father's side, Marianne Thornton, was the daughter of a banker whose household had been the centre of one of the most influential social movements of the early nineteenth century. Marianne Thornton was devoted to her fatherless great-nephew; she died when he was eight, but in those early years he was the predominant interest of her strong personality. In her correspondence she constantly referred to him as 'the important one', and she bequeathed him the private income which was to enable him to go to Cambridge and to become a professional writer. He acknowledged his debt to her by publishing her biography in 1955.

The title of this book is *Marianne Thornton: a Domestic Biography*; this indicates that the subject is Marianne's personal life rather than the public interest of that circle of reformers of which her father, Henry Thornton, had been the central though not the most famous figure. Nonetheless he gives us his impressions of the standpoint and outlook of the circle, and those impressions are important when we assess his own standpoint and outlook as a writer: his writings show himself as strongly aware of himself as a product of the English upper-middle class, and of the force with which that class had impressed itself on the English national character, for good and ill, in the period of his own youth.

Henry Thornton lived from 1760 to 1815. He had strong personality and intelligence; by profession he was not only a banker but a Member of Parliament, and author of a pamphlet on paper credit which is still respected by economists. His abilities, moreover, were reinforced and given direction by his religious convictions: he belonged to the evangelical movement, which originated in the influence of John Wesley in the mid-eighteenth century, though it remained in the Church of England. He lived in a large house called Battersea Rise on Clapham Common, and this became the focus for the body of reformers called 'the Clapham Sect'. Its most famous member was Henry's second cousin, William Wilberforce, celebrated for his successful campaign to abolish the slave trade in 1807. Other members included Hannah More, whose tracts led to the foundation of the Religious Tract Society by John Venn, another member of the circle; John Shore, first President of the British and Foreign Bible Society; Zachary Macaulay, father of the historian, and the Stephen family, forebears of Forster's friend Virginia Woolf.

The impression Forster gives of the sect is not at all of the primness and repressiveness which we tend to associate with the later Victorian Evangelicals; its character seems to have been that of the Thornton household which was its focus. Forster writes of them:

> Surely there never was such a house, so full of intellect and piety and active benevolence. They lived in such uninterrupted harmony with each other, were so full of their separate pursuits, enjoyed with such interest and vivacity all the pleasures of their beautiful home, or wholly laid aside all the forms of society that were irksome, that young or old one felt oneself in a brighter and happier world . . .

It was a large family of nine children, of whom Marianne was the eldest. To read about them in Forster's words is to be reminded of Jane Austen's family life half a generation before: the Austens were not Evangelicals, though the father was a clergyman, but the family—also a large one—seems to have had a comparable bond of affection, liveliness in individual activity, and confident assurance. This was the period (the end of the eighteenth century and opening of the nineteenth) when the middle class was enjoying the beginning of its golden age, vigorous with its sense of promise and not yet arrogant with power or shadowed by the conflicts and doubts which darkened the Victorian era and imbued it with the need for defensiveness and repression. Such large families seem to have thriven above all by their capacity to give and receive family love. The sorrow of death brought this out conspicuously, and Forster contrasts their response to bereavement with our own: 'People today love each other from moment to moment much as their ancestors did, but loyalty of soul, such as the elder Thorntons possessed, is on the decrease.' This, too, recalls Jane Austen: the loyalty within her own family, and the stress which she lays on that virtue in her novels.

And yet Forster does not depict the period of Thornton greatness as a golden age: he sees the limitations of the Clapham circle to have been as strong as its virtues were positive. On the one hand, it was an inclusive and embracing society: it entertained an American Indian and West Africans, and

> . . . little black boys would wander over Clapham Common and be beckoned into houses by the delighted inhabitants. The great world was expanding.

But on the other hand:

> It brought no mystery, no feeling for poetry. But it was an

E.M. Forster's great-grandfather, Henry Thornton M.P. by John Hoppner (c 1814)

increasing field for curiosity and missionary effort.

Summing up the relationship between Marianne and her father, he writes:

> For Marianne, as for her father, the terrestrial world became entirely tangible and behind it, equally reliable in another and superior way, stood God. For her, as for him, imagination is dangerous because it makes us behave in an unreal way to people, which may hurt them.

One must be kind to people, in other words, but one must not disturb them. It was an attitude which Matthew Arnold was later to denominate 'philistinism', and it tended to produce complacency about indigenous social values. About these, Henry Thornton exhibited a curiously divided mind; he could sympathise with the sufferings of industrial workers, but he could not condemn the system which caused the sufferings since it was also producing the wealth of which he and his kind were making such good use. After a tour with his wife of an industrial area in the north, he writes:

> We ... have been learning to feel for those who dig in Mines, who toil in Quarries, perspire in Salt works, wear out their Eyes looking at Furnaces, or pass their morning noon and Even in the limited Employment of putting on the head of a Pin, or drawing over and over the same pattern on a piece of China.

In fact, he had been witnessing that industrial victimisation which half a century later was to throw John Ruskin into eloquent rage. Thornton, however, temperately remarks that such sights are very educative, and goes on:

> It has not a little entertained Mrs T. & I trust that the View which we have taken of our fellow creatures has inspired some thankfulness for the temporal as well as spiritual Advantages of our condition.

On this letter, Forster comments that Marianne's parents 'would have behaved very differently if they had encountered a slave gang .... When the slavery was industrial they did nothing and had no thought of doing anything ... to encounter it was an educational experience, and an opportunity for smug thankfulness.'

The Clapham Sect values were inherited and transmitted by the new public school system originated by Thomas Arnold, the famous headmaster of Rugby from 1828 to 1842. But by institutionalising such values as a system in single-sex schools, Thomas Arnold and his successors aggravated their negative influence—philistinism and suspicion of the imagination—without the available compensations afforded by an organic family such as the Battersea Rise household. In

'Notes on the English Character', written in 1920 and published in *Abinger Harvest*, Forster assesses the consequences of this development. He begins by stating that the character of the English is essentially middle class, and that this is understandable because, since the end of the eighteenth century (when the Clapham Sect was at the height of its influence), the middle classes had dominated English society. He goes on to remark that the heart of the middle class had been the Public School. This educational training enforced discipline of character in such a way that the characteristic English defect is 'the undeveloped heart'—'not that the Englishman can't feel' but that 'he is afraid to feel'.

Thus Forster's assessment of the qualities of his ancestry are ambivalent. A stuntedness of feeling beyond a given circle of relationships, suspicion of imagination because of the disturbances that it can arouse, a disposition to disconnect such human relationships as are inconvenient—all these constitute one strand of its legacy. All the same, his biography of Marianne Thornton acknowledges wistfully not only the rich, abundant family life at Battersea Rise, but the rootedness of the family in that beautiful, spacious, seemingly indestructible house, which, as he sadly relates, has passed away, together with the style of family which it sheltered. In his own life he was denied both, and in much of it he seems to have been in quest for such a house and a substitute for such a family.

2 Childhood

To compare Forster's childhood with that of Marianne Thornton is in some ways to see her world stood upon its head. Instead of being one of a large family of brothers and sisters, he was an only child; instead of having a strong and rich father, he was fatherless, and surrounded by women—his mother, his father's sister Laura, his great-aunt and his Whichelo grandmother. Besides, there was never much money, although always a sufficiency thanks to the Thornton wealth and Marianne's generosity. Instead of being rooted in one place—a secure, material home—his was a childhood of shifting residences; for only one of these did he and his mother feel deep affection, and that one they had to abandon like all the others.

Nonetheless, his childhood resembled his great-aunt's in two respects. First, his infancy was sheltered by deep love, which established early in him a strong self-confidence; this was badly shaken by his school and by self-questioning, but he never entirely lost it, and it was to flower and fade again and again in the changing circumstances of his life. Second, like Marianne he grew up in a circle which took for granted its middle-class status, and cultivated what its members considered the 'right' social relationships; his mother was capable of refusing to see her landlord because he called at her back-door—as though, in her opinion, he was not regarding her as a social equal. But even this resemblance contained a contrast, for in Marianne's childhood there had been no problem about her family knowing 'the right people'; they were only too anxious to know her family, whereas Forster's mother found herself shrinking towards the fringes of the circles she cultivated.

An only child, fatherless and brought up by a devoted mother, with other female relatives eager to assume the role of motherhood when the opportunity offered, is likely to undergo an exceptional development for better and worse. His great-aunt, in accordance with a practice two generations gone, insisted that he wore Little Lord Fauntleroy suits and his curly hair down to his shoulders, so that he looked what she dubbed him—the 'Important One'—the rich little king surrounded by adorers. His self-will luxuriated in pleasure-seeking, unchecked by the competition of equals in sex, age and social station, since his playmates were chiefly an admiring servant-girl and garden-boys who seem to have accepted him uncritically. He was, of course, 'spoilt'—given to wild rages when frustrated—and over-protected, especially because his father's early death increased his mother's anxiety for him. But the most conspicuous trait of a well-endowed child brought up in such circumstances is likely to be precocity. His intelligence and

Forster's great-aunt, Marianne Thornton

imagination developed freely, richly and comically. He discovered that he could read, without being taught, at the age of four, and thereafter read voraciously. He also wrote what he called 'long stories about things that never happened inside my head' with titles like 'Chattering Hassocks', 'Scream', 'Scuffles in the Wardrobe', and 'The Earring in the Keyhole'. His information for such a small child seems to have been extraordinary; when he was six, his mother reported that he was drawing a map of South America and worrying that the maid, who was helping him, 'won't think it matters a bit whether I put Patagonia in place of Ecuador'.

His relationship with his mother was always paramount, and probably it was over-intense. His biographer, P.N. Furbank, records that a love affair sprang up between them in his infancy; it 'made Forster's childhood a radiantly happy one, and it went on, in a sense, for the rest of both their lives'. She died when he was sixty-six, leaving him for a time desolate and bewildered: 'I partly died', he was to write, 'when my mother did, and must smell sometimes of the grave.' Not that the relationship was always harmonious; she grew impatient with his physical awkwardness and unpracticality in adolescence, and later in life seems to have partly withdrawn herself from him. Perhaps it is fair to sum up their relationship in his own words to his friend and admirer, J.R. Ackerley:

> Although my mother has been intermittently tiresome for the last thirty years, cramped and warped my genius, hindered my career, blocked and buggered up my house, and boycotted my beloved, I have to admit that she has provided a sort of rich subsoil where I have been able to rest and grow.

She gave him roots.

But Forster needed another sort of rootedness, one which would perhaps have made the sustaining relationship with his mother more secure: an environment which they could both love, feel possession of and be possessed by—a house which was itself rooted in an intelligible past and through which he could have related himself physically to the tradition of English culture. He and his mother lived in such a house from 1883 when he was five until 1893, when they left it so that he could be near his public school at Tonbridge. It was called Rooksnest, and was situated near Stevenage in Hertfordshire, a county for which, in consequence, he kept a lasting affection, feeling it to be in its shy way representative of essential England. It was old but unpretentious, and he depicted it as Howards End in the novel with that title, including the wych-elm in its garden, with the mysterious fangs embedded in its bark, a relic of local superstition. He is reported to have said that if he could have continued to live there, he would have married and had children.

Forster, aged 5, with his mother

Rooksnest was not, however, the only house to have captured his imagination in his youth. His aunt Laura lived in a house near Abinger in Surrey, where his mother had spent happy girlhood years before her marriage, although already under the patronage of Marianne Thornton. The house had been built for his aunt by his father, and it had a further connection with the past by Laura using it and its garden to establish links with the long-lost Thornton home, Battersea Rise. The young Forster learnt to know the neighbourhood intimately, describing it in the last of the essays in *Two Cheers for Democracy*, and he commemorated the place in the title of his first collection, *Abinger Harvest*.

Thus three houses dominated his imagination in his youth: Rooksnest, West Hackhurst near Abinger, and—though known only by family reminiscence—Battersea Rise. They seem to have impregnated him with that deep feeling for place evident in his writings, and a constituent of his values. To be without it was for Forster to lack one of the relationships which are essential to full humanity, and his possession of it is one of the marks that characterise him as transitional between an older England and our own, in which we have come to accept frequent removals and disruptive urbanisation as normal features of our lives and environments. He saw the tendencies with foreboding; so he writes in *Howards End*:

> London was but a foretaste of this nomadic civilization which is altering human nature so profoundly, and throws upon personal relations a stress greater than they have ever borne before. Under cosmopolitanism, if it comes, we shall receive no help from the earth. Trees and meadows and mountains will only be a spectacle, and the binding force that they once exercised on character must be entrusted to Love alone. May Love be equal to the task!
>
> (*Chapter 31*)

The house represents continuity and resuscitation of life in the midst of this deadening flux, but like Rooksnest, its original near Stevenage, it is in the home counties and itself under menace:

> '... There are moments when I feel Howards End peculiarly our own.'
>
> 'All the same, London's creeping.'
>
> She pointed over the meadow—over eight or nine meadows, but at the end of them was a red dust.
>
> 'You see that in Surrey and even Hampshire now,' she continued. I can see it from the Purbeck Downs. And London is only part of something else, I'm afraid. Life's going to be melted down, all over the world.' (*Chapter 44*)

There are no invulnerable fortresses in Forster's writings; all the same, he refused the easy retreat into pessimism.

3 Education

In 1890, when he was eleven, Forster was sent to a preparatory boarding school. It was his unhappiness there which caused his mother to leave Rooksnest and move to Tonbridge, so that he could attend his public school there as a dayboy.

He was to typify Tonbridge in his third novel, *The Longest Journey*. Sawston, in that novel, had had a history similar to that of many English minor public schools. Tradesmen had founded it in the seventeenth century for tradesmen's sons, and it had continued in that style until the nineteenth.

> Then two things happened. Firstly, the school's property rose in value, and it became rich. Secondly, for no obvious reason, it suddenly emitted a quantity of bishops. The bishops, like the stars from a Roman candle, were of all colours, and flew in all directions, some high, some low, some to distant colonies, one into the Church of Rome. But many a father traced their course in the papers; many a mother wondered whether her son, if properly ignited, might not burn as bright; many a family moved to the place where living and education were so cheap, where day-boys were not looked down upon, and where the orthodox and up-to-date were said to be combined. The school doubled its numbers. It built new class-rooms, laboratories, and a gymnasium. It dropped the prefix 'Grammar'. It coaxed the sons of the local tradesmen into a new foundation, the 'Commercial School', built a couple of miles away. And it started boarding-houses ... Where traditions served, it clung to them. Where new departures seemed desirable, they were made. It aimed at producing the average Englishman, and, to a very great extent, it succeeded.   (*Chapter 4*)

Forster is aware, of course, that 'the average Englishman' is a term which has meaning only in statistics, and that this statistical abstraction was more likely to be found among the tradesmen's sons. For the school, however, the term expressed a qualitative standard, and in 'Notes on the English Character' he describes its products as going forth into the world

> with well-developed bodies, fairly developed minds, and undeveloped hearts ....

In every novel, these 'average' Englishmen are contrasted to the sensitive ones, but it would be a mistake to assume that Forster felt only hostility and contempt for the 'average Englishman' of the upper middle class who dominated English society until his late middle age.

He felt appropriate respect for the virtues of 'the average' and his aim is not to eliminate the class but to convert it. A good example is the relationship between the Schlegels and the Wilcoxes in *Howards End*. The Schlegel family are the 'sensitives' and, significantly, it is their German father from whom they derive their respect for culture; the Wilcoxes are 'the average'. But we are not allowed to forget that the Schlegels, who have a comfortable private income, owe it to the energies of such people as the Wilcoxes. If Wilcoxes are too often blind to the values of Schlegels, then Schlegels too easily ignore their dependence on Wilcoxes. The well-known epigraph to the novel is— 'Only connect . . .'.

But Forster was himself irremediably unaverage, and what Tonbridge did for him was to change him from a volatile, beautiful, eloquent child into an awkward, diffident, repressed adolescent. Brought up as he had been by affectionate women who indulged him, and then educated at a school where he was unappreciated, he might himself have never managed to make any 'connections'; the world where he was at home and that where he was an alien might have remained estranged systems, as they have for so many twentieth-century artists, instead of becoming hemispheres of the one system to which they truly belong. But Cambridge—more specifically, King's College—enabled him to go far towards overcoming such a disjunction in himself. It was itself a restricted world, for, as his biographer remarks, it nourished in him the prejudice that 'it was scholars and civil servants, not business men, who ran Britain', but it had two major influences upon him. First, it enabled him to cultivate a sceptical but caring disinterestedness towards all systems of value, especially towards any systems which projected themselves as absolute and final. The second influence of the place is best epitomised in his own words, as he expressed it in his biography of Goldsworthy Lowes Dickinson, published in 1934:

> As Cambridge filled up with friends it acquired a magic quality. Body and spirit, reason and emotion, work and play, architecture and scenery, laughter and seriousness, life and art—these pairs which are elsewhere contrasted were there fused into one.

He had already experienced some of these fusions in the world of women in which he had spent his childhood. But that had been a world of innocence, in which relationships, however fond, had seldom been free. They had become dissociated at school, where relationships were neither free nor fond, and by the time he came to Cambridge he must have learnt that they are not often associated in the world at large—particularly that world of 'telegrams and anger' of the *Howards End* Wilcoxes. Cambridge brought the fusion to him through the freedoms of friendship, and especially those friendships associated with the famous and exclusive discussion circle known as 'the Apostles'.

The Apostles

It was a long-established society, founded in 1820, and although it had never been large it had included in its membership such famous names as those of the poet Tennyson, his friend Arthur Hallam, the Christian Socialist F.D. Maurice, the physicist James Clerk-Maxwell, and the philosopher Henry Sidgwick. Sidgwick's description of its aims was 'the pursuit of truth with absolute devotion and unreserve by a group of intimate friends'. Forster became a member in his fourth year, and his immediate contemporaries in the circle included men of great future distinction: Maynard Keynes, Roger Fry, Leonard Woolf, Desmond MacCarthy. Thoby Stephen, who died young, the brilliant brother of the novelist Virginia Woolf, was also a member; Lytton Strachey, Bertrand Russell and Alfred North Whitehead joined a little later.

The original name of the circle had been the 'Conversazione Society' (or simply 'the Society'), and the three names together suggest its special and complex character. It was informal ('Conversazione') and yet very serious—'conversazione' implies a tradition of serious dialogue as distinct from the possibly casual exchange of mere 'conversation'. Membership was by election, but it required no specific qualifications, social or academic, except that women were excluded. Yet it was very select; candidates underwent scrutiny for two or three terms before admission. It maintained critical scepticism of all institutions with their rituals, but it was itself an institution with its own rituals: undergraduate members of the Apostles were denominated 'Active Brethren', and senior members were denominated 'Angels'; early defectors were subjected to a formal 'curse'; members were assumed to practise the intimacy of the Society in their daily lives, but they met on Saturday evenings when a formal paper was read. By its nature, it could not exert continuity of subject from generation to generation in such discussions, but tendencies persisted over given periods. In Forster's time, the dominating influence was that of the philosopher G.E. Moore (author of the *Principia Ethica*), and the papers were especially philosophical; Forster's own mind was not disposed to philosophical analysis, and he approved of a new direction under the influence of Strachey and Keynes, after he left Cambridge, into more mundane material. However, the central tenets of Moore's ethical principles must have appealed to him, although apparently he never read the *Principia*. Moore taught that 'the truth' is not an esoteric pursuit requiring special powers of the intellect and a specific language for its expression, but that it necessitated complete honesty in rigorous thinking, and that its attainment was registered in good states of mind, signified by admiration of things of beauty and by good relationship with other minds.

For Forster, it was the honesty and the relationship that mattered most in the Apostles, but their exclusiveness became a trouble to him. Brought up in a circle of adoring women, then alienated by the exclusively male environment of his schools, he found in Cambridge the experience of deep male friendships which complemented the female over-balance of his childhood. It was a circle that, for a time, completely satisfied him, and yet it could not be a permanent satisfaction, for there was still the outer world. He was not made for a career in the University; his academic record (second classes in Classics and History) was inadequate to earn him one. Apart from that, there was the question whether such academic exclusiveness was in itself desirable or even estimable.

It is at this point in his career that P.N. Furbank, in his biography, points to the relevance of a paper read to the Apostles by John Tresidder Sheppard, later Provost of King's, in 1903, two years after Forster had left university. Sheppard distinguishes two attitudes to relationships: one, which he associates with Trinity College, insists on meticulous discrimination in relationships, on the grounds that the unreality of most individuals is such that significant relationship with them is impossible; and the other, that of King's College, which requires acceptance of all individuals with positive appreciation. One of the motives which Sheppard gives for delivering his paper is 'the evident grief with which our brother Forster speaks of the cleavage', and he ends by rejecting the Trinity attitude with a quotation from Shelley's *Epipsychidion*, which begins

> I never was attached to that great sect
> Whose doctrine is, that each one should select
> Out of the world a mistress or a friend,
> And all the rest, though fair and wise, commend
> To cold oblivion

and ends:

> With one chained friend, perhaps a jealous foe,
> The dreariest and the longest journey go.

The last line takes us to Forster's second novel, *The Longest Journey*, and Furbank supposes that Forster may himself have suggested Shelley's lines to Sheppard.

The beginning of the novel illustrates Forster's state of mind about the problem. It opens in a college room with a philosophical discussion, to which the central character, Rickie Elliot, is paying scant attention—as Forster seems to have attended scantily to Apostolic discussions—although he is happy to be in the circle of his friends. The quiet scene is suddenly disrupted by Agnes Pembroke, the

George Moore (1873–1958)

22

young sister of Rickie's guardian. The circle of philosophers disperses, except for its leader, Stuart Ansell, who perplexingly ignores Agnes when Rickie attempts to introduce them, as though she were not there. The philosophical discussion had in fact been on the question whether an object can be said to be real unless its reality is corroborated by an observer, and when Ansell later explains his rudeness to Agnes, he insists that Agnes had not been truly real when introduced; she existed as a phenomenon, in semblance only. In the meantime the reader has been given sufficient clues as to what Ansell means; Agnes, despite her vivacity and physical attractiveness, is an unreal person, with no genuine feelings, her behaviour derived chiefly from second-hand social codes. The novel's theme has been set: what does it mean for a person to be 'real', and how does he or she achieve or sustain this reality?

The interest of this opening, for diagnosing Forster's problem, extends further, and it lies in the name and character of Ansell. He has been identified as a blend of two of Forster's contemporaries in the Apostles circle—H.O. Meredith (who introduced him to it) and A.R. Ainsworth; thus, through Ansell, Forster seems to be presenting what Sheppard calls the 'Trinity' view of human relationship. But Ansell was also the name of one of the gardening boys with whom Forster had been allowed to play as a child—his sole outlet then to the male world and to a different social one. Moreover, Ansell in the novel, though devoted to Cambridge and his hopes dedicated to a career there, comes from a very modest background to which he is entirely loyal, and humanly he is the link between Forster's self-portrayal as Rickie Elliot and Rickie's half-brother, Stephen Wonham, a rough-mannered rustic. Neither the gardening boy nor the fictional Ansell belong to the select humanity which the Trinity point of view—such as Lytton Strachey's—wanted to recognise as the 'real' people. *Ansell*, finally, is the title of an early story by Forster (written in 1902 or 1903 and included in *The Life to Come*) about another such as Stephen Wonham, who 'appropriates' the author, depriving him of his academic prospects. These characters show Forster treating the problem in Sheppard's paper in his own way. Yes, Trinity is right: people are real and unreal, and in their unreality they are unacceptable; but, yes, King's is also right: reality and unreality have to be measured by criteria different from such as Strachey and his kin had to offer.

Cambridge, King's, the Apostles opened to Forster new vistas of human relationship, but they might have entrapped him and he evaded the trap. All his novels, and indeed the rest of his life, were given to further explorations of human relationship.

4 After Cambridge

When he left Cambridge, Forster was able to keep an open mind about his prospects, thanks to the legacy of £8000 left him by Marianne Thornton. After a year of travel with his mother, he took to part-time adult education, first teaching Latin in 1902 at the Working Men's College (founded in 1854 by F.D. Maurice, a former Apostle) in Bloomsbury, and later (1904) lecturing on Italian art and history for the Cambridge Local Lectures Board. In the spring and summer of 1905 he tutored the children of Elizabeth, Countess von Arnim, in Germany. She was an Englishwoman, aunt of one of his friends, and at the time a famous novelist. Rich, whimsical, dominating, she liked to patronise her tutors and governesses, and the slightly-built, apparently diffident young Forster seemed at first a suitable victim for her teasing condescension. By degrees she realised that he was too dangerous; when she remarked to him that certain acquaintances of hers seemed to dislike her, he replied 'I know.' Then superiority dissolved into respect when she read an article by him in the new *Independent Review*, and recognised that not only was he a fellow writer, but a talented one. All the same she did not like *Where Angels Fear to Tread*, the proofs of which arrived during his stay, but she greatly admired his second novel, *The Longest Journey*, when it came out in 1907.

In fact literature was clearly Forster's true vocation by the time he left Cambridge. At first it was a vague aspiration, but it became definite during his tour of Italy in 1901, when 'The Story of a Panic' came to him with sudden inspiration. Meanwhile he contributed short articles and sketches to the *Independent*, and then his first novel was well received.

Whatever Forster's difficulties as a writer, he was not one of those who had to struggle against early lack of appreciation. Such a struggle may be due to the lack of a literary community to encourage a writer at the beginning of his career, and it was Forster's good fortune to have one. When the *Independent* was founded in 1903, several of his friends were on the editorial board, including Lowes Dickinson, the historian G.M. Trevelyan, and Nathaniel Wedd, who had been his tutor at King's and one of his most inspiring influences there; Trevelyan remarked with satisfaction that 'There is a majority of Apostles on the Committee.' Indeed Forster did not truly leave Cambridge when he had finished with it academically, and its academic contribution to his education had never been the most important, though it was the pretext for all that was. His personal relations formed there were not interrupted; not only did he visit Cambridge frequently in the succeeding years, but they continued in his London milieu, known in cultural history as 'the Bloomsbury Group'.

It is difficult in a short space to give a coherent account of the Bloomsbury Group. Nobody doubts that it existed, and that it owed its name to the district of London in the neighbourhood of the British Museum (with its comprehensive library) and London University where intellectuals were disposed to live, as artists lived in Chelsea. On the other hand it was not a 'movement', although it is sometimes called one, for it had little coherence and no specific sense of direction. Again, no one doubts the identities of its central nucleus: Virginia Woolf, her husband Leonard, the economist Maynard Keynes, the biographer Lytton Strachey, Virginia's sister Vanessa Bell and Duncan Grant—both painters—the art critics Clive Bell and Roger Fry; these were the most famous names, but beyond them there were other less famous fringe members and aspirants to the circle; it is among the fringe that Forster is often included, as is T.S. Eliot. It started from that nucleus and extended itself until it lost its original centre, and an account of it depends on the opinion as to the point at which its dissemination destroyed it. Michael Holroyd, in his book *Lytton Strachey and the Bloomsbury Group*, cites Vanessa Bell as dating the beginnings of the group from 1904 and its disruption at the beginning of the war; Leonard Woolf, on the other hand, is cited as dating the beginnings from 1912 to 1914, with the implication that it continued until much later. He married Virginia Stephen in 1912, and their house in Gordon Square became the group's central meeting place. Both include Forster's name among the original members.

The most intelligible way to describe the Bloomsbury Group is perhaps to say that it was a climate of cultural opinion which had prestige in the first quarter of this century. Many of its male members (Keynes, Strachey, Woolf, Forster and others) had been Apostles at Cambridge and carried the spirit of the Society into the more amorphous Group. The exclusive maleness of the Apostles angered Virginia Woolf and Vanessa Bell, whom Roy Harrod has described as 'Apostles to their finger-tips'. The inclusion of women must have made a great difference; the Apostles, despite their self-declared freedom, had their taboos in discussion, and sexuality was one; this could scarcely continue in a circle which proclaimed equal freedom and included women. Moreover, the women had their own communal source: the need to emancipate themselves from the domination of their father, Leslie Stephen, the philosopher and literary critic. Emancipation was the essence of the climate: at a time when English society was at its most philistine, its values subjected to the interests and policies of the commercially rich, Bloomsbury stood for independence of mind and culture, for liberation of the critical faculties, for 'civilisation' in short, and the arrogance often attributed to it arose partly from its collective will to sustain itself in a world of massive antagonistic forces. Admittedly their ideas of civilisation included the refinements of luxury, though few of them were rich, so that when Clive Bell wrote his book on civilisation Virginia Woolf herself remarked that it sounded very much like a 'lunch party at no. 50 Gordon Square'. Chief among these refinements was wittily intellectual talk, and the human irritations of such talk are indicated by the Bloomsbury-style lunch party in chapter 8 of *Howards End*, to which Mrs Wilcox is invited but fails to play her part. But Bloomsbury was not merely self-indulgent; one of its creative achievements was the Hogarth Press, a publishing firm run by Leonard and Virginia Woolf with no capital and against great difficulties, but a progressive force in contemporary literature after the 1914–18 war. A negative tribute to the importance of Bloomsbury must be the degree of hostility which it aroused; nothing that lacks significance is likely to be strongly opposed, and its violent opponents included such forceful figures as the painter and writer Wyndham Lewis, who hated the effeminacy of its culture, the novelist L.H. Myers who criticised its indifference to moral values, the critic F.R. Leavis who considered it pretentious and shallow, and D.H. Lawrence who loathed their talk for the sake of talk. As he said to one of them (David Garnett): 'they talk endlessly—and never, never a good thing said. They are cased each in a hard little shell of his own and out of this they talk words.' Francis King in his *E.M. Forster and his World* records that years later the socialist reformer, Beatrice Webb, asked Forster 'why he did not write another great novel ... giving the essence of the current conflict all over the world between those who aim at exquisite relationships within the closed circle of the 'elect' and those who aim at hygienic and scientific improvement of the whole of the race?' Presumably, King remarks, she is distinguishing Forster and the 'Bloomsberries' from such as herself. But Forster, although he believed in the 'elect' ('the aristocracy of the sensitive' as he put it in 'What I Believe'), did not assume that they were all in Bloomsbury, and he certainly did not believe that the race was susceptible to the Webb ideas for its improvement.

It may be a fair judgement that the real importance of Bloomsbury was the encouragement and stimulus it gave to the work of its individual members, and in the instance of Forster it seems plain that this fruitfulness derived more from his relationships within the circle than with the circle as a whole. He had an especially warm friendship with Roger Fry, whom, as his obituary note in *Abinger Harvest* shows, he regarded as setting a standard for cultured liberalism. He also became a close friend of Leonard Woolf whose practical advice he greatly appreciated. With Virginia he was more reserved; she recorded in her diary in 1919 that 'I always feel him shrinking sensitively from me, as a woman, a clever woman, an up-to-date woman', and this accords with his disparagement of her feminism in his essay on her in *Two Cheers*, but his friendship with her husband drew them together,

Leonard Woolf (1880–1969) as an undergraduate at Cambridge, contemporary with Forster

and they had a further professional bond as two of the new novelists; she certainly valued his criticism although there is less evidence that he felt similarly rewarded by hers. To Lytton Strachey he was introduced by G.M. Trevelyan when they were undergraduates, and Forster found him disconcerting. However, if the character of Risley in *Maurice* is based on Strachey, this may indicate that Forster from the first found him also enlivening, and the following extract from *Maurice* gives us a more favourable aspect of Bloomsbury talk than we get from chapter 8 in *Howards End*:

> Risley was not egotistic, though he always talked about himself. He did not interrupt. Nor did he feign indifference. Gambolling like a dolphin, he accompanied them whithersoever they went, without hindering their course. He was at play, but seriously. It was as important to him to go to and fro as to them to go forward, and he loved keeping near them. A few months ago Maurice would have agreed with Chapman, but now he was sure the man had an inside, and wondered whether he should see more of him.
>
> (*Chapter 5*)

Strachey's own response to Forster seems to have been a reserved one for years. It was Strachey who invented the nickname 'taupe'— 'mole'—for him, to express Forster's elusiveness and self-effacement, interrupted by sudden appearances focusing the attention of those about him. Keynes seems to have shared Strachey's puzzlement, but while he and Forster only remained friends at a distance, Strachey became a close friend from about 1915. He admired *Maurice*, and Forster respected his criticism.

Forster valued Bloomsbury because it continued and extended some of the Cambridge values that meant most to him, but he was reaching into relationships with individuals beyond the Bloomsbury ken, and they meant more to him than Bloomsbury, as a milieu, did.

Other relationships

Throughout his life Forster had a number of friends among contemporary writers, Forrest Reid and T.E. Lawrence—'Lawrence of Arabia'—among them. Most of these relationships were easy and genial, but one in particular was complex and challenging, and perhaps, if only for that reason, the most interesting of them all. This was with D.H. Lawrence. It began well; Forster records their first meeting in a letter to Reid (who did not like Lawrence's writings) in January 1915:

> O my dear Reid, I have been in the most awful gloom lately, and who do you think raised me from it? You will be so contemptuous of me. D.H. Lawrence. Not the words, but their author, a sandy

haired passionate Nibelung, whom I met last Thursday at a dinner party. He is really extraordinarily nice.

The dinner party was given by Lady Ottoline Morrell, a rich, lavish, eccentric woman who made it her vocation to be a patroness of the arts in the Renaissance style, and who had decided to 'launch' Lawrence and his wife Frieda in cultured society; Lawrence himself was not yet well known, though he had published *The White Peacock* and *Sons and Lovers*. He and Forster took to each other mutually; each found in the other that inner reality which Forster did not always find in Bloomsbury and Lawrence never did; in Furbank's words, Lawrence was 'so human, so personal; he *lived* his views, with none of that pose of detachment that bored him in Cambridge philosophizing'.

Then they quarrelled. Lawrence believed in home truths, thought that Forster was denying by his way of life his own essential reality, and told him so at length. Forster listened grimly, and then asked Lawrence if there was anything at all he could praise in his works, and Lawrence conceded the character of Leonard Bast in *Howards End*. It is interesting that by doing so he picked on a character whose social circumstances were close to his own but outside Forster's. It is a type that features in the work of other novelists of the period, notably H.G. Wells's *Mr Polly*. Wells attempted, as Forster did, to show how such a character might overcome his deprivations, not in the conventional way by promoting himself in the social structure, but by realising his own inner freedom. Wells, however, attempted this by a stratagem not far from fantasy, whereas Forster shows Bast's struggle and achievement as desperate and tragic, and Lawrence may have felt that the character had analogy with his own self-portrait as Paul Morel in *Sons and Lovers*. If so, one can diagnose part of the barrier between the two men; Forster had endured his own deprivations, but they were not social ones; by entering Bast's world he had invaded foreign territory, as Lawrence was a foreigner to Forster's own.

Both Frieda and Lady Ottoline tried to make peace between them, and peace was made, but the friendship did not grow, though both continued to feel concern with and interest in each other. Lawrence continued to believe that Forster was denying essential life in himself; as we shall see, even *A Passage to India* did not convert him. However, his impact on Forster was positive inasmuch as it made him more aware of the deviousness and shyness in his own nature, and he became more outspoken about his feelings. He himself admired Lawrence's writings increasingly—on his death in 1930, Forster was one of the very few writers publicly to lament the loss to contemporary literature. But he thought that Lawrence blinded himself to his own homosexual

At Lady Ottoline's, 1917–18. From left to right: Ottoline Morrell, Maria Nys, Lytton Strachey, Duncan Grant, Vanessa Bell

side. This was probably not true; the suppressed opening chapter to *Women in Love* (in Phoenix II) shows that Lawrence was very much aware of his own sexual ambivalence. However, Lawrence himself seems to have been curiously blind to Forster's homosexuality, or at least to the strength of it. 'He tries to dodge himself', he wrote to Bertrand Russell; 'But why can't he act? Why can't he take a woman and fight clear to his own basic primal being?'

> Because he knows that self-realisation is not his ultimate desire. His ultimate desire is for the continued action which has been called the social passion—the love for humanity—the desire to work for humanity.

The diagnosis is strangely wrong, and yet it has remarkable truth in it as well. It is wrong chiefly because it shows no understanding of the extent to which Forster felt that his homosexuality crippled him at the same time as he felt it to be irremediable. In 1904 he registered his condition, as he felt it then, in his diary:

> I'd better eat my soul for I certainly shan't have it. I'm going to be a minority [the term he used for homosexuality] if not a solitary, and I'd best make copy out of my position. There is nothing contemptible or cynical in this. I too have sweet waters though I shall never drink them. So I can understand the drought of others, though they will not understand my abstinence.

The secret confession points up the ways in which Lawrence both understood and misunderstood him. He was one of those who could not understand the cause of Forster's 'abstinence', but he saw clearly that though he could not free himself he had the deepest concern for the freedom of others—the 'social passion'—though Forster himself would never have called it that. Social passions usually go with political passions, and in 'What I Believe' he showed his detestation of those. But all his writings reveal the still deeper faith that the individual must find himself, that he can only do so through other individuals, and that he must affirm and assert what he finds.

That he believed himself to be irremediably crippled is evident from his self-portrait in Rickie Elliot (*The Longest Journey*) who is—for no reason obvious to a reader who does not know Forster's secret—a physical cripple. Perhaps it also helps to explain his special interest in Herman Melville's *Billy Budd*, which he praises in *Aspects of the Novel* ('Prophecy'), and which Benjamin Britten made into one of his finest operas in 1949, with Eric Crozier and Forster as librettists. As Forster describes Billy in *Aspects*, he is 'a handsome young sailor' with

> goodness of the glowing aggressive sort which cannot exist unless it has evil to consume. He is not himself aggressive. It is the light within him that irritates and explodes. On the surface he is a pleasant, merry, rather insensitive lad, whose physique is marred by one slight defect, a stammer which finally destroys him.

His antagonist is one of the petty officers, Claggart, whose evil nature deeply resents Billy's natural goodness. He accuses Billy of inciting mutiny, and Billy is so outraged at the lie that his stammer overcomes him; unable to speak, he strikes Claggart with such force that he kills him, and is subsequently executed for murder. What impressed Forster about the story was that Melville's 'apprehensions are free from personal worry, so that we become bigger not smaller after sharing them'. He has, in fact, a disinterestedness which rises above what is personal in the petty sense so as to raise the personal to a tragic plane of dignity. It is not that Forster identifies with Billy as he does with his own character, Rickie, though it is interesting that Billy too is crippled by a physical defect; Billy is on the contrary mentally and physically Forster's antithesis, more what he wished to show in Stephen Wonham, Rickie's half-brother. But it is precisely moral sympathy with what is physically and psychologically antithetic to oneself that promotes Melville's kind of disinterestedness, by the emancipation from 'personal worry'. To a homosexual temperament, such a contrast may indeed have a physical appeal corresponding to the difference of sex in a heterosexual relationship, and Forster was subject to that too; it is the cause of artistic weakness in both *The Longest Journey* and *Maurice*. But that tendency need not invalidate the disinterestedness of friendship. Biographically, Forster seems to have had a number of such passionately disinterested friendships with other men, notably with Bob Buckingham, the policeman turned probation officer who was his friend in later life, and earlier with the Moslem lawyer Masood, who was the basis for the character of Aziz in *A Passage to India*.

The mention of both men takes us well away from the Apostles and Bloomsbury. Both circles were élites, and Forster believed in élites— 'the aristocracy of the sensitive'—but the exclusiveness evident in their confidence of superiority did not satisfy what he meant by an élite; their human foundations were too narrow for what they arrogated to themselves. To be worthy of a truly human élite, an individual must enlarge himself beyond such congenial shelters, and such enlargement came to Forster by his travels and familiarisation, beyond not only Bloomsbury but England, with alien cultures. This, for him, was the 'action' that Lawrence desired for him, though he took it in his own, not Lawrence's way.

Travels

'Travel narrows the mind' is one of G.K. Chesterton's aphorisms, reversing the cliché; he meant that most travellers carry with them their national prepossessions, see what confirms these, and return more bigoted than when they set out. Even Forster may not have been exempt from the charge, but on the whole he was the genuine traveller, whose mind travels further than his body and assimilates what he cannot receive from the scope of his native culture.

His important travels corresponded with the most important period of his literary achievement—the twenty years from 1901 to 1921. His visits to Italy in 1901 and to Greece in 1902 sparked his creative fiction, as we shall see in the section on his stories. Such fertilisation was possible to him because he went to those countries not in the spirit of visiting museums of European art, nor as an Englishman disposed to abase himself beneath or arrogate himself above countries whose past grandeur had dwindled into present poverty. Nor did he make the futile gesture of trying to forget that he was English at all. All these mistakes are in fact picked out for satire in his fiction. His Englishness remained, but he opened it to the native Italian and Greek virtues both of the past and of the present, so as to enlarge his sympathies and to awaken his mind to new imaginative possibilities. Thus he developed one of his distinctive characteristics as a novelist: his use of criteria for living still available in certain foreign cultures but lost to, or dormant in our own, so establishing a critical standpoint for assessing English ways of life. It is thus that he uses Italy in *Where Angels Fear to Tread* and *A Room with a View*, and Greece in some of his stories, notably 'The Road to Colonus'. Germany, which, as we have seen, he visited in 1905 as tutor to Elizabeth von Arnim's children, meant less to him, and yet that too may have contributed to his portrayal of the Schlegel family in *Howards End*, in which a Germanic view of culture is contrasted with English philistinism. Still more important, however, than these European visits were the longer ones beyond Europe.

From late in 1915 until early in 1919 he did war-service for the Red Cross in Egypt, where he learnt to dislike British methods of imperial government, developed an important literary friendship with the Greek poet Cavafy whose work he made known to the British public on his return, and had his first serious homosexual relationship with an Egyptian tram driver, Mohammed-el-Adl, with whom he kept up friendship after he left. He wrote an attractive guide book to Alexandria while he was there, and some essays published under the title of *Pharos and Pharillon* in 1923. The long stay in Egypt was important to him chiefly because it meant emancipation from ties with Britain and his mother, enabling him to achieve a new independence in body and mind, but it was not so important as his two visits to India in 1912 and 1921. *The Hill of Devi*, published in 1953, is composed from letters linked by comment and written during both visits, but especially the second.

The first visit was one of pleasure, motivated partly by his friendship with Masood, whom he had met in England in 1910. He went out in the company of three friends from his Cambridge days, one of whom, Goldsworthy Lowes Dickinson, was a fellow of King's and had been one of Forster's mentors there. Dickinson came out to see India in its political and social conditions, but Forster wanted to get to know Indians and to explore their imaginative universe. Accordingly he parted from his friends on arrival, travelling north to visit Masood at Aligarh, where Masood's grandfather had founded a famous Moslem college. There he found himself immediately immersed in Moslem politics, since the college had become a centre of Moslem nationalism. But he did not only meet Moslems; he went on to travel extensively in north and north-west India as far as Peshawar, sometimes with friends he had made in England, such as Malcolm Darling who was working in Lahore as a magistrate, and also meeting Hindus. Notable among these were two Maharajahs—of Dewas Senior, a unique, unstable personality with whom he was to develop one of his strong attachments, and of Chhaturpur, who had a passionate though ingenuous interest in religion and western philosophy. He saw some of the great Indian sights as well as others less known, such as the Barabar caves near Bankipore in Bengal, which he was to transmute into the Marabar caves of *A Passage to India*. That they needed transmutation is evident from his letter describing them, which shows his impression of them to be rather less unusual than that made by the caves in the novel:

The caves are cut out of the solid granite; a small square doorway and an oval hall inside. This sounds dull, but the granite has been so

Goldsworthy Lowes Dickinson (1862–1932), Fellow of King's when Forster was undergraduate, and later one of his closest friends

splendidly polished that they rank very high among caves for cheerfulness. Date—250 B.C.; as early as anything in India. One of them has a frieze of elephants over the door, but in the rest the only decoration is the fine Pali inscriptions on the sides of the entrance tunnel. Standing inside one sees them in the strong sunlight, and beyond the view. We lit candles which showed the grain of the granite and its reds and greys. The nephews also tried to wake the echoes, but whatever was said and in whatever voice the cave only returned a dignified roar.

He finished his tour with a visit to the great central state of Hyderabad, partly hosted by May Wyld, an enterprising Englishwoman who ran a school for Indian girls. Her reports on him show that he may not have been entirely immune to Chesterton's gibe. She told him that he misunderstood and underrated the difficulties of English officials in their relations with Indians, and reported:

Morgan had got a few introductions to Indian homes in north India. Later on I heard one or two comments on his visits. They had wondered what the English visitor wanted to know. They did not find him as easy to talk to as the Englishmen who lived in India.

(P.N. Furbank, *E.M. Forster: A Life*, vol. 1)

Forster was far from being a unique example of an English liberal failing to communicate where the type-cast 'oppressive' official is more successful. On the other hand the official relationship is often conducted in a code of language and behaviour acceptable to both parties; the liberal refuses a code of the official kind, and cannot be held to blame for any perplexity he arouses in consequence.

Forster was certainly not a superficial traveller, but he travelled in his own way. Not only did he confirm his long friendship with Masood, but he made new friends with Indians, both Moslem and Hindu, and where other liberals investigated the political surface of India, he explored its culture and its literature. The visit inspired *A Passage to India*, but what sort of novel it would have produced we cannot know, for the war came, and after it his second visit, both of which changed the character of his writing, causing him to write the novel in a different way.

In 1921 he went in a different capacity. On his first visit he had met more Moslems; now he wished to cultivate the Hindus, and he was to be private secretary to the Maharajah of Dewas Senior in the temporary absence of the previous secretary, Colonel Leslie. Dewas Senior was a small state in Central India, comically intertwined with its neighbour, Dewas Junior, which was ruled by another branch of the same family. It seems appropriate almost to improbability that a man of Forster's idiosyncrasy should be employed in a state so freakish in its geographical structure, and in the service of a ruler whose own character was unique and self-contradictory. The society was hierarchical, with four grades of nobles, Forster ranking with the lowest; its affairs were overseen by two British officials, the Agent to the Governor-General and the Political Agent, in relationship to both of whom Forster was to regard himself as an Indian. His own duties were, however, not political; it was his function to supervise the palace garden and tennis courts, the garages and the palace electricity supply, the mail and the guest-house; above all he was to serve as the Maharajah's personal companion. Such a role gave him intimacy with this Hindu microcosm exactly as he wanted, but the duties were not as easy as they seemed, chiefly because the Maharajah was an incorrigible muddler. He inhabited the New Palace, the tasteless construction of which had been begun during Forster's previous visit, and yet it was not only unfinished but in parts falling down. Moreover the finances of the country were in confusion, and its ruler burdened with increasing debt. Intrigue was as insidious and ubiquitous as the snakes. On the other hand the Maharajah was a charming host who entertained Masood like a visiting prince, and deeply understood Forster's nature including his homosexuality. His absence of taste embarrassed Forster, and the confusion of his affairs distressed him, but his friendship compensated for very much, and so did the religious festivals, especially that of Gokul Ashtami—the Feast of Krishna—which is clearly the basis for the religious festival in chapter 33 of *A Passage to India*, its climactic episode as it was of Forster's stay in Dewas. Nevertheless the material difficulties forced him to terminate the stay after eight months; he did not feel competent to help his employer who so much needed help. He could not even see how he could be helped; nor, apparently, could anybody else. He summed up the relationship in a letter to his mother in November 1921:

I hated leaving him, but it is his tragedy not to know how to employ people, and I could not feel it any use to go on muddling with work that gave no satisfaction, and was of no essential importance to him. The things of this life mean so little to him—mean something so different any way—I never feel certain what he likes, or even whether he likes me: consideration for others so often simulates affection in him. I only know that he is one of the sweetest and saintliest men I have ever known . . . .

He spent the last two months in a different human climate, in company with Masood and his Moslem friends. This was a world he again understood; he wrote in another letter that, standing on a minaret of the Taj Mahal

I knew at all events *where* I stood and *what* I heard; it was a land that was not merely atmosphere but had definite outlines and horizons. So with the Mohammedan friends of Masood whom I am meeting now. They may not be as subtle or suggestive as the Hindus, but I can follow what they are saying.

The sage

Forster returned to England early in 1922; in 1924 *A Passage to India* was published and acclaimed. He was only forty-six, and he lived to the age of ninety-two, but his career as a novelist was at an end. It is true that he did not cease to write. He accomplished two fine biographies, issued two volumes of essays of wide range, and a famous serious of lectures on the art of the novel; he wrote the greater part of the libretto of *Billy Budd*. This is to mention only his salient work. Of his literary journalism, the literary editor of *The Listener*, J.H. Ackerley, remarked: 'If you could land him for an article, or a book-review, you landed the whale and were the envy of every other literary editor in London.' His high reputation also brought him into public activity; in 1934 he became the first President of the National Council of Civil Liberties; in 1935 he headed the British delegation to the International Congress of Writers in Paris; he became a noted broadcaster. He was also prominent in the activities of PEN—the International Association of Poets, Playwrights, Editors, Essayists and Novelists—presiding over its conference in London in 1944 and going on its behalf on his third and last visit to India in 1945. He received public honours—was offered a knighthood in 1949, but refused it, and received the Order of Merit in 1969.

Such a record is evidence, first, of the continuance of a valuable literary career, and secondly, of high reputation, but it suggests puzzles. The writings, however valuable, were after all no longer of the first distinction; one might expect, on their evidence alone, a gradual fading of prestige; instead it was remarked that Forster became more and more famous with every book he did not write. The fact is that Forster attained the reputation of being the great liberal sage of the inter-war and post-war periods. What exactly is implied by that status must await consideration until we have given attention to the English liberal tradition which he sustained, and to the characteristics of his critical writings which were the products of it. What we can notice here is that the growth of his reputation had much to do with the consistency of his development, with the freshness and youthfulness which never deserted either his personality or his writings, and with his ability to sustain community with the reading public without the vulgarity of cultivating a popular style and without adulterating his beliefs. The Bloomsbury generation and its contemporaries had had prestige but they had also provoked a sense of distance in the common reader; Forster had shared the prestige but never seemed remote. Moreover, many of the writers important in the first quarter of the century had come to seem, to the generations of the thirties and after, either naive in their leftism, like Shaw and Wells, or politically irresponsible in their cultural liberalism, like Bloomsbury, or at the unacceptable end of the political spectrum, like Eliot and Wyndham Lewis. Forster shared Bloomsbury liberalism without communicating the impression they conveyed that culture resembles the ownership of a private estate, and he never compromised his liberalism by flirting with either wing of political extremism. This made him not only respected by but congenial to the new generation of left-wing writers—Auden, Isherwood, Spender, MacNeice, Day Lewis and Calder Marshall—who felt homeless without a doctrine, and yet could see that he was standing firmer on his shifting sands than they were. Thus he was able to preserve continuities in the last fifty years of his life to an extent that few leading British personalities achieved in that half century of dissolution.

The continuities were symbolised by his own living places. In 1925 he moved with his mother to West Hackhurst, the house built by the father he never knew for his favourite aunt Laura. He held the house under a lease which was continued till his mother's death in 1945; then King's, the college where he had first found his true identity, made him an Honorary Fellow, and he lived there for the rest of his life. It was an unusual step, though not unprecedented at King's, especially because the position entailed no duties: 'I hold no College office,' he remarked in a speech, 'I attend no committee; I sit on no body, however solid, not even on the Annual Congregation; I co-opt not, neither am I co-opted; I teach not, neither do I think . . . .' However, he was personally accessible as anything but a literary mandarin; still proud to be a member of an élite, but refusing exclusiveness and rejecting worship.

He lived on for twenty-five years, and in the first ten of these he continued active, collaborating in the libretto for *Billy Budd*, writing the life of Marianne Thornton and lecturing in America. Thereafter he became quiescent; his most conspicuous public appearance was at the court case on *Lady Chatterley's Lover* in 1960, in which his evidence against the charge of obscenity had his characteristic force and lucidity. But he never became a mere monument, nor did his personality fade from public memory; his vitality in relationship continued to the end.

5 Breaking the circles: the short stories

In his lifetime, Forster issued two volumes of short stories: *The Celestial Omnibus* in 1911 and *The Eternal Moment* in 1928; a third volume, *The Life to Come*, containing hitherto unpublished work, some of it early and the remainder written between 1922 and 1958, came out after his death, in 1972.

Unlike the stories of some of his distinguished contemporaries—Lawrence, Joyce, James, Conrad, Wells—Forster's do not contain some of his best work; if he had not written the novels, the stories would very likely be forgotten. This, however, is not to say that they are negligible; they have the freshness and wit that all readers find in his novels, and, although they are much slighter in substance, they have the interest of epitomising his developing thought in a simplified form, so that they become a helpful preface to his longer and more subtle work. The earliest of them are especially helpful, since they reveal his fictional imagination as it begins to take shape in practice. We shall consider four: 'The Story of a Panic' (1902), 'The Road from Colonus' (1903), 'The Eternal Moment' (1904), and 'The Machine Stops' (1908). The first of these has already been mentioned; it deserves particular attention not only because it was Forster's first authentic inspiration but because it foreshadows themes which he was to develop more fully and more deviously in the novels.

'The Story of a Panic'

'The Story of a Panic' is told from the point of view of its fictional narrator; he is a prim, sincere, but decidedly muddled English tourist called Mr Tytler, staying at an inn in Ravello with his wife and daughter. His fellow English tourists are an amateur painter, Mr Leyland; a fourteen-year-old boy called Eustace Robinson; Eustace's two aunts; and his tutor—a curate called Mr Sandbach. Eustace is the centre of the story, and he seems to have some of the characteristics of Forster himself as an adolescent: he is clumsy and withdrawn and not at all the type approved of by public schools such as Tonbridge—'he neither played hard nor worked hard' is Mr Tytler's comment on him, and he is over-indulged by his aunts. While his elders lay out 'a not very nice' picnic (prepared by the unsatisfactory temporary waiter Gennaro) at the head of the valley, Eustace sulkily withdraws to cut for himself a whistle from the bark of one of the trees. The picnic is finished, the tourists grow somnolent, and then Eustace blows his whistle.

Leyland, who had apparently been asleep, sat up. 'It is astonishing how blind a boy is to anything that is elevating or beautiful,' he observed. 'I should not have thought he could have found the wherewithal out here to spoil our pleasure like this.' Then the terrible silence fell on us again. I was now standing up and watching a cat's paw of wind that was running down one of the ridges opposite, turning the light green to dark as it travelled. A fanciful feeling of foreboding came over me; so I turned away, to find to my amazement, that all the others were also on their feet, watching it too.

Then the panic begins. The tourists suddenly take to flight—all except Eustace. And what has happened to him?

This much seems to have come to Forster in the same valley in the May of 1902—the story that 'seemed unfinished' so that he expanded it to three times its length. The expansion shows that what was a panic for his elders was a release for Eustace, who becomes a physically joyous being; his friendship with Gennaro, the fisherman turned waiter, who alone understands him; and the attempts of Mr Tytler and the other tourists to restrain him once more in the straitjacket of his repressions; his escape, and the death of Gennaro after Mr Tytler has subjected him to obtuse maltreatment. The story becomes too explicit, explaining more than can be explained; it is the first chapter which has power and which reveals most about Forster's inspiration. This shows itself in two ways—his attitude to character and to culture, and the nature of the 'panic'.

The characterisation in this early story is inevitably sketchy, and yet Tytler, Leyland and Sandbach are shrewdly differentiated. All three are typically English middle class, but each is a distinct type within that category. Tytler describes himself as 'a plain, simple man, with no pretensions to literary style', but it is clear that he considers his limitations to be virtues and that he has small respect for virtues beyond his compass. He despises the artist, Leyland, who enjoys exposing the ignorance and philistinism of the rest of the company and inveighs against the commercial despoliation of the environment:

And because these few trees were cut down, Leyland burst into a petty indictment of the proprietor.

'All the poetry is going from Nature,' he cried, 'her lakes and marshes are drained, her seas banked up, her forests cut down. Everywhere we see the vulgarity of desolation spreading.'

I have had some experience of estates, and answered that cutting was very necessary for the health of the larger trees. Besides, it was unreasonable to expect the proprietor to derive no income from his lands.

'If you take the commercial side of landscape, you may feel

pleasure in the owner's activity. But to me the mere thought that a tree is convertible into cash is disgusting.'

'I see no reason,' I observed politely, 'to despise the gifts of Nature because they are of value.'

The brief argument foreshows what is to be a characteristic of discussions in the novels. Both men are right in their statements, but both are wrong in the points of view from which they make them. Facts are not truths when the statement of them is wrongly motivated; it is cultural vanity which motivates Leyland, and self-satisfaction which motivates the practical but morally short-sighted Tytler. And now Mr Sandbach, the curate, removes the conversation one stage further from the truth:

> 'Pan!' cried Mr Sandbach, his mellow voice filling the valley as if it had been a great green church, 'Pan is dead. That is why the woods do not shelter him.'

In imaginative terms, he is expressing what religious believers and unbelievers might equally accept as a spiritual fact. But the 'fact' is not a truth because it is his gift for exposition that concerns him, not what he is expounding.

These are the dominant figures in the circle surrounding the gauche, repressed, sullen boy Eustace. His aunts appear to be silly women whose indulgence cushions his isolation without releasing him from it. All the adults are settled in assurances of their own personal adequacy afforded by their society; only Tytler's still unformed daughter Rose shows a glimmer of insight into what has happened, and only the primitive Gennaro has full understanding of how Eustace has been shocked by the 'panic' into life.

And how are we meant to understand this event? Its stimulus in the menacingly still, hot, noonday landscape is evidently Eustace's whistle: 'I have never heard' (remarks Mr Tytler) 'any instrument give forth so ear-splitting and discordant a sound.' It is followed by the 'cat's paw of wind' approaching over the forest, and it is this which precipitates the general flight. The shock is as great for Eustace: when they return, they find him physically prostrated, but then he astonishes the adults by waking from his trance irradiated by a manic joy. Poetically speaking, he is possessed by the god Pan, whom Sandbach and Leyland have just been unctuously mourning, but the story is not just a poetic whimsy. Nature—including human nature—has forces of which the English tourists, typically shielded by their comfortable fortress, refuse to take cognisance, and cognisance of such forces is central to the possession of a valid culture. The Greeks, who had one, gave the name of Pan to such forces; that we have discovered no other names for them was Forster's pretext for his fantasy. Eustace's transformation is at first meaningless to the adults, and then a menace:

they are unable at first to conceive, and then to tolerate a force of influence beyond the circle—and the circles within that circle—which have secured them their factitious identities, and this is true not only of Tytler whose world is that of common sense, but also of Leyland and Sandbach who only profess to believe in other worlds.

'The Road from Colonus'

'The Road from Colonus', written a year later, has a comparable but more subtle theme and is better executed. An elderly man, Mr Lucas, is walking in Greece; getting ahead of his party, he finds himself at a lonely *khan* or country inn. For the first time he finds himself at peace, in enjoyment of the scene. Hitherto he had been disappointed:

> Forty years ago he had caught the fever of Hellenism, and all his life he had felt that could he but visit that land, he would not have lived in vain. But Athens had been dusty, Delphi hot, Thermopylae flat, and he had listened with amazement and cynicism to the rapturous exclamations of his companions. Greece was like England; it was a man growing old, and it made no difference whether that man looked at the Thames or the Eurotas. It was his last hope of contradicting that logic of experience, and it was failing.

All the same, the experience had not been so negative as he was supposing: 'It had made him discontented, and there are stirrings of life in discontent.' Standing among the plane trees that surround the inn, he decides that he will fight back against his atrophy, and recover the sources of his life. Then he notices a hollow tree from out of which a spring of water is gushing; what looks like a miracle has been acknowledged to be such by the country people, who have cut a shrine to the virgin into its rind. He steps into the tree and reclines back within it.

> There was meaning in the stoop of the old woman over her work, and in the quick motions of the little pig, and in her diminishing globe of wool. A young man came singing over the streams on a mule, and there was beauty in his pose and sincerity in his greeting. The sun made no accidental patterns upon the spreading roots of the trees, and there was intention in the nodding clumps of asphodel, and in the music of the water. To Mr Lucas, who, in a brief space of time, had discovered not only Greece, but England and all the world and life, there seemed nothing ludicrous in the desire to hang within the tree another votive offering—a little model of an entire man.
>
> 'Why, here's papa, playing at being Merlin.'

This is the voice of his manageering daughter, Ethel, who appears with the rest of Mr Lucas's party. They are in raptures at the beauty of the place, and laugh at the stiff and formal phrases with which he tries to

43

express his appreciation of it. The truth is that they are not sharing the same experience: theirs is a touristic delight; his has been religious.

It is when he tries to insist on staying at the inn that conflict begins: Ethel declares it to be quite impossible—the beds have bugs in them. Mr Lucas is tricked away, and once gone, he returns to his elderly peevishness and hopelessness.

The last episode is back in England. Mr Lucas is complaining about his bad night, and Ethel, weary but as ever dutiful, listens patiently. Then she reads an old Greek newspaper that has been sent to them, and learns that on the very night of their visit to the inn, the building had been crushed by the huge hollow tree falling upon it.

> 'Such a marvellous deliverance does make one believe in Providence.'
>
> Mr Lucas, who was still composing his letter to the landlord, did not reply.

The title of the story relates it to the play by Sophocles, written when he was himself an old man, *Oedipus at Colonus*. The aged, blind Oedipus, at the end of his terrible life, comes with the aid of his daughter to a sacred place, from which he is taken up to their abode by the gods. They redeem him not because he has been guiltless, nor because they have been excessively ruthless to his guilt, but because, through all his sufferings, he has never closed his heart to them. In the story, Mr Lucas' daughter leads her father away from redemption, and afterwards she rejoices at saving the life of a useless and life-weary old man, whom she does not love, because she is locked within the circle of her conventional sense of filial duty. Forster's first story had been about successful escape from adolescent repression; his second was about failure to break out of elderly depression. In both, Forster is concerned with the sources of life, and he is equating these with the sources of a living culture.

When Forster was writing 'The Eternal Moment' in 1904, he was already engaged on his first novel. He had by now subdued his tendency to fantasy, though he returned to it later in such stories as 'The Celestial Omnibus', 'The Machine Stops' and 'The Point of It'. Fantasy, dominant in 'The Story of a Panic', is only implicit in 'The Road from Colonus', and is absent from this new story.

'The Eternal Moment'

An elderly novelist, Miss Raby, pays a visit with her maid and a male friend, Colonel Leyland, to an Italian village which had been the setting for her first novel, with the same title as Forster's story. The novel had been a best-seller (though she now despises its immaturity) and had made the fortune of the village, transforming it into a tourist centre. She is dismayed by the resulting opulent vulgarity of the place, and disgusted to find that a rivalry has existed between the now neglected Albergo Biscione, once the only inn, where she had put up as a young woman, and the ostentatious Grand Hôtel des Alpes, owned by the son of the proprietess of the Albergo. She recognises the fat and competent concierge of the Grand Hôtel to be the Italian peasant boy, formerly employed by the Albergo, who had once made love to her

> For she realised that only now was she not in love with him: that the incident on the mountain had been one of the greatest moments of her life—perhaps the greatest, certainly the most enduring: that she had drawn unacknowledged power and inspiration from it, just as trees draw vigour from a subterranean spring.

To his understandable embarrassment, she forces the concierge to recognise her and tries to persuade him to allow her to adopt his youngest son. He is tempted by the profit he might hope from this, but then he realises the possible scandal and refuses. Colonel Leyland misunderstands the relationship, supposing that she is still in love with the concierge. On perceiving this, she sees through the Colonel:

> Here was a man who was well born and well educated, who had all those things called advantages, who imagined himself full of insight and cultivation and knowledge of mankind. And he had proved himself to be at the exact spiritual level of the man who had no advantages, who was poor and had been made vulgar, whose early virtue had been destroyed by circumstance, whose manliness and simplicity had perished in serving the rich.

Nonetheless, for Miss Raby, the renewed encounter is not mere disillusionment:

> In that moment of final failure, there had been vouchsafed to her a vision of herself, and she saw that she had lived worthily. She was conscious of a triumph over experience and earthly facts, a triumph magnificent, cold, hardly human, whose existence no one but herself would ever surmise.

'The Eternal Moment' is more sophisticated but less well achieved than the other two stories. Forster does not show us quite enough: Colonel Leyland's mistake is understandable and his concern for proprieties more reasonable than Forster wishes us to believe. All the same, the story represents an advance. He is not now concerned with the immature human being whose need is to overcome the restraints against his development, but with the mature being whose escape is far in the past, and who is capable of meeting the challenge of disillusionment. Only in the last two of the novels published in his lifetime does Forster return to this difficult but far-reaching theme.

One characteristic the three stories share: the transfiguring experience which in religious history has been known as the 'epiphany'. Forster's own description of how the first two stories came to him (Introduction to *The Collected Short Stories*) shows his belief that the epiphanic experience has, or can have, much to do with the act of literary creation, but the novels treat its influence in ordinary lives. In strictly religious terms, the epiphany is a supernatural experience; it is so presented in 'The Story of a Panic' and—less distinctly—in 'The Road from Colonus'; in 'The Eternal Moment' the supernatural is eliminated, but Miss Raby's experience has not been the less intense to her for that reason. Forster lost his faith in orthodox Christianity at Cambridge and became an agnostic, but the loss was intellectual rather than emotional. His sense of a religious dimension to living is implicit in all his novels, and becomes explicit in *A Passage to India*.

'*The Machine Stops*'

This sense of a religious dimension to life is indeed explicit in the last story we shall consider: 'The Machine Stops'. This is his best known, probably because of the current popularity of science fiction, and for Forster it constituted, as he says in his Introduction to *The Collected Short Stories*, 'a reaction to one of the earlier heavens of H.G. Wells'. Its immediate stimulus, however, was not Wells's writing but a technological achievement: on January 13, 1908, Henri Farman succeeded in flying an aircraft over a circuit of one kilometre in one and a half minutes. The event depressed Forster deeply, as his biographer records by a passage from his diary:

> It is coming quickly, and if I live to be old I shall see the sky as pestilential as the roads. I have been born at the end of the age of peace and can't expect to feel anything but despair. Science, instead of freeing man—the Greeks nearly freed him by right feeling—is enslaving him to machines ... Man may get a new and perhaps a greater soul for the new condition. But such a soul as mine will be crushed out.

In the story he depicts a world, many civilisations in the future, in which human beings are seeking to achieve this 'new and greater soul' by living entirely in terms of ideas; 'direct experience', like the sunlight, becomes abhorrent, and as the story proceeds even first-hand ideas come to be seen as undesirable; not only are second-hand ones preferable but tenth-hand ones far better still. Humanity, its physicality reduced as far as compatibility with survival allows, becomes a system of ideas, living by and worshipping the one great Idea, which is the Machine.

The entire population of this world—no longer differentiated by race or nationality—lives beneath the surface of the earth in a vast network of galleries, each individual in a separate cell which is provided with a communication system to any other individual with whom he or she may wish to relate: 'She knew several thousand people; in certain directions human intercourse had advanced enormously.' Personal confrontations, except, as we would say, televisually, are rare, and physical contact is taboo. It is not missed, since the mechanised communications are almost instantaneous. Physical needs are provided for with equal mechanical efficiency although the satisfaction is standardised, as are the human images:

> ... the Machine did not transmit nuances of expression. It only gave a general idea of people—an idea that was good enough for all practical purposes, Vashti thought. The imponderable bloom, declared by a discredited philosophy to be the actual essence of intercourse, was rightly ignored by the Machine, just as the imponderable bloom of the grape was ignored by the manufacturers of artificial fruit. Something 'good enough' had long since been accepted by our race.

Everything, in short, is manufactured, including the atmosphere. Visits to the earth's surface are allowed, but only by special egression permits, and they are rare and require respirators. However, a network of airborne machines still operates over the globe, not so much because it is needed as because it is intrinsic to the system. The surface has been abandoned as uninhabitable and without appeal; even air travel offers no excitement:

> 'No ideas here,' murmured Vashti, and hid the Caucasus behind a metal blind.

Except when she is travelling by airship, Vashti, the character representative of this civilisation, is content: she broadcasts lectures, is an audience for them, listens to music, exchanges ideas and lives for them. However, her son Kuno is a nonconformist; he breaks on to the earth's surface without an egression permit, and he sees 'the man in the sky' (the constellation of Orion) which inspires him with the beginnings of religious feelings. He also conceives that the Machine will one day stop. This is unimaginable to his mother, whose own religious instincts are satisfied by the Book of the Machine—the only book available to its inhabitants. He is nevertheless proved right: the Machine functions with increasing inefficiency, and the great anonymous committees which are supposed to govern it lose control. Only Kuno correctly diagnoses the sources of the breakdown. 'Cannot you see,' he asks his mother,

> cannot all you lecturers see, that it is we that are dying, and that down here the only thing that really lives is the Machine? We created the Machine, to do our will, but we cannot make it do our will now. It has robbed us of the sense of space and the sense of touch, it has blurred every human relation and narrowed down love to a carnal act, it has paralysed our bodies and our wills, and now it compels us to worship it. The Machine develops—but not on our lines. The Machine proceeds—but not to our goal. We only exist as

the blood corpuscles that course through its arteries, and if it could work without us, it would let us die.

This scarcely convinces as colloquial speech, but as rhetoric about an aspect of the human predicament in the twentieth century it is still more persuasive now than it can have seemed in 1908. Forster was writing before the age of broadcasting, well before television, and long before the silicon chip, and yet he anticipates the possible consequences of such technology although he understood nothing about the technology itself. He was not indeed unique in his foresight; H.G. Wells, who knew far more science and was by no means the mechanical optimist that Forster and kindred spirits seem to have thought him, was far his superior as a progenitor of science fiction. Forster, however, knew better than Wells what values in the human condition were vulnerable to technological forces, and in that sense 'The Machine Stops' is worth more than any of Wells's better informed works of imagination. And yet we have the irony that this story, which is in essence a diatribe against living by ideas instead of by direct experience, should itself depend for its interest on the ideas that it presents.

'It does not strike me as a very good idea, but it is certainly original,' Vashti remarks, when Kuno describes to her his glimpse of Orion, 'the man in the sky'. For us, it is not even original; it is the child's conception of the Christian God, a concept outworn for most modern adults, and original for Vashti only because it had been relegated long before her time as a dead superstition not even worth study by the disciples of the Machine. But for Forster the image seems to have been important, and despite his agnosticism he is not afraid of renewing it. In *Howards End* he repeats the image in reference to the dismal anonymity of London's crowds:

> London is religion's opportunity—not the decorous religion of the theologians, but anthropomorphic, crude. Yes, the continuous flow would be tolerable if a man of our own sort—not anyone pompous or tearful—were caring for us up in the sky.
>
> (*chapter 13*)

The crowds of London and the cellular inhabitants of the Machine seem dissimilar, but they are alike in the absence of mutual physical and emotional contact between individual and individual. The universe, for Forster, must be both physically and psychically a communion, or it is meaningless. The only meaning in breaking the circles is to enable the growth of valid circles that are meaningful in personal terms. The later stories included in *The Life to Come* attempt to envisage such personal release along his homosexual bias, as he was also to do in *Maurice*. They have their distinction, but, as in that novel, he wrote them more to himself than to the common reader, with whom, in all his best fiction, he seeks the truly personal relationship.

Part Two
The Intellectual Setting

6 The liberal tradition

In his essay 'The Challenge of Our Time', Forster describes himself as belonging to 'the fag-end of Victorian Liberalism'. But the American critic, Lionel Trilling, states about him that 'For all his long commitment to the doctrines of liberalism, Forster was at war with the liberal imagination.' Trilling goes on to explain, persuasively, what he means by his judgement, but he is writing for an American public in the light of American liberal assumptions. English readers may find it more helpful to see both statements—Forster's and Trilling's—in a historical perspective. We need to ask, first, what it meant to be a Victorian liberal, and next, what sort of imagination belonged to such liberals, and what it might mean to be a liberal and yet at war with it.

Nowadays we use the word 'liberal' so loosely that, like many familiar terms, we understand it more by what it suggests than as a definition. Thus it is helpful to remember that, in the context of politics or other forms of thought, the word is a foreign import, deriving from the French Revolution with its uncompromising slogan 'Liberty, Equality, Brotherhood, or Death.' So, in the early nineteenth century when the word made its first appearance for this context in our thought, a liberal was identified as a revolutionary thinker, more usually known as a 'radical' because he attacked social institutions at their roots, with the aim of either reforming them altogether or else abolishing them and establishing new ones. The radical movement was especially inspired by the ideas of the lawyer Jeremy Bentham who died in 1832, and from him the most energetic part of it was labelled 'Utilitarian', because, as his disciple John Stuart Mill put it, he asked about any institution or idea the practical question 'What is the use of it?' and decided the correctness of policy in accordance with the answer.

This was the phase of early Victorian liberalism in the second quarter of the nineteenth century. Thereafter the movement underwent two further phases: the second in the mid-Victorian period of the third quarter, and the third, during Forster's youth, in the last quarter of the nineteenth century and the first decade of the twentieth.

In the mid-Victorian period, liberalism no longer denoted a radical minority but was adopted by one of the two great political parties. It was now rather more than the merely political philosophy of a large proportion of the British industrial and commercial middle classes, who felt behind them the force of history as manifested by the laws of nature, and by the laws of political economy which they took to be an extension of natural law. The early liberals had pushed for change in the name of reform against the inertia of stagnant tradition; the mid-

Victorians welcomed change because they equated it with material progress, and they considered progress to be caused by the release of the energies of the individual. Other large sections of the upper and middle classes accepted liberal philosophy more passively: industry needed investment, and they provided it. They flourished on investment without interesting themselves much in the sources of their wealth, content to believe that what was good for themselves was good for others, even if the immediate effects—exploitation of human need, huge, dirty and hideous urbanisation—on those others were extremely disagreeable. Consciences were appeased by a fairly easy accord with Protestant evangelical ethics, of a more passive sort than such as had inspired Forster's own forebears in the Clapham Sect. This new liberalism did not suit an old-fashioned radical like Mill, who saw that the new liberals were concerned to advance their own interests with indifference to reforms which did not advance them, such as the emancipation of women which he himself advocated.

However, changes in political and economic circumstances gradually modified mid-Victorian optimism in the last quarter of the century. Other nations, especially the Germans and the Americans, were feeling that history was on their side, and were proving successful competitors; economic organisation, besides, was becoming larger and more impersonal, more indifferent to the enterprising individual with his faith that his personal prosperity lay within the scope of his own efforts. Liberals who sought security began to change their allegiance to the Conservatives, and radical liberals, following the example of Mill who died in 1873, began to seek revival in association with the new socialist reformers, especially the Fabian Socialists who advocated socialism by legislative reform and not by revolution. These were the circles in which Forster moved, and when some of his friends founded the liberal *Independent Review* in 1903, it was there that he published his first essays and stories. Recalling the period in his biography of Lowes Dickinson he wrote:

> Those who were Liberals felt that the heavy, stocky body of their party was about to grow wings and leave the ground. Those who were not Liberals were equally filled with hope: they saw avenues opening into literature, philosophy, human relationships, and the road of the future passing through not insurmountable changes to a possible Utopia. Can you imagine decency touched with poetry? It was thus the 'Independent' appeared to us—a light rather than a fire, but a light that penetrated the emotions.

As this implies, the *Independent* was not merely political but a 'progressive' journal containing work on many subjects. Forster and Hilaire Belloc, the Catholic apologist, were its chief contributors of imaginative work, and the fact that his name was mistaken by some readers for a pseudonym of Belloc's shows how little political bias

THE INDEPENDENT REVIEW

. NO. 2

NOV. 190

CONTENTS

THE MORAL ISSUE

LABOUR AND FREE TRADE
JOHN BURNS, M.P.

PROTECTION AND LABOUR IN GERMANY   EDOUARD BERNSTEIN

PROTECTION AND THE COTTON INDUSTRY   ELIJAH HELM

"TO FOLLOW THE FISHERMAN"
A. W. VERRALL

THE BUSINESS OF THE ARMY
"SUPPLY"

ARE THE ANGLO-SAXONS DYING OUT?   HAVELOOK ELLIS

THE ECCENTRIC AUTHOR OF "SANDFORD AND MERTON"
JOHN FYVIE

MACOLNIA SHOPS
E. M. FORSTER

MR. BURDEN.   Chap. II
HILAIRE BELLOO

MR. MORLEY'S "GLADSTONE"
GEO. W. E. RUSSELL

OTHER REVIEWS

LONDON·PUBLISHED·BY
T·FISHER·UNWIN·

TWO SHILLINGS AND SIXPENCE NET

his contributions contained. In fact, Forster's liberalism always concentrated on what politicians ignored, and could not afford to ignore, in their thinking. But this emphasis was not peculiar to himself; liberalism, from near its start, had always had such liberal critics.

Mill and Arnold

The greatest of the Victorian Liberals, John Stuart Mill, came himself to see the severe limitations of liberal thought in the writings of Jeremy Bentham, the progenitor of the whole movement, and he exposed them in a famous essay in 1838. Bentham's principles were very simple: life is composed of pleasures and pains; any policy or behaviour which increased the pleasures and reduced the pains was good; what did the reverse was bad, and must be eliminated. The fallacy in this of course is that what brings pleasure is not necessarily good in its unforeseeable consequences, and pain is not necessarily bad if it produces good effects on the character of the sufferer. Mill puts the point succinctly:

> All he [Bentham] can do is but to indicate means by which, in any given state of the national mind, the material interests of society can be protected; saving the question, of which others must judge, whether the use of those means would have, on the national character, any injurious influence.
>
> (*Essay on Bentham*)

The question had to be saved for others, in Mill's opinion, because Bentham was inherently incapable of understanding any influence not assessable by practical reason. He was ignorant of, or chose to ignore:

> The sense of *honour*, and personal dignity—that feeling of personal exaltation and degradation which acts independently of other people's opinion, or even in defiance of it; the love of *beauty*, the passion of the artist; the love of *order*, of congruity, of consistency in all things, and conformity to their end; the love of *power*, not in the limited form of power over other human beings, but abstract power, the power of making our volitions effectual; the love of *action*, the thirst for movement and activity, a principle scarcely of less influence in human life than its opposite, the love of ease . . .
>
> (*Essay on Bentham*)

In short, all that an individual values within himself, as distinct from what can be calculated about his external conduct. It was a criticism which could be levelled not merely at Bentham but at many of his liberal successors, and it stands in accord with Forster's own evaluation of what is personal above what is public. However, to recognise the

Previous page *Cover of the liberal 'Independent Review' including one of Forster's earliest contributions* reality of the culture of the human spirit is one thing; to see how to nourish that culture without abandoning the demands of practical politics may be another matter. Mill himself remained fundamentally a utilitarian liberal, though with a much broader and deeper understanding of society than Bentham's, believing that the urgency of practical reform in Victorian society was so great that the more nebulous questions affecting national character would have to be postponed.

Nonetheless, another great Victorian liberal, sixteen years younger than Mill, believed that politics and culture ought not to be so divided, and that if either must take precedence in that age, then it should be the latter. This was Matthew Arnold, who described himself as 'a liberal of the future'. In his indignation against social injustice, and his resentment against the mid-Victorian Liberals for neglecting it and preferring the strengthening of their own interests, Arnold was a radical liberal and resembled Mill. He particularly despised the current tendency to push responsibility for behaviour on to the individual, often on the pretext of religious piety, without consideration of the material conditions in which an individual had to conduct himself. Thus, in his most serious critique of society, *Culture and Anarchy*, published in 1869, he writes:

> I remember, only the other day, a good man looking with me upon a multitude of children who were gathered before us in one of the most miserable regions of London,—children eaten up with disease, half-sized, half-fed, half-clothed, neglected by their parents, without health, without home, without hope,—said to me: 'The one thing really needful is to teach these little ones to succour one another, if only with a cup of cold water; but now, from one end of the country to the other, one hears nothing but the cry for Knowledge, knowledge, knowledge!' And yet surely, so long as these children are there in these festering masses, without health, without home, without hope, and so long as their multitude is perpetually swelling, charged with misery they must still be for themselves, charged with misery they must still be for us, whether they help one another with a cup of cold water or no; and the knowledge how to prevent their accumulating is necessary, even to give their moral life and growth a fair chance!

The passage comes in a chapter entitled 'Our Liberal Practitioners'; Arnold is making the criticism on the one hand that the Liberal leaders accept social misery as one of the inevitable consequences of the operation of the laws of political economy, itself regarded as one of the laws of nature, and on the other hand that the ethical leaders submit to these liberal assumptions, offering only an ethical code which may suffice for the individual but disclaims responsibility for the social evils. For a society to advance, it needs more than the knowledge of a set of

John Stuart Mill (1806–1873) by G.F. Watts

theories explaining the working of commerce, and it needs an ethic that does more than accommodate the individual to his immediate circumstances. In these respects, Arnold took a different approach to society from Mill's, and the difference can be seen in their ideas on the uses of criticism. In the greatest of his essays, 'On Liberty' (1859), Mill lays down that the importance of criticism is to ensure freedom—not merely against the state, but against the majority: every attitude, belief, dogma or prejudice must be subjected to criticism at all times to ensure that the human mind continues to grow and that society never lapses into lethargy. Arnold, on the other hand, in his essay 'The Function of Criticism' (1865), maintains that this function is to establish 'the best that is known and thought in the world', and this, in *Culture and Anarchy*, constitutes his definition of Culture. Only by a wide and rich culture can a society acquire the knowledge it needs to limit the force of self-interested theorisers and to achieve an ethic which will recognise those social evils that are unacceptable.

Thus, while Mill lays emphasis on the individual, Arnold stresses society; he went so far as to affirm a doctrine of the state according to which the state should be regarded as 'the union of our best selves'. However, it would be a serious misunderstanding of Arnold to suppose that he was in a political or any other sense what we would nowadays call a totalitarian. His own gospel preached that social redemption must come through the individual. He did not condemn the Victorian cultivation of the private conscience, which he called 'hebraism' (in allusion to the Old Testament Hebrews) and defined as 'strictness of conscience', but he thought it needed supplementing. The culture with which he wished to supplement hebraism he called 'hellenism' in allusion to the ancient Greeks, and defined it as 'spontaneity of consciousness'.

A consciousness cannot, of course, be spontaneous if it is a mere submission to doctrines of enlightenment imposed from without in the name of education. Arnold was by profession an Inspector of Schools as well as a writer, and he certainly believed, as did Mill, in more and better education. But he did not want education to impose ideas, but to make available to as many as possible 'the best that is known and thought in the world', so that individual consciousness might be liberated, and a state might arise in which 'the whole of society is in the fullest measure permeated by thought, sensible to beauty, intelligent and alive'. He was not so naive as to suppose that every individual could be so permeated, but he complained of Victorian Britain that no class in it was cultured in such a sense. He typified the three social classes as, respectively: Barbarians—the upper class—who cultivated the values of the body but not those of the mind; Philistines—the middle class—who ignored both; and Populace—the working class—who were deprived of both. Like Mill, who in later life became a socialist, he was opposed to social division, declaring that culture 'seeks to do away with classes'. On the other hand we may infer that he wanted another sort of differentiation—a true aristocracy in its original sense of 'government by the best'—not far perhaps from Forster's 'aristocracy of the sensitive' which he desiderates in his essay 'What I Believe'.

We can indeed find much in Forster to accord with Arnold's thought. For instance, Arnold's idea of culture is an idea of order, but order discovered and created and not imposed, in contrast to the disorder masquerading as order imposed by the Victorian state. So Forster writes:

> In the world of daily life, the world we perforce inhabit, there is much talk about order, particularly from statesmen and politicians. They tend, however, to confuse order with orders, just as they confuse creation with regulations. Order, I suggest, is something evolved from within, not something imposed from without; it is an internal stability, a vital harmony, and in the social and political category it has never existed except for the convenience of historians.

This is from 'Art for Art's Sake' in *Two Cheers*, and in 'The Challenge of Our Time' in the same collection, he writes:

> Art is valuable not because it is educational (though it may be), not because it is recreative (though it may be), not because everybody enjoys it (for everybody does not), not even because it has to do with beauty. It is valuable because it has to do with order, and creates little worlds of its own, possessing internal harmony, in the bosom of this disordered planet.

Forster surely found congenial, too, Arnold's stigmatisation of the middle classes as 'philistine', and philistinism as the prevailing spirit of society. Philistinism—though Forster does not give himself to the word—is the object of much of his attack in his first four novels. Leonard Bast, too, in *Howards End*, is a representative of Arnold's 'populace' in his painful search for culture without being afforded 'spontaneity of consciousness', and the British administrators in *A Passage to India* are examples of middle class philistines working by hebraist 'strictness of conscience' at the same time as they frustrate themselves by their blindness to the Indian cultures which they dominate.

And yet, when we come to Arnold's key-word, 'Culture', we find Forster in disagreement. It is not only that culture snobbery as well as philistinism is under attack in his novels, nor that he praises the cultured Schlegels in *Howards End* for not mistaking culture as an end. He also severely qualifies Arnold's gospel of culture in 'A Note on the Way' (*Abinger Harvest*):

But the help won't be given as directly, as crudely, as Matthew Arnold thought. An educationist as well as a poet, he believed one could 'turn' to writers—to Homer, Epictetus and Sophocles in his own case—and by quoting their beauties or remembering their thoughts could steel oneself against injustice or cruelty. I don't think they are going to bring their help that way. Their gifts are received less consciously and often provoke no thanks. But it is a great mistake to assume that nothing is going on . . . .

This in itself sounds a little crude: Arnold meant nothing so simple by culture as Forster represents. To do the passage justice, however, we have to remember some of the important changes that had occurred between the time of Arnold's death in 1888 and 1934 when Forster wrote it. Possibly the exploitation of cultural exclusiveness to achieve a status of factitious superiority was a commoner tendency at least in Forster's youth than it was in Arnold's day; Bloomsbury was not a Victorian phenomenon, though it had anticipations then. A more important change was that a commercialised sub-culture had grown up in the twentieth century beyond Arnold's expectations, though he himself lived in a period of declining aesthetic standards vulgarised by cheap technology. The sub-culture had its many adherents who had known nothing better, and they were not only from Arnold's 'populace'. Only an ingenuous educator could suppose them to be easily converted. Thus, in the essay 'Does Culture Matter?' Forster caricatures the Arnoldian prophet of culture of his own day:

Today people are coming to the top who are, in some ways, more clear-sighted and honest than the ruling classes of the past, and they refuse to pay for what they don't want; judging by the noises through the floor, our neighbour in the flat above doesn't want books, pictures, tunes, runes, anyhow doesn't want the sorts we recommend. Ought we to bother him? When he is hurrying to lead his own life, ought we to get in his way like a maiden aunt, our arms, as it were, full of parcels, and say to him: 'I was given these specially to hand on to you . . . Sophocles, Velasquez, Henry James . . . I'm afraid they're a little heavy, but you'll get to love them in time, and if you don't take them off my hands I don't know who will . . . please . . . please . . . they're really important, they're culture.'

More important still, the twentieth century has seen a development which Arnold could not have foreseen—the immense growth in power of the twentieth-century state. When he advocated that the state should be seen as the 'union of our best selves', he was writing at a time when state machinery was inadequate for bare efficiency; Forster wrote in a period of immense bureaucracies in half the states of

Europe, with unprecedented powers of police and propaganda at their service. No century before our own has so flattered the individual and at the same time manipulated him with such subtle forces of terror and deceit, either driving him into irresponsible privacy or stamping him into a unit of a regimented mass. Arnold's doctrine of culture, with its demands on individual responsiveness and self-discipline, stands little chance against such flattery and intimidation enforced by the powerful technology of our age.

Forster understood this very well, and believed that the only hope of influencing the individual in such circumstances is constantly to remind him that he is just that: an individual with an inalienable right to remain one.

> I have no mystic faith in the people. I have in the individual. He seems to me a divine achievement and I mistrust any view that belittles him. If anyone calls you a wretched little individual—and I have been called that—don't you take it lying down. You are important because everyone else is an individual too—including the person who criticizes you. In asserting your personality you are playing for your side.
>
> ('*The Challenge of Our Time*')

Thus, in Forster's view, the individual is perfectly right to repel any 'maiden aunt' who tries to unburden on him the load of culture. This does not mean that in his view culture does not matter; it means only that if the individual cannot use it to create the inner order of his own mind, then it is better for him to reject it; otherwise he will submit to it in the spirit of yet another of the 'orders' imposed on him from without. Arnold saw 'the road of the future' (Forster's phrase) to lead from the individual's spontaneity of consciousness to what he described as a society 'permeated by thought, sensible to beauty, intelligent and alive'. Forster saw that road blocked by a landfall of rubble. By what circuitous track, then, did Forster see the individual advancing? For, after all, reinforcing the individual's sense of personal identity is plainly, by itself, insufficient.

In the same short essay in which Forster disparages Arnold's prose message, he praises what he sees to be his true message in his poetry: 'His poetry stands up in the middle of the nineteenth century as a beacon to the twentieth'. He values the poetry for the reason that, as a poet, Arnold 'writes to us because he is not writing about us'. The remark recalls another (quoted by John Colmer in his book on Forster) that he made to Indian students, warning them against cultivating literature in order to give themselves status—'a book is really talk, glorified talk . . . you must read it with the knowledge that the writer is talking to you'. The remark implies, perhaps, that if a book does not

Matthew Arnold (1822–1888)

'talk' as one reads it—if the reader cannot hear the writer's personal voice—then there is something wrong with either the book or the reader. At all events it reminds us that Forster always 'talks'—in his novels and in his critical writings—and we hear his personal message as we hear the conversation of a friend. But this conversational method is not merely a quality of style; it is also a clue to Forster's declared 'mystic faith in the individual', and that he should have found a truer message in Arnold's poetry than in his prose is another clue.

It seems strange to uphold the poems as 'a beacon to the twentieth' century, and Arnold himself would have felt it strange, for, almost without exception, they are laments for the loneliness of the individual, for his internal division and alienation from nature. They do not 'animate' the reader, as Arnold was the first to complain, because they invite him to resignation rather than to action, and indeed it is from a poem entitled 'Resignation' that Forster quotes admiringly the concluding quatrain:

> Not milder to the general lot
> Because our spirits have forgot,
> In action's dizzying eddy whirl'd
> The something that infects the world.

The 'something' emanates from the enduring natural environment; it can be remembered through seeing and not through doing, and, Arnold implies, it can recover the sense of wholeness which a life of action and aspiration merely disperses.

Plainly, we are back now with a mode of thought which lies outside the tradition of liberal rationalism—Bentham's, Mill's or Arnold's. Mill and Arnold, differently, discern the simplifications current in the main stream of that rationalism: precisely where it is most in control it betrays what it cannot achieve; its sum of good and bad—pleasures and pains—takes in too little of good and misconstrues bad. Yet Mill and Arnold still focus on the good–bad contrast, and on the task of eliminating 'bad', whereas human complexity is inextricably involved in both—good and bad. It is in that knot that the life of the individual struggles and grows, and untying the knot does not free the human spirit, it only releases ideas. Forster's case against Arnold might be put by saying that, while in his poetry he acknowledges the knot, in his prose he is concerned to release an idea, as a pretext for initiating the liberal action of reform.

Forster and Carpenter

This mode of thought, outside liberalism, also has its Victorian tradition, one which emanates more from the Romantic poets than, as does the liberal tradition, from the eighteenth-century enlightenment.

Mill acknowledged its importance in his essay on Coleridge (1840), and from Coleridge it proceeded through Carlyle and Ruskin to the romantic socialists of Forster's own day—William Morris and the now neglected Edward Carpenter. It was also a tradition of reform, but one that differed from liberalism in that it started farther back in its thinking—from the nature of the human being instead of from the individual in society. This starting-point inclined it to a neo-religious interpretation of experience, and we do not find Forster in those regions; its concern with human nature, on the other hand, may have supplied what he felt to be missing in liberal individualism, which takes so much about human nature for granted.

At all events—as John Colmer points out—Carpenter was not merely a personal friend of Forster's; Forster acknowledged much influence from him. Carpenter was born in 1844 and died in 1929; he advocated the 'simple life' in accord with the natural environment, in contrast to the artificial life of modern society, alienated from nature. Although he is now little read, his numerous essays had wide appeal in his lifetime. One in particular, 'Civilisation: Its Cause and Cure', was famous for its radical argument that the effects of civilisation—not merely industrialisation—have been to divorce man from nature by creating his self-consciousness, which must now be used to undo the process so as to restore the human sense of wholeness. Essential to this wholeness would be the sense in the individual of belonging as much to his species as to himself, so that it would be impossible to feel himself alienated from fellow-individuals. He argues as follows:

The modern notion, and which has evidently in a very subtle way penetrated the whole thought of today, is that the essential fact of life is the existence of innumerable external forces, which, by a very delicate balance and difficult to maintain, concur to produce Man—who in consequence may be destroyed again by the non-concurrence of those forces. The older notion apparently is that the essential fact of life *is* Man himself; and that the external forces, so-called, are in some way subsidiary to this fact—that they may aid his expression or manifestation, or that they may hinder it, but that they can neither create nor annihilate the Man. Probably both ways of looking at the subject are important; there is a man that can be destroyed, and there is a man that cannot be destroyed. The old words, soul and body, indicate this contrast; but like all words they are subject to the defect that they are an attempt to draw a line where no line can ultimately be drawn; they mark a contrast where in fact there is only continuity—for between the little mortal man who dwells here and now, and the divine and universal Man who also forms a part of our consciousness, is there not a perfect gradation of being, and where (if anywhere) is there a gulf fixed? Together they form a unit, and each is necessary to the other: the first cannot do without the second, and the second cannot get along without the first.

Carpenter himself speaks of the rage with which 'Civilisation' was received when it was read to the Fabian Society as a lecture. In *Two Cheers*, Forster includes an essay on Sidney and Beatrice Webb, the Fabian leaders. He writes of them with respect, describing his only meeting with them, but he says he could never have become intimate with them: 'only those who worked with them could be that, and my own schemes for improving society run upon different lines'. He also has an essay on Carpenter. Speaking of Carpenter's love for the poetry of Whitman, he says: 'They expressed . . . his love for the individual and nature. These were the only two things he cared about . . .', and goes on: 'He demands from society the furtherance of these two things; all else is nonsense.' The Webbs stemmed from the great Victorian tradition of Millite liberalism, and Forster had respect for it and gave it half his allegiance. The other half seems to have gone to the alternative tradition. Carpenter's influence on Forster was no doubt even stronger through personal friendship than through his writings, but even a slight reading of these help us to understand Forster's 'mystic faith' in the individual. The passage from 'Civilisation' is an example: through the individual, with that faith, by accepting human complexities and projecting his own sympathies, Forster felt he was reaching beyond the isolated reader; to promote the sense of Man (in Carpenter's terms) in a single reader was to promote the sense of human society beyond the reach of radical liberals and socialists.

'A liberal at war with the liberal imagination'. Trilling goes on to justify the statement by showing how Forster overcame the simplifications of the liberal reformers by accepting the paradoxes of human nature and stimulating a sense of order in spite of them.

> The way of human action of course does not satisfy him, but he does not believe there are any new virtues to be discovered; not by becoming better, he says, but by ordering and distributing his native goodness can man live as befits him.
>
> (Lionel Trilling, *E.M. Forster*)

This section has been an attempt to show how Forster's intellectual antecedents made it natural for him to reach such a conclusion.

As we shall see when we come to the essays, Forster's later liberalism was not expressed directly in political terms—scarcely even in social ones. It focused on the areas of human experience which are usually ignored by politicians and sociologists alike—the personal links by which the individual relates himself to his environment in such a way as to make politics and social science humanly intelligible.

Edward Carpenter by Roger Fry

7   The art of the novel

It is helpful to the study of any writer to try to place him or her in relationship to other practitioners of the same form. Much as when we approach a high mountain from a great distance it seems at first to be an isolated object, and only when we draw closer do we find that it is one of a chain from which it derives its individual shape and form, so deeper knowledge shows us how much writers derive from and contribute to other writers, without losing their individuality. Minor writers are sometimes reduced by the process, but any significant writer only becomes more intelligible, much as we know a human being better through meeting the company he keeps, without necessarily valuing him any less.

It is natural to look first at a writer's own period, though many of his affinities may be outside it.

Forster grew up in a generation which made greater claims for the novel as a serious form of art than had previously been the case in this country. Although the major novelists had written as seriously as any other literary artists, discriminating critics—Arnold and Mill among them—had been inclined to regard the novel, by comparison with poetry or drama, as entertainment, and even the serious novelists had conceded this view by making their fiction as accessible to the general reader as possible. Then, with the advent of the late Victorian novelists—in particular Henry James and Joseph Conrad, both of foreign extraction—intelligent readers, under the influence of the claims that the new novelists were making for themselves, began to distinguish between the art novel and the conservative form, the latter being sometimes allowed the same seriousness as political journalism. The distinction made for a distinction in style: the novelist as artist now handled his material with fewer concessions to his readers than hitherto; if the reader found the work difficult, the responsibility was left to him to struggle with it or abandon it. The conservative novelist, on the other hand, continued to make his work accessible to the casual reader, on the older assumption that, whether or not he was able to do justice to the message, it was still the first duty of the novelist to relax him into a mood of pleasure. Thus, in Forster's novel-writing period, he had on the one hand the 'artists'—James, Conrad, Joyce, Lawrence, Woolf—and on the other hand the 'conservatives'—Wells, Bennett, Galsworthy, Kipling, Chesterton. However, if we try to fit Forster's own work into either camp, we find, typically, that he is not so easy to place.

Our first impression is likely to be that he belongs to the second; few eminent novelists have employed such an easy, conversational idiom, so that we are clear that we are reading an informal novelist concerned to entertain us restfully. And yet, by the time he has finished the book—and much sooner if he is reading *Howards End* or *A Passage to India*—the reader is jolted from his easy reading by uncertainties. *A Room with a View* provides one slight example: Lucy Honeychurch becomes engaged to the culture-snob, Cecil Vyse; he turns out to be unpleasantly supercilious and a comic bore, and the reader anticipates pleasurably his just repudiation by Lucy. It comes, but why in that scene does it happen that he is made to exhibit his hidden better side, whereas Lucy is made out awkward and wrong? Because, Forster is reminding us, people are not simple but complex, and in such a crisis they do not necessarily reveal themselves at their best because they are right, or at their worst because they are wrong. Consequently we are alerted to watch every detail of a character's speech and gesture as closely as we read Henry James's complex prose, rich in every sentence with implications. In *Howards End* and *A Passage to India* we become aware of the recurrence of very ordinary phenomena, such as swords and umbrellas in the former, and we suspect that they are not to be ignored. Forster's fictions cease to glide through our minds like pleasant dreams; not only is the characterisation paradoxical, but the narrative is patterned with themes like a musical score. Above all, we notice that his light and pleasing comedy is in fact like a butterfly equipped with the sting of a wasp. What kind of influence stimulated this comedy which, despite its apparent lightness, stimulates serious reflections?

Austen and Forster

We go, of course, to his literary essays and lectures for clues, and we find them there. When, for instance, we read in the essay 'In my Library' that Jane Austen is the only one among the three writers (the other two being Shakespeare and Gibbon) that he would spontaneously reach for at any moment, we justifiably expect her work to offer affinities with his own. There are, besides, parallels in their places in literary history. Jane Austen carried against the movement of early nineteenth-century Romanticism much of the spirit of the previous Augustan period of Pope and Johnson, and Forster recommended the virtues of the Victorian era to a twentieth century disposed to empty its consciousness of Victorianism wholesale. Another resemblance is that both achieved large reputations by a small number of novels, and another that both tended to restrict their settings to a narrow compass through which they communicated deeply about their life and times. But their strongest affinity is their common disposition to treat the surfaces of their material in the spirit of comedy, allowing sombre experience to emerge by degrees.

In his lectures, *Aspects of the Novel*, Forster resists historical treatment of his subject, preferring to pair passages from writers of different periods in order to show their affinities across the chronological gaps; Richardson is paired with James, Woolf with Sterne, Wells with Dickens. The game can be played with Austen and Forster likewise:

'... Oh! I am delighted with the book! I should like to spend my whole life reading it, I assure you; if it had not been to meet you, I would not have come away from it for all the world.'

'Dear creature! how much I am obliged to you; and when you have finished "Udolpho", we will read "The Italian" together; and I have made a list of ten or twelve more of the same kind for you.'

'Have you indeed? How glad I am! What are they all?'

'I will read you their names directly; here they are in my pocket-book: "Castle of Wolfenbach", "Clermont", "Mysterious Warnings", "Necromancer of the Black Forest", "Midnight Bell", "Orphan of the Rhine", and "Horrid Mysteries" ... Those will last us some time.'

'Yes; pretty well; but are they all horrid? Are you sure they are all horrid?'

'Yes, quite sure; for a particular friend of mine, a Miss Andrews, a sweet girl, one of the sweetest creatures in the world, has read every one of them. I wish you knew Miss Andrews, you would be delighted with her. She is netting herself the sweetest cloak you can conceive. I think her as beautiful as an angel, and I am so vexed with the men for not admiring her! I scold them all amazingly about it.'

'Scold them! Do you scold them for not admiring her?'

'Yes, that I do. There is nothing I would not do for those who are really my friends. I have no notion of loving people by halves; it is not my nature. My attachments are always excessively strong. I told Captain Hunt, at one of our assemblies this winter, that if he was to tease me all night, I would not dance with him, unless he would allow Miss Andrews to be as beautiful as an angel. The men think us incapable of real friendship, you know; and I am determined to show them the difference. Now if I were to hear anybody speak slightingly of you, I should fire up in a moment: but that is not at all likely, for *you* are just the kind of girl to be a great favourite with the men.'

'Oh dear!' cried Catherine, colouring, 'how can you say so?'

'A smell! a true Florentine smell! Every city, let me teach you, has its own smell.'

'Is it a very nice smell?' said Lucy, who had inherited from her mother a distaste for dirt.

'One doesn't come to Italy for niceness,' was the retort, 'one comes for life. Look at that adorable wine-cart! How the driver stares at us, dear simple soul!'

So Miss Lavish proceeded through the streets of Florence, short, fidgety, and playful as a kitten, though without a kitten's grace. It was a treat for the girl to be with anyone so clever and cheerful; and a blue military cloak, such as an Italian officer wears, only increased the sense of festivity.

'Buon giorno! Take the word of an old woman, Miss Lucy: you will never repent of a little civility to your inferiors. *That* is true democracy. Though I am a real Radical as well. There, now you're shocked.'

'Indeed I'm not!' exclaimed Lucy. 'We are Radicals, too, out and out. My father always voted for Mr Gladstone, until he was so dreadful about Ireland.'

'I see, I see. And now you have gone over to the enemy.'

'Oh please—! If my father was alive, I'm sure he would vote Radical again, now that Ireland is all right. And as it is, the glass over our front door was broken last election, and Freddy is sure it was the Tories; but mother says nonsense, a tramp.'

'Shameful! A manufacturing district I suppose?'

'No—in the Surrey hills. About five miles from Dorking, looking over the Weald.'

Miss Lavish seemed interested, and slackened her trot.

'What a delightful part; I know it so well. It is full of the very nicest people. Do you know Sir Harry Otway—a Radical if ever there was?'

'Very well indeed.'

'And old Mrs Butterworth the philanthropist?'

'Why, she rents a field from us! How funny!'

Miss Lavish looked at the narrow ribbon of sky, and murmured: 'Oh you have property in Surrey?'

'Hardly any,' said Lucy, fearful of being thought a snob. 'Only thirty acres—just the garden, all downhill, and some fields.'

Miss Lavish was not disgusted, and said it was just the size of her aunt's Suffolk estate.

The episodes have a good deal in common. Catherine Morland in the first passage, from *Northanger Abbey* (chapter 6), has been having her first introduction to smart society on a visit to Bath; in the second, from *A Room with a View* (chapter 2), Lucy Honeychurch is receiving her first taste of sophisticated culture on a visit to Florence. Both are being taken in hand by foolish, disingenuous, affected older women— Isabella Thorpe and Eleanor Lavish respectively. Isabella cultivates the fashionable romantic horror fiction now known as 'gothic novels' to which she has introduced Catherine, and from these she has derived the cult of romantic friendship, although in fact she is incapable of genuine affection and is chiefly interested in making a display of herself. Eleanor Lavish is likewise an exhibitionist; she pretends to an advanced taste for the 'real Italy' behind the guidebooks, with which she associates her pretension to radicalism although in fact she is a snob; like Isabella, she enjoys making a show of real feeling, although she is incapable of any. Catherine and Lucy are the same sort of girl— inexperienced, ignorant and easily impressed, but as yet unspoilt and capable of much more genuine feeling than their companions; we see pretentious silliness, verging on viciousness, imposing on naive silliness, redeemed by the charm of innocence. Both novelists depend on dialogue to make their points, although Forster is much more inclined than Jane Austen to enforce his with authorial interpolations; both use comedy as a means of distinguishing the genuine from the factitious by a technique that is light and yet leads into serious judgements.

When we look further into the two novels, we continue to find similarities between them, but eventually we find a contrast which is also revealing about Forster.

They are alike in having heroines who eventually marry the right man, despite obstacles which make this prospect unlikely, and they are similar also in having critical experiences which teach them necessary lessons. Catherine is invited to stay at the Abbey, home of General Tilney, father of Henry Tilney whom she eventually marries. Obsessed with her gothic novels, Catherine expects this gothic mansion to be a place of mystery and evil, and she conjectures that the General, a widower, has done away with his wife. She searches a bureau in her room in the hope of finding incriminating papers, finds a roll, and goes to bed with it in an ecstasy of dread. But when she reads it at first light, she discovers it to contain laundry and farrier's bills. This is the first of the lessons she receives to teach her that romantic literature does not so often tell the truth as betray it: the General is indeed a scheming and unscrupulous man, but not at all in the way she has supposed. Lucy's lesson is quite different. Searching for her elders and protectors during a picnic above Florence, she is misled by the young Italian driver of their vehicle on to a hillside rich with violets, into the arms of a young man not considered quite respectable by her circle, who kisses her. She is outwardly shocked, but inwardly unsettled: her spontaneous self, straitlaced by conventionality, rejoices, whereas her conventional self is outraged. For some time she allows the latter to dictate her behaviour, but in the end her spontaneity triumphs, and she marries the young man.

The difference between the two episodes seems plain; Jane Austen's handling of hers shows her to be anti-romantic, whereas Forster's treatment of his is romantic. This in fact is what we might expect from the ways in which both writers advocate the traditions of their antecedent epochs: since Jane Austen is a witness to the virtues of Augustan reason, we expect her to counteract Romantic extravagance of feeling, and since Forster is a self-confessed Victorian, it is natural that he should resist the disposition of his own generation to regard sentimentality as a worse vice than cynicism. However, the difference is not as simple as that. It is not romanticism in the sense that it implies freedom of feeling that Austen is criticising, but literary romanticism of the vulgar sort with which Catherine has become infatuated. Her spontaneity is never brought into judgement; what is questioned is whether her environment will allow it genuine expression, or will poison it down to its source by first vulgarising her feelings with sensationalism and then falsifying them with artifice. So far Forster must be in agreement; Eleanor Lavish is just such a literary vulgariser as is Isabella Thorpe, and he stigmatises her just as comically. But Lucy's predicament is much more complicated, and the complication is consequent on a much deeper confusion of values in the world in which she is growing up. Superficially the vices of her world and Catherine's are similar: both girls are surrounded by people who at best suffer confusion without awareness of it, and at worst flaunt a display of insincere values divorced from any truth of feeling or fact. However, beyond her immediate environment, Catherine lives in a civilisation which still values proportion and good sense spacious enough to accommodate deep feeling, whereas Lucy's world is much more deceitful. Lucy's world offers her much greater appearance of freedom and much wider scope of expectation than Catherine's, but its expectations of her are equally constraining, and its surface order overlies a confusion of social and chauvinistic prejudices, defences and inhibitions. Whereas Catherine daydreams of an agreeably shocking freedom which is really licence, and awakens to a state of mind in which reason and feeling complement each other in a true order, Lucy is an unconscious prisoner of a disorder masquerading as order. She has to be shocked into a freedom of which she has hitherto only been conscious through music: 'If Miss Honeychurch ever takes to live as she plays,' remarks the intelligent vicar, Mr Beebe, 'it will be very exciting—both for us and for her.' Mr Beebe, in fact, finds that outcome altogether too exciting.

Narrative organisation

Music was always very important to Forster, and whenever it occurs in his novels—Lucy's playing in *A Room with a View*, Beethoven's Fifth Symphony in *Howards End*, the opera in *Where Angels Fear to Tread*—it connotes emancipation from constraints. In the opening sentence of 'The Raison d'Etre of Criticism' (*Two Cheers*), he describes it as 'the deepest of the arts and deep beneath the arts'. The statement is troubling; it raises the question whether any art can be said to be 'deeper' than any other art, and even less, as itself an art, 'deep beneath the arts'. It is, in fact, a 'romantic' view of music—one which expresses the experience of it as enlarging beyond the other artistic media which are more obviously tied to practical experience, as the verbal arts are leashed to the language we daily use and the visual ones to the shapes and colours we daily observe. However, as we read on in the same essay (and others on music—'Not Listening to Music' and 'The C Minor of that Life') we find that Forster's response to music was dual: to some he responds for its power of suggestion and its stimulus to revery; to other styles of it he responds with an interest in its form, and this interest he carries back into his concern with form in the novel.

It is this kind of interest in narrative organisation which, in one aspect of his work, shows Forster to be among the innovators in English fiction, as opposed to the conservatives who relied on the familiar formal constituents—story and plot. In his lectures entitled *Aspects of the Novel* he discusses both, regarding them as almost indispensable, though he regrets the indispensability of the first. Only in the last lecture does he discuss 'Pattern and Rhythm', both of them terms which the ordinary novel reader would probably not think of using, and for examples of which he refers to contemporary writers—Anatole France and Henry James for pattern, and Marcel Proust for rhythm. Pattern, of course, has a visual connotation for him, and his interest in it is limited by his feeling that it may constrict the life of a novel, at least when it is 'rigid':

> It may externalise the atmosphere, spring naturally from the plot, but it shuts the doors on life and leaves the novelist doing exercises, generally in the drawing-room ... To most readers of fiction the sensation from a pattern is not intense enough to justify the sacrifices that made it, and their verdict is 'Beautifully done, but not worth doing.'

We seem to be back with Forster the conservative, but his attitude to rhythm is different.

He illustrates rhythm from Proust's nine-volume novel *A la Recherche du Temps Perdu* (*Remembrance of Things Past*), uncompleted at the time of Forster's lecture. He sees the unity of Proust's work to be internal, independent of the patent devices of story and plot. Rhythm is produced by the repetition in different contexts within the story of details which accrue significance of increasing complexity as the variations of context accumulate, much as a phrase in a musical composition may be repeated, varied and amplified. He gives, as a specific example from Proust, a musical phrase by an unknown composer, Vinteuil:

> The little phrase crosses the book again and again, but as an echo, a memory, we like to encounter it, but it has no binding power. Then, hundreds and hundreds of pages on, when Vinteuil has become a national possession, and there is talk of raising a statue to him in the town where he has been so wretched and so obscure, another work

of his is performed—a posthumous sextet. The hero listens—he is in an unknown rather terrible universe while a sinister dawn reddens the sea. Suddenly for him and for the reader too, the little phrase of the sonata recurs—half heard, changed but giving complete orientation, so that he is back in the country of childhood with the knowledge that it belongs to things unknown.

('*Pattern and Rhythm*')

The example reflects not only Forster's interest in Proust but his dual interest in music—in its power of intimate suggestion, and in the subtlety of organisation available to musical composers.

Certainly, Proust and music were interests which Forster exploited in order to express what he felt to be the centre of truth in the human reality he expounded in his novels. Like other novelists of his time, he saw human character in two aspects. It is social, subject to social pressures and constraints of which it is often unconscious and from which it must free itself if it is to grow; this is the province of comedy and the art of Jane Austen which he so much relished. But the other aspect is intimate, elusive, often inexpressible by direct means; it makes itself felt in details of experience which may be shared by different individuals unawares to themselves, as the wasp which is loved by Mrs Moore at the end of chapter 3 of *A Passage to India* is united with her in an act of love by Professor Godbole at the end of chapter 33, or it may differentiate them crucially, as the attitude to the possession of umbrellas differentiates Helen Schlegel from Leonard Bast in *Howards End*. Jane Austen and Marcel Proust represent the polar opposites of Forster as a novelist. The influence of the former is overt and the resemblance easy to detect; that of the latter is evident chiefly in the last two novels and often not at first reading.

Butler and Forster

Between polar opposites, however, there is a lot of space. A novelist may be interested not merely in aspects of human experience and how these are to be rendered, but in secondary devices of narrative technique; in what produces a succession of events, or changes in a character's outlook, in such a way that the reader is not merely convinced by the plausibility of the development but startled by it, so as to be brought to the verge of incredulity, and yet forced to accept what happens almost as though it has happened to himself. Two such writers seem to have had this sort of influence on Forster, both of them Victorians: Samuel Butler and George Meredith.

Butler was born in 1835 and died in 1902, and his best-known book is his utopian narrative *Erewhon* (1872)—'Nowhere' reversed. Its hero is a bland mid-Victorian believer in a convenient blend of evangelical and commercial imperialism. He has discovered the unknown country, which he hopes to exploit, in the middle of a mountainous region, the whereabouts of which he does not disclose in case richer entrepreneurs might take advantage of him. The society he finds in it proves to be—like Swift's Brobdingnag and Lilliput—in many ways like his own, but with differences the significance of which the reader is meant to understand, although the obtusely self-righteous hero, like Gulliver, does not. He discovers, for instance, that it is an offence to possess a watch; machines have been banned, because they generate machines which will eventually achieve such complexity and power that they will take control of their human inventors. It is likewise an offence to catch a cold, although crimes such as embezzlement are regarded as illnesses deserving sympathy; their cure is as disagreeable as a European penal code, however—it is only the social attitude that is different. He also finds, besides the usual financial institutions, that there are 'musical banks', the currency of which is much esteemed although it has no exchange value; this is satire on the conventional attitude to religion in Europe, which encourages the devout to build up spiritual credit accounts on analogous principles to those of the businessman making investments. So Butler builds up a view of a society which might as well belong to nineteenth-century Europe, except that it has developed out of different assumptions which are in no obvious way less viable than those which Europeans accept as the only valid ones. His implication is that what we accept as rational behaviour is in fact an imposition on the individual, who is thus reduced to a moral stereotype when he supposes himself both rational and free.

It seems not to have been so much the aptness of the satire which appealed to Forster in *Erewhon*, as the humane humour and the cunning contrivances with which the satire is rendered. He pays tribute to it in the essay 'A Book that Influenced Me' in *Two Cheers*, and in giving his reasons he makes a number of self-revealing remarks. It is not, he acknowledges, a 'great' book, in the sense that Tolstoy's *War and Peace*, Gibbon's *Decline and Fall*, and Dante's *Divine Comedy* are great, but these have not influenced him because he could not imagine himself writing them. At the same time, he prefers *Erewhon* to other books concerned with human conduct, because these have a ruthlessness which he does not wish to emulate. He enjoys Butler's book because it is 'a serious book not written too seriously', because he himself has 'the sort of mind which likes to be taken unawares', and because it has relevance to his own technique:

> I like that idea of fantasy, of muddling up the actual and the impossible until the reader isn't sure which is which, and I have sometimes tried to do it when writing myself.
>
> ('*A Book that Influenced Me*')

(Presumably he is referring to his short stories.)

All this is explicit, but to some extent it may be open to

misunderstanding, and it is worth clearing up that possibility, not so much to do Forster justice as because in doing so we can find in his remarks further indications of his character as a writer. The misunderstanding might be to suppose that Forster does not want 'greatness' in a writer: that he is overawed by Tolstoy's spaciousness and by Swift's energy. The nineteenth and twentieth centuries have resounded with loud voices, as indeed has every age of European history, but the last two centuries have also seen the rise of the common man to a status in which he has an acknowledged entitlement to contribute his own small voice to the movement of opinion. However, the common man has difficulty in making his voice heard in the din, and of advocating the value of his virtues in defiance of extremists. We have seen how resolutely Forster asserts the dignity of the modest individual in 'The Challenge of Our Time', and that, although he is not egalitarian, he requires discrimination, in 'What I Believe', not as a hierarchy of superior abilities but as an 'aristocracy of the sensitive'. He acknowledges greatness—in Tolstoy, Dante, Gibbon—but he sees his mission (as he finds it in Butler) in revealing the moral sanity which the individual needs within such greatness, and he rejects whatever he finds distorting to that sanity:

> I know that St Augustine's *Confessions* is a 'good' book, and I want to be good. But not in St Augustine's way. I don't want the goodness which entails an asceticism close to cruelty. I prefer the goodness of William Blake. And Macchiavelli—he is clever—and unlike some of my compatriots I want to be clever. But not with Macchiavelli's cold, inhuman cleverness. I prefer the cleverness of Voltaire. And indignation—Swift's indignation in *Gulliver* is too savage for me; I prefer Butler's in *Erewhon*. And strength—yes, I want to be strong, but not with the strength of Carlyle's dictator heroes, who foreshadow Hitler. I prefer the strength of Antigone.
>
> ('*A Book that Influenced Me*')

Butler is, in literary quality, a lesser figure than Swift, but Blake, Voltaire and Sophocles are by no means the literary inferiors of those to whom Forster is opposing them. His concern in the essay is not essentially with the greatness of genius, but with the moral greatness attainable by every individual, and with such literature as he sees helping the individual to attain it. His admiration for Butler's technique is thus more than tribute to a congenial artistic method; it is recognition of a congenial language.

Meredith and Forster

An important part of this language is the renunciation of self-conscious rhetoric, such as, among the Victorian 'sages', Carlyle used and

Arnold and Butler abjured. And yet George Meredith, the other Victorian novelist who is generally accepted as an influence on Forster, wrote in a style conspicuous for its artifice and mannered eloquence. In *Aspects of the Novel*, Forster acknowledges this:

> His philosophy has not worn well. His heavy attacks on sentimentality—they bore the present generation, which pursues the same quarry with neater instruments, and is apt to suspect anyone carrying a blunderbuss of being a sentimentalist himself . . . When he gets serious and noble-minded there is a strident overtone, a bullying that becomes distressing. I feel indeed that he was like Tennyson in one respect: through not taking himself quietly enough he strained his inside.
>
> ('*The Plot*')

And yet, when Forster has had his say against Meredith, he goes on to pay him the tribute that

> He is the finest contriver that English fiction has ever produced, and any lecture on plot must do homage to him.
>
> ('*The Plot*')

George Meredith lived from 1828 to 1909, and his numerous novels were published in the last forty years of the nineteenth century. These dates mark him—like Hardy—as chronologically spanning the gap between the great mid-Victorians (Dickens and George Eliot) and writers such as James and Conrad who wrote into the twentieth century. When Forster was beginning to write, Meredith's reputation was at its peak; his witty and abstruse style made readers find George Eliot's plain-spoken moralising seem flat-footed and sermonising, and the deviousness of his plots showed up those of Dickens as melo-dramatically simple. Only when respect grew for the precision of James's style and the authenticity of Conrad's tragic intensity did Meredith come to seem comparatively meretricious, and this change of opinion reflects Forster's own. But he excepts Meredith's organisation in the following terms:

> A Meredithian plot is not a temple to the tragic or even to the comic Muse, but rather resembles a series of kiosks most artfully placed among wooded slopes, which his people reach by their own impetus, and from which they emerge with altered aspect. Incident springs out of character, and having occurred it alters that character. People and events are closely connected, and he does it by means of contrivances. They are often delightful, sometimes touching, always unexpected. This shock, followed by the feeling, 'Oh, that's all right,' is a sign that all is well with the plot:

George Meredith (1828–1909) by G.F. Watts

characters, to be real, ought to run smoothly, but a plot ought to cause surprise.

('*The Plot*')

The high value Forster attaches to surprise recalls his admiration for Butler's *Erewhon*, but now we have its association with character, emphasis on which is one of the best known features of his discussion of the novel in *Aspects*.

In his two lectures on 'People', Forster distinguishes fictional characters as either 'flat' or 'round'. 'Flat' characters are recognisable for embodying single characteristics to which they adhere consistently. In Dickens' *David Copperfield*, Mrs Micawber early declares that she will never desert Mr Micawber; she never does, and that is her character. 'Round' characters, on the other hand, are recognisable not so much because, like real people, they embody a complexity of qualities, as because, for this reason, they are capable of causing surprise. By doing so they become agents of the plot which, as Forster says, ought to be surprising. They must not of course be incredibly inconsistent since that will make them unreal to the mind of the reader—they will not 'run smoothly'—but if they show themselves in a new but intelligible aspect they will provide that necessary shock which changes a reader's passive acceptance into active interest.

Forster's example from Meredith is Laetitia Dale's refusal of Sir Willoughby Patterne's final offer of marriage (after twice jilting her) in *The Egoist*. The reader has become accustomed to Laetitia as an adorer of the egoist, Sir Willoughby; she appears to be a weak, sentimentally poetical flat character incapable of saying 'no' to him, and when she surprisingly but intelligibly does (completing his downfall) the reader is shocked, but the shock is followed by the reaction Forster deems desirable—'Oh, that's all right'—which is a compound of gratification at seeing justice done to the egoist's monstrous assumptions about himself, and satisfaction that Laetitia, for all her apparent insipidity, has turned out to be a real person, with a dignity of her own and a mind to sustain it.

One example among others of Forster's use of the same technique is the behaviour of Charlotte Bartlett at the end of *A Room with a View*. Throughout the novel Miss Bartlett has been a flat character, though an amusing one in a deadly way. She has been a stuffy, emotionally deprived spinster, encumbering Lucy with inhibitions and pro-hibitions so as to represent the chief obstacle between the girl and the freedom she eventually achieves. The suddenness of this achievement is due to an unexpected encounter with Mr Emerson, father of the young man who kissed her on the hillside and for whom she has been trying not to admit her love, although she has taken an unconscious step in his direction by breaking with her fiancé, Cecil Vyse. The meeting with Mr Emerson forces Lucy to recognise the truth of her feelings, but the real surprise awaits the reader in the last chapter, when she is already married to George Emerson; it is that Charlotte Bartlett has connived at that crucial meeting. That she should do so is at first astonishing, just as it is astonishing that it is the enlightened, unconventional Mr Beebe and not Charlotte who is scandalised by Lucy's violent reversal of all she has professed to feel. Our surprise causes us to reconsider these characters as they have been presented, and when we do we are likely to realise that they are not as simple—as 'flat'—as we have supposed. Mr Beebe's genial freedom of attitude overlies an aversion for heterosexual passion and a militant faith in the value of order and consistency of conduct, whereas Miss Bartlett's timid primness covers a deep desire for emotional release, no longer available for herself but desired for the girl who has been her protegée, provided that Charlotte herself does not have to admit overt responsibility for it. Thus, at the very end of the novel, the character-dimensions are abruptly enriched: we are made aware that the agents of constraint in society are not necessarily what they seem to be, but profounder and more devious in their operation.

In *Aspects of the Novel* Forster demonstrates clearly the ways in which Meredith influenced him and the extent to which he no longer respects him. However, he goes an unexpected stage further. He compares Thomas Hardy's organisation of plot unfavourably with that of Meredith, and then goes on to admit his greater admiration for Hardy as a novelist: 'the work of Hardy is my home and that of Meredith cannot be'. The unexpectedness of this is that it is at first difficult to find association between Forster's outlook on and treatment of human experience and Hardy's. This is no reason against his admiring Hardy's work, but if a novelist declares the work of another to be 'his home', one does expect to find affinities between the two. Only when we learn from Forster's biography of his deep desire to find a home in English soil, when we reflect on his deep love for Abinger evident in the last essay in *Two Cheers for Democracy*, when we remember that *Howards End* is based on his maternal home of Rooksnest, and when we note all the evidence that he had a nostalgia amounting to envy for pastoral types of humanity, can we see how he might feel peculiarly at home in Hardy's fiction. In tracing the characteristics of an outstanding novelist we often have to look further than those who have left clear traces upon him. Similarly, when we learn about his strong admiration for Herman Melville in his lecture on 'Prophecy' in *Aspects of the Novel*, we realise that Forster was not so domestic in his approach to the scope of fiction as he seems to be if we restrict ourselves to his more immediate influences; we realise that there is evidence for sources of inspiration for the near-mysticism of *A Passage to India*.

But the immediate prevailing influence on Forster's work—Austen, Butler, Meredith—remains the tradition of comedy. This tradition had gone decadent by Forster's lifetime. In its popular form in the

music-halls it gave release, but in its sophisticated form it chiefly offered distraction to the bored; the wit of Oscar Wilde did not go very deep, and even that of Bernard Shaw did not go as deep as he meant it to. The great tradition of European comedy had had its last epoch in the eighteenth century, and the mention of that inevitably evokes the name of Voltaire. Of him, in his essay 'Voltaire and Frederick the Great' (*Two Cheers*), Forster writes:

> If I had to name two people to speak for Europe at the Last Judgement I should choose Shakespeare and Voltaire— Shakespeare for his creative genius, Voltaire for his critical genius and humanity. Voltaire cared for the truth, he believed in toler- ance, he pitied the oppressed, and since he was a forceful character he was able to drive his ideas home. They happen to be my own ideas, and like many other small people I am thankful when a great person comes along and says for me what I can't say properly for myself. Voltaire speaks for the thousands and thousands of us who hate injustice and work for a better world.

Voltaire used comedy to undermine the pretentious structures of authoritarian power in his own age, the more effectively because it is in the nature of authentic comedy to renounce pretensions. The re- nunciation of pretensions with the aim of revealing the greatness that has no need of pretensions is the nearest we can get to epitomising the motivation of Forster's art.

Thomas Hardy (1840–1928)

8   Essays and criticism

We have grown used to the term 'sage' in its application to certain Victorian writers—notably Carlyle, Ruskin, Arnold and Mill—who were critical commentators on their society, dissatisfied with the standards by which it lived and anxious to explore and establish new ones. The term has an unpleasant pomposity which seems particularly inappropriate to Forster and which he would certainly not have arrogated to himself. And yet it is sometimes applied to him, to comprehend the kind of influence he increasingly exercised after he ceased publishing novels in early middle age but did not cease to write.

The Victorians framed the questions about our civilisation to which the twentieth century has been seeking answers with increasing urgency and difficulty. 'Sages' are no longer in fashion, because we find it harder to believe that a single mind can comprehend either the complexity of our problems or the conflict of hopes to which their solution might give rise; we prefer the 'experts', who, however, betray our confidence by their disagreements. Nonetheless sage figures have arisen, though few of them have aspired to the function, and have achieved respect and confidence, because they have, almost accidentally, fulfilled tasks of clarification similar to those attempted by the Victorian sages. Forster was among these, especially in his influence on the writers we have come to associate with the 1930s. A convenient piece of evidence is the sonnet dedicated to him by W.H. Auden, in his book written in collaboration with Christopher Isherwood—*Journey to a War*, published in 1939. The book concerns a visit to China during the Sino-Japanese war of the 1930s, and the sonnet is as follows:

> Though Italy and King's are far away,
> And Truth a subject only bombs discuss,
> Our ears unfriendly, still you speak to us,
> Insisting that the inner life can pay.
>
> As we dash down the slope of hate with gladness
> You trip us up like an unnoticed stone,
> And, just when we are closeted with madness,
> You interrupt us like the telephone.
>
> Yes, we are Lucy, Turton, Philip; we
> Wish international evil, are delighted
> To join the jolly ranks of the benighted
>
> Where reason is denied and love ignored,
> But, as we swear our lie, Miss Avery
> Comes out into the garden with a sword.

In the third stanza, Auden identifies himself and his friends with those of Forster's characters who, well-disposed but in the clinches of their social and insular prejudices, court disaster until—if they do—they achieve self-recognition; in the last, he introduces the shadowy but strongly symbolic figure in *Howards End*, who lives independently of contemporary social assumptions and stands for incontrovertible human truth. To understand the emotional context of the sonnet, and consequently its meaning, we have to understand how, in the 1930s, the literary generations were generally divided by political and religious sympathies. The older writers—Eliot, Pound, Wyndham Lewis, Lawrence (though he died in 1930), the Bloomsbury Group, even Shaw—were rooted in the experiences surrounding the previous war, and either tended (like the first four) towards the political right, or were too sceptical and detached in their commitments to satisfy the young generation (Auden, Day Lewis, MacNeice, Orwell) who were on the left. Forster was himself of the older generation and politically detached (though slightly disposed towards the younger writers' attraction to Communism) but he commanded not only their respect but their sympathies to an unusual degree. This was owing to his example in the crisis of identity which afflicted the younger generation, arising from a sense of loss in social continuities. Up till 1930 the middle class, though with increasing shakiness, had continued its Victorian tradition of upholding national standards in politics and culture, but the immensity of the financial crisis in that year caused it to lose much of what remained of its confidence, and at the same time exposed social injustice to a public less inclined to avert its attention. The younger writers aligned themselves with the working class, but they could not identify with it as they wished to, both because they were themselves of middle-class origin and because they well knew that they were read by a middle-class public. This would have mattered less if other traditions had survived; if, for instance, a great religious spirit throughout English culture had offered a home to their minds and feelings; but where such a spirit lived (as in the later work of T.S. Eliot) they found it politically suspect, and elsewhere the churches had long lost their intellectual independence of the secular state. In such confusion, how could they sustain their integrity? But this is Forster's central theme in all his work. It is true he provides no systematic philosophy for its attainment, but his subject is the search for it, and in his presentation of the search he exhibits it. This is Auden's tribute to him in the sonnet; he alludes only to the novels, but what is implicit in them is often explicit, in a necessarily more fragmented way, in the other writings.

For instance, the poem was written in the same year as Forster's most famous essay, 'What I Believe' in *Two Cheers for Democracy*; that pre-war year of 1938, when the democracies were wavering most in confidence and the voices of the totalitarians were loudest and most menacing. Without reference to the essay, which he may not have known at the time of writing, Auden epitomises much of what it says. Let us consider, for instance, Forster's second and third paragraphs. In the first, having uncompromisingly rejected belief in Belief, he has gone on to admit the necessity of formulating one in self-defence against the current fanaticisms. In fact he formulates not one but several: in personal relations, in Democracy, in the necessity for the containment of force, in the 'aristocracy of the sensitive', and in the individual. Such beliefs are not unusual; they are indeed those of traditional liberalism; nonetheless Forster makes them unusual in his expression of them:

> I have, however, to live in an Age of Faith—the sort of epoch I used to hear praised when I was a boy. It is extremely unpleasant really. It is bloody in every sense of the word. And I have to keep my end up in it. Where do I start?
>
> With personal relationships. Here is something comparatively solid in a world full of violence and cruelty. Not absolutely solid, for Psychology has split and shattered the idea of a 'Person', and has shown that there is something incalculable in each of us, which may at any moment rise to the surface and destroy our normal balance. We don't know what we are like. We can't know what other people are like. How, then, can we put any trust in personal relationships, or cling to them in the gathering political storm? In theory we cannot. But in practice we can and do. Though A is not unchangeably A, or B unchangeably B, there can still be love and loyalty between the two. For the purpose of living one has to assume that the personality is solid, and the 'self' is an entity, and to ignore all contrary evidence. And since to ignore evidence is one of the characteristics of faith, I certainly can proclaim that I believe in personal relationships.

The unusualness of such a statement is its combination of scepticism with affirmation. Mere scepticism dissolves faith; mere affirmation blinds it. Either by itself results in evasion, the former by seeming to exempt the individual from responsibilities which are still inescapable, the latter by moving the responsibilities elsewhere, so that he feels himself licensed to commit crimes guiltlessly. The fusion of the two results in an affirmation of responsibility by the assertion of moral independence. Not many intellectuals of our century at a time of urgent crisis have shown Forster's capacity to expose his vulnerability so candidly while affirming his responsibilities so uncompromisingly; the standpoint requires a fusion of intellectual lucidity and moral courage which is the keynote to a valid culture.

Auden's poem confesses the human desire for certainties; Forster agrees that certainties are needed, but he will not allow them too cheaply. Auden refers to the certainties that run away with the passions—'the slope of hate'—and glamorise the individual in doing so, but Forster insists that glamour is not necessarily an attribute of certainty: it would be gratifying to give *three* cheers for Democracy, but it does not certainly deserve them. Much of the technique of the essays as well as of the novels depends on the view that life and people are notably uncertain; uncertainty is our element, so that even our certainties, when we reach them, may well bear evidence of uncertainty. In 'The Raison d'Etre of Criticism' Forster acknowledges his over-use of the conjunction 'but', intervening in a statement with an objection or a qualification, and we can suppose that his 'buts' are representatively the 'unnoticed stones' which Auden refers to in his second stanza. Nonetheless, Forster insists on his certainties, not writing so as to impose them on the reader but so as to convince him that he has the obligation to find his own certainties in his own 'inner life'; this is the indispensable price of remaining an individual—the one belief which, at the end of the essay, he refuses to qualify.

To be an individual is to achieve character, and the kind of character one admires in Forster is expressed in his tribute to his recently dead friend Roger Fry in *Abinger Harvest*:

> If you said to him, 'This must be right, all the experts say so, all the Trustees of the National Gallery say so, Hitler says so, Marx says so, Christ says so, *The Times* says so,' he would reply in effect, 'Well I wonder. Let's see.' He would see and make you see. You would always come away realising that an opinion may be influentially backed and yet be tripe.

This is to a great extent Forster's own quality. He does not set out to refute authority, but we recognise his judgements as those of the whole man, attained by his feeling and his reason with equal force. This conjunction reveals another merit of the essays: he avoids convenient generalities which persuade the reader mentally but not emotionally because he does not know precisely into what he is being persuaded; he is always particular, so that we find ourselves in the situation which has provoked the argument. The essay 'Me, Them and You' in *Abinger Harvest* illustrates the method. Forster is attacking the blindness of social arrogance:

> I entered the exhibition, and found myself almost immediately in the presence of a family servant.
> 'Wretched weather,' I remarked civilly. There was no reply, the forehead swelled, the lips contracted haughtily. I had begun my tour with a very serious mistake, and had addressed a portrait of Lord Curzon. His face had misled me into thinking him a family servant. I ought to have looked only at the clothes, which were blue and blazing, and which he clutched with a blue-veined hand. They

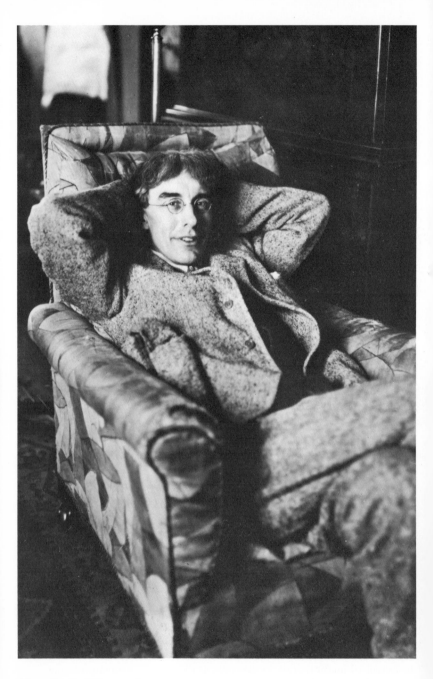

Roger Fry (1866–1934)

cost a hundred pounds perhaps. How cheap did my own costume seem now, and how impossible it was to imagine that Lord Curzon continues beneath his clothes, that he, too (if I may venture on the parallel), was a Me.

So far the satire is gentle; only Forster himself, the middle-class man, is the object of disparagement by the upper class, and the implicit point, that display can lie about realities, is not pressed. Later, however, he does press it, because now he is indignant:

> You had been plentiful enough in the snow outside (your proper place), but I had not expected to find You here in the place of honour, too. Yours was by far the largest picture in the show. You were hung between Lady Cowdray and the Hon. Mrs Langman, and You were entitled 'Gassed'. You were of godlike beauty—for the upper classes only allow the lower classes to appear in art on condition that they wash themselves and have classical features. These conditions you fulfilled. A line of golden-haired Apollos moved along a duck-board from left to right with bandages over their eyes. They had been blinded by mustard-gas. Others sat peacefully in the foreground, others approached through the middle distance. The battlefield was sad but tidy. No one complained, no one looked lousy or over-tired, and the aeroplanes overhead struck the necessary note of the majesty of England. It was all that a great war picture should be, and it was modern because it managed to tell a new sort of lie.

Forster makes his point as a novelist through a particular example, and it is from particulars, not from generalities, that true indignation arises. What follows from the particulars, in the formation of beliefs, must depend on the direct experience of other particulars which must be weighed against one another. As he says in his note on Orwell (*Two Cheers*):

> A true liberal, he hoped to help through small things. Programmes mean pogroms.

This is the lesson which Auden is taking to heart in his sonnet.

Collections of essays often give the impression of being desultory; the essays have been written at different times under various pretexts, so that connections from one to another are apt to be tenuous. Forster's first collection, *Abinger Harvest* (1936) seems more desultory than *Two Cheers for Democracy* because the essays in it were written over a wider period, and those of the later volume (1951) have more unity of tone through being mainly composed in the shadow of war. He offers some sort of order to *Abinger Harvest* by grouping the essays under headings—'The Present', 'Books', 'The Past', 'The East'. The first has some unity from the theme of social criticism; the second has the bond of literary criticism, and the fourth relates to India. It is when we come to 'The Past' that the charge of desultoriness seems most applicable. It is not surprising to find themes related to his own ancestral background in the essays on Hannah More and Battersea Rise, and the biographical sketches on Gibbon, Voltaire, Coleridge and Keats are connected to those by period if not in other ways. None, however, seem to have much connection with the sketch set in ancient Rome, 'Macolnia Shops', or his visit to the ancient Greek site of Cnidus in murky weather, nor do his studies of the Renaissance figures Gemisthus Pletho and Cardan. The subjects are indeed fairly random. And yet Forster's treatment of them does offer a bond, and this is the same sense of the particular that we have been considering, though he refers to it as 'actuality'. The opening essay, 'The Consolations of History', gives the clue:

> If only the sense of actuality can be lulled—and it sleeps for ever in most historians—there is no passion that cannot be gratified in the past. The past is devoid of all dangers, social and moral, and one can meet with perfect ease not only Kings, but people who are even rarer on one's visiting list.

It is the sense of actuality that Forster does not lull but arouses. He was never tempted to assume roles for which he had no professional qualification, and he does not undertake to be a historian; on the other hand he was a biographer and a novelist, and it is the biographical and novelistic techniques he uses to give the past the actuality of the present. The past is actual to us not so much when we meet great figures at their great moments as when minor ones, more like ourselves, are brought to life from it, or when we are made to feel mundane aspects of the lives of the great, as though an invisible window were opened to reveal that a landscape we had supposed gone is still with us, part of our own reality. The effect is historically creative: through small actualities, larger realities come home to us. Gemisthus Pletho, for instance, was a late Byzantine scholar with a boring theory about Greek paganism which he sought to revive, and he also took part in a mission to Florence the purpose of which was the unification of eastern and western Christianity. So obscure a figure is not likely to excite an unscholarly reader, and yet Forster not only makes his career convincingly alive, but demonstrates a perennial truth about cultural history—how a scholarly theorist (Pletho) may mislead himself away from the life of his study while an ignorant but creative society (the Florentine) may resurrect it. In each of the essays, Forster uses an individual or a place as a focus for the development of such an idea; the idea is on the whole left to the reader to seize out of the actuality depicted, and as the depiction is vivid, so the idea is fresh and reviving. We learn that our study of the past not only need never be boring but should always be more than consolatory. Undoubtedly Forster is following the lead of his friend, the famous biographer Lytton Strachey, but he is also in tune with another contemporary, T.S. Eliot. Like Eliot, Forster believed that we survive, if we do, in a living tradition, and that tradition survives in the life of its particulars, just as much as the present.

As we might expect from essays mainly written just before, during and just after the war, the opening sections of *Two Cheers for Democracy* have a grimness not much present in those of *Abinger Harvest*, but in both volumes we find a relaxation of tone in the succeeding sections— 'Books' in the latter, 'Art in General' and 'The Arts in Action' in the former. In fact, when writing or lecturing on the arts, Forster is always relaxed, and we can infer that this is not because his thought about them is less serious than on other subjects, but partly because he considered that the appropriate address on the subject must be persuasive, and partly—owing no doubt to the influence of academic Cambridge upon him—because he thought of himself, in criticism, as an amateur. Besides, he seems to have felt reserve about the value of its function. In the 'Raison d'Etre of Criticism' he pays a general tribute to it:

> We can readily agree that criticism has educational and cultural value; the critic helps to civilise the community, builds up standards, forms theories, stimulates, dissects, encourages the individual to enjoy the world into which he has been born; and on the destructive side he exposes fraud and pretentiousness and checks conceit. These are substantial achievements.

When, however, he discusses these functions in more detail—and he does not discuss them all, omitting, for instance, to say anything about the central activity of 'building up standards'—the effect is oddly disqualifying:

> The construction of aesthetic theories and their comparison are desirable cultural exercises; the theories themselves are unlikely to spread far or to hinder or help.

(What, then, can be the value of formulating them?) He ends by denying that a critic can have any community with an artist in the generation of a work of art, finally declaring that 'The only activity which can establish such a raison d'être is love.' We are back with persuasiveness.

It is not surprising, then, that Forster does not rank among the great critics of his generation. He could not re-order assumptions on the poetic tradition as Eliot did, nor vitalise conceptions of the relationship of art to life like Lawrence, nor establish literature as the central discipline for the training of human judgement like Leavis.

Nevertheless, he could talk to the reader on equal terms without trivialisation better than most writers of his time. His distinctiveness is often that he will begin with an easily recognisable approach and proceed, with an air of mischief, to an unfamiliar slant. Thus in the essay on Virginia Woolf (*Two Cheers*) he first makes the acceptable statement: 'She is a poet, who wants to write something as near a novel as possible.' The statement is acceptable rather than quite explanatory, for it begs the question why she wrote fiction rather than poetry. But he goes on:

What concerns me now is the material itself, her interests, her opinions. And, not to be too vague, I will begin with food.

It is the typical Forsterian approach of always introducing the particular as a stimulus to generalities, and it seems to risk the charge of trivialisation. The charge would not be valid, however: earlier he has distinguished 'two sorts of life in fiction: life on the page, and life eternal'; it is the former which he sees as representing Virginia Woolf's talent, and he could not demonstrate it better than by singling out such an unpoetical feature. We can see that Virginia Woolf is a novelist after all.

Another characteristic of his critical writing is similar to his method in writing about the past: he brings life to the critical comment by giving life to character and place in association with it. This is similar to the method of Virginia Woolf in her critical essays and it is very unfashionable nowadays, but it is not hard to justify, and it is an appealing approach to readers who do not profess scholarship. Imaginative writers, after all, are people; like other people they have experiences unique to themselves but not beyond understanding, and they grow up in their own environments. What makes them imaginative creators is a mystery, and one in which, according to Forster, the critic cannot participate. All the same, the more we understand about the writer as a man and the closer we can get to his environment as he knew it, the stronger our sympathies are likely to be with him; and without sympathy—so at least Forster believed—our responses will be weaker than they should be. At least the approach as he used it produced valuable insights. His essay on Ibsen in *Abinger Harvest*, for instance, is entitled 'Ibsen the Romantic'—a very unexpected description of that dramatist when he wrote it in 1928, but one which he justifies by relating Ibsen to the landscape of western Norway, and which has received general recognition since. Similarly, in the essay on Conrad in the same volume he brings out Conrad's distinction as a writer by emphasising how personal it is; the result is not to stimulate a legend of the man obscuring the merits of the writing, as has happened with many critics who have used the biographical approach, but to elucidate precisely what is individual in Conrad's work. Likewise he counteracts the depressingly desultory impression produced by 'occasional' writing. Several of the essays on individual writers were lectures devised for special occasions, like those on Crabbe and Skelton in *Two Cheers* originally given at Aldeburgh, both poets having been natives of the region, or they may have been stimulated by personal occasions, like the essay on Eliot in *Abinger Harvest*, which opens with his reactions to Eliot's first volume in the circumstances of war. But Forster persuades us that 'occasional' does not mean 'casual'; occasions are particularities of life, and bring to life particularities of literary experience.

From a critic so concerned with approach to universals through particulars one does not expect theorising, but *Two Cheers for Democracy*, in the section entitled 'Art in General', does in fact contain essays on the theory of art. They are, however, characteristically personal, stimulated by a personal need to validate individual responses, not academic doctrines. Thus one of the best, 'Anonymity: an Enquiry', opens with the simple question 'Do you like to know who a book's by?' and proceeds by lucid and ingenious analysis to a primary literary truth:

> We decided pretty easily that information ought to be signed; common sense leads to this conclusion, and newspapers which are largely unsigned have gained by that device their undesirable influence over civilization. Creation—that we found a more difficult matter. 'Literature wants not to be signed,' I suggested. Creation comes from the depths—the mystic will say from God. The signature, the name, belongs to the surface-personality, and pertains to the world of information, it is a ticket, not the spirit of life. While the author wrote he forgot his name; while we read him we forget both his name and our own.

The essay is dated earliest of those in the book (1925), just after the publication of his masterpiece *A Passage to India*, and this conclusion has the authority of the artist who realises that he has just excelled his apparent limits. Its distinction between the language of information and that of creation has elementary value for any reader and does not show individual bias. The others in the same section candidly do; they are openings for discussion, but of a profitable sort. As a theoriser, Forster has the virtue of being frankly provisional; he is without the disabling diffidence which frustrates discussion by its vagueness, but he is also without the intimidating arrogance which seems to defy it.

This is the virtue of his best-known work of critical thought, the Clark lectures delivered at Cambridge in 1927 under the title *Aspects of the Novel*. The permanence of their importance is debatable: critics have complained of Forster's wilful amateurism of tone, of the whimsicality with which he makes his points, of the partiality and even the superficiality of some of his judgements. On the other hand, few discussions of the novel have so combined entertainment with discernment, and few works of specialised criticism have achieved such wide currency. Forster's distinction between 'story' and 'plot'—

'The king died and then the queen died,' is a story. 'The king died, and then the queen died of grief' is a plot.

—simplifies the question monstrously, and yet it is a convenient starting-point for any reader, who can go on to elaborate the complexities for himself. His distinction between flat and round characters similarly ignores many questions about characterisation, and yet it has become currency for many writers who have found it a useful provisional tool. It may be that the chief value of *Aspects* now is that it is a useful introduction to Forster's own novels; at the time of delivery, when the quantity of critical theory about the novel was painfully slight, it was a valuable initiative for discussion beyond the ingenuous and hackneyed assumptions about fiction common not only among general readers but in academic circles. It has kept much of that value because Forster was not afraid to be rudimentary, and at the same time was facing problems in the novel which he himself had experienced as a leading practitioner. We are taken back to Virginia Woolf's tribute already quoted:

> Morgan has the artist's mind; he says the simple things that clever people don't say; I find him the best of critics for that reason.

The last section of *Abinger Harvest* is called 'The East'; that of *Two Cheers*, 'Places'. Together, though not consistently, they illustrate the contrasting aspects of Forster's very strong emotions about environment. On the one hand, the environment both enfolds the individual and shapes him, absorbing him with itself into a state of mind, as in 'The Last of Abinger' in *Two Cheers*, a series of jottings from his private commonplace book:

> BUNCH OF SENSATIONS. Listening in the late dusk to gramophone records I did not know; smoking; the quarter-moon shone as the light faded, and brought out sections of my books; motors coming down the Felday road shone through the window and flung the tulip-tree—and pane—shadows on the wallpaper near the fireplace. When the music stopped I felt something had arrived in the room; the sense of a world that asks to be noticed rather than explained was again upon me.

On the other hand, environment can estrange the individual, confusing him and threatening with disintegration his most intimate self. This is more evident in 'The East', for instance in 'Adrift in India', describing a bewildering visit to an ancient site:

> One confusion enveloped Ujjain and all things. Why differentiate? I asked the driver what kind of trees those were, and he answered 'Trees'; what was the name of that bird, and he said 'Bird'; and the plain, interminable, murmured, 'Old buildings are buildings, ruins are ruins.'

*t Hackhurst, Abinger, Surrey, designed for Forster's aunt, Laura Forster,
is father. Forster inherited the lease in 1924, and lived there with his
er till her death in 1945.*

Both are important; it is as necessary to be unsettled at times as it is to
feel settled at others. Nor is it predictable where either experience may
occur: he remembers feeling peace and happiness in a mosque in Cairo
while he is aware of sinister evil in a particular corner of Surrey. What
is unforgivable is insensibility to environment as in insensitive architecture, illustrated by this example from 'London is a Muddle':

> If you want a muddle, look around you as you walk from Piccadilly
> Circus to Oxford Circus. Here are ornaments that do not adorn,
> features that feature nothing, flatness, meanness, uniformity with-
> out harmony, bigness without size. Even when the shops are built at
> the same moment and by architects of equal fatuity, they manage to
> contradict one another. Here is the heart of the Empire, and the
> best it can do. Regent Street exhibits, in its most depressing aspect,
> the Spirit of London.

Forster's treatment of environment in the essays echoes much more in
the novels than just 'the spirit of place'.

But as much can probably be said of all Forster's non-fictional writings. His reputation as a novelist, when he ceased publishing fiction, was special if not unique. He was not just a leading exemplar of the art of the novel, nor a novelist who, as H.G. Wells declared of himself to Henry James, esteemed the role of journalist above that of artist. He belonged to the former class in valuing new techniques in rendering experience, surprising the reader out of his habitual responses, but also to the latter inasmuch as he was equally concerned not to estrange the reader but on the contrary to share the complexities of experience with him. He felt deeply that the experience of life in literature was that of life outside it, but simplified so as to elucidate the deeper complexities without belying them. The essays and biographies reproduce the insights of the fiction and make them explicit.

This does not mean that they are a mere substitute for the fiction; the reproduction is always partial, never reaches the same emotional depths, and can never—by its nature—make as strong appeal to the imagination. But these writings sustained the wisdom of the novels by other means, and help to explain them. Perhaps the most revealing of the essays in this explanatory function is 'Art for Art's Sake' (1949) in *Two Cheers*. In that essay Forster adopts a phrase that had become unfashionable since it had been an aesthetic slogan of the 1890s in protest against technological philistinism, and was felt to be redundant by the sophisticated artists of the twentieth century who cared as little for the narrowness of the aesthetes as they did for the ignorance of the philistines. Forster uses the expression in a new way: he postulates that order is indispensable to human sanity, and that the course of history is unlikely to produce it by any means except by art. He refers to Shelley's dictum that poets are 'the unacknowledged legislators of the world', and goes on:

> What laws did Shelley propose to pass? None. The legislation of the artist is never formulated at the time, though it is sometimes discerned by future generations. He legislates through creating. And he creates through his sensitiveness and his power to impose form. Without form the sensitiveness vanishes. And form is as important today, when the human race is trying to ride the whirlwind, as it ever was in those less agitating days of the past, when the earth seemed solid and the stars fixed, and the discoveries of science were made slowly, slowly. Form is not tradition. It alters from generation to generation. Artists always seek a new technique, and will continue to do so as long as their work excites them. But form of some kind is imperative. It is the surface crust of the internal harmony, it is the outward evidence of order.

We must now examine the form of Forster's own novels, so as to explore his version of that internal order, the search for which gave him his reputation as a 'sage'.

Part Three
The Novels

9 The sage and the artist: *Where Angels Fear to Tread*

The first and the last of the five novels published in Forster's lifetime differ from the other three in one respect: the endings are open; the problems have not been resolved. This by itself is of course no indication of merit; a 'happy' ending is not necessarily an artistically bad one. Nevertheless the open ending may have a closer relation to life, since in life only minor problems have solutions; major ones open into new problems, or perpetuate themselves by changing their forms. The happy ending is more likely to be a dangerous temptation, either because the author is seeking to gratify his audience—not a temptation to which Forster was liable—or because the resolution enables him to drive home a lesson which an open ending is more likely to leave in doubt. Being the sort of novelist he was—that is to say concerned to expose realities ignored by his society, in order to improve its civilisation—Forster was inclined to the second temptation. He was a truth-seeker, aware of the ways in which societies can cheat individuals and individuals can cheat themselves, but he was also a sage, disposed to demonstrate that wisdom can overcome lies. The function of a sage is not that of an artist, so that the two roles sometimes conflict in Forster's work. It is because the artist wins in the first novel, as he does in the last, that it seems sensible to begin the study of his novels with a close look at it. This is not to say that it is comparable to *A Passage to India*, so very much greater in depth and scope, nor even that it is his second best, since it lacks the breadth of interest of *Howards End*, but its comparative simplicity makes it suitable for demonstrating some of Forster's salient qualities, and its artistic purity frees us from the more debatable sage-like qualities, to which we must come later.

To begin with, the novel illustrates Forster's characteristic use of settings. These are two, each of them representing a quite different climate of civilisation—a circle, dictating the assumptions and habits of its human components. Sawston is an English town in the home counties dominated by the complacent middle-class which is philistine more by indifference to the arts than by hostility to them. The other setting is the Italian hill town of Monteriano, beautiful, but by Sawston standards plebeian and primitive. Its primitiveness, however, is much more complex than snobbish Sawston is able to appreciate; it is primitive in preserving older and coarser social customs, such as the total subjection of wives to husbands, but it is primitive also in its emotional freedom and spontaneity, in its instinctive outgoing courtesy to strangers who must be received with hospitality unless they come as overt enemies, and above all in its delight in the arts—or at least in the prevailing popular art of opera.

The two settings are initially connected by a secondary character, Lilia, the main pretext for the plot. She is vulgar, foolish and headstrong, widow to the elder son of Mrs Herriton (also a widow) who keeps her at Sawston so as to ensure that Lilia's little daughter shall be brought up a good Herriton and not such another as her mother. To keep Lilia from making an undesirable second marriage, Mrs Herriton sends her off to Italy in the charge of Caroline Abbott, ten years younger, but a boringly reliable do-gooder who can be depended upon to keep her companion out of trouble. The two women land up in Monteriano, from which Mrs Herriton is horrified to receive a telegram announcing that Lilia is about to marry a stranger whom she has met there. Philip, the surviving Herriton son and the 'clever' one, is despatched to prevent the marriage, but he arrives too late. Lilia has made a most undesirable match with Gino Cariola, son of a local dentist. The mystery is how Caroline Abbott could ever have allowed it.

The chief characters

Thus the plot is launched, and the main characters are established. Typically, Forster cheats the reader's expectations by removing Lilia who, with all her defects is a very positive character and seems at first certain to be a leading one; however, she dies in giving birth to her child by Gino. It is this which carries the plot forward, for Mrs Herriton is made to feel that she must adopt the baby. Philip, his stupid sister Harriet, and Caroline Abbott go out on this errand of redemption, but Philip and Caroline decide that it cannot be accomplished. Harriet, however, kidnaps the baby, who is killed in an accident on the way to the station. Caroline, Philip and Gino are left to face one another in the stark light of this tragedy.

The four main characters turn out to be Mrs Herriton and Gino flanking Philip and Caroline Abbott. The first two frame the action by embodying the values of their two so dissimilar societies.

Every individual is of course shaped by his or her society, and such conditioning is inevitably at a deep level unconscious, but it is possible to become conscious that such is the case, and that realisation can produce change in the character, making him critical first of the society and then of himself. Total commitment to the assumptions that condition him or her will, on the contrary, make such a change impossible. This is the difference that distinguishes the flanking characters from the two leaders. Mrs Herriton allows no moral obstruction to her central aim of sustaining the social eminence of her family in Sawston, but within the limits of that society she is amusing, intelligent and, above all, well-bred. Her breeding is her conscience;

she has no other, but it is the conscience of Sawston. Gino likewise has no conscience of his own, but he shares one with his community and this communal conscience is also a product of breeding, although the breeding of the two places is so different that neither would recognise it in the other. Sawston is proud, but it has very little sense of local identity; its pride is national, and especially the pride of a social class which believes itself identifiable with the nation. Monteriano, on the contrary, has no important social distinctions, but it has immense pride in itself and in its long and violent history. Enemies have been ruthless and cunning, so that cunning and ruthlessness are inbred in the Monteriano character, but friends have been indispensable against the enemies, so that joy in friendship and courtesy to strangers (who are friends until they prove themselves enemies) are equally instinctive to it. It is also a particularly masculine society, since violence must give precedence to the male, whereas the security and orderliness of Sawston gives precedence to the ladies, so long as they remain ladylike. Thus Gino compounds in himself the Monteriano characteristics just as Mrs Herriton compounds the Sawston ones. Both are intriguers, but Gino's intrigues, though skilful, are naked and exposed where Mrs Herriton's are concealed, since in the Sawston code naked intrigue is vulgar. Both possess good manners of their own sort, but Mrs Herriton cultivates politeness in the set forms of her class, whereas Gino's courtesy is intrinsic to his delight in friendship. Both have great family pride, but Gino's assumes feminine subservience to his paternity, whereas Mrs Herriton is a matriarch. Gino is a male in a masculine society indifferent to social rank; Mrs Herriton is a woman in a society which demands that women shall be ladies.

Her son Philip has a far more individual nature, but, until the end of the novel, he is without the strength of an individuality capable of resisting his mother's social identity. He is too intelligent to be satisfied by Sawston, and from the first page his infection by Italy and by its people, not merely by its museum culture, gives him a standpoint for criticism of Sawston values. On the other hand he is in practice a victim of them. He has financial independence enabling him to pursue his profession in the law at the pleasure of his own ease, and his freedom from responsibility and passive acceptance of the social *status quo* leave him entirely at the disposal of his strong-willed mother. He is what he comes to see himself as being, when he describes himself in chapter 8:

> 'I seem fated to pass through the world without colliding with it or moving it—and I'm sure I can't tell you whether the fate's good or evil'.

Caroline Abbott is more complex and self-contradictory still. She lives with her father, serving his needs, and spends her ample leisure in relieving the needs of Sawston's less privileged inhabitants. Such safe conscientious rectitude makes her an ideal choice for Mrs Herriton when Caroline decides—and the decision is our first clue to her hidden peculiarity—to spend a year in Italy: she will be chaperone to the tiresome daughter-in-law Lilia. The fact that she allows the marriage is at first seen as evidence that she is not as sensible as she is respectable, and her behaviour to Philip when he comes over, too late, to stop the marriage confirms the impression. However, the lapse does not significantly alter the Herriton bored respect for her; she is still, apparently, the dull, conformist Sawston do-gooder. Then, midway in the novel, she has a conversation with Philip in a train to London which changes his impression of her, and changes the reader's impression still more.

She begins by confessing that she did not merely allow the marriage, but incited Lilia to it. This makes him indignant, but his indignation changes to surprised interest when she goes on to give her explanation:

'I hated Sawston, you see.'

He was delighted. 'So did and do I. That's splendid. Go on.'

'I hated the idleness, the stupidity, the respectability, the petty unselfishness.'

'Petty selfishness,' he corrected. Sawston psychology had long been his speciality.

'Petty unselfishness,' she repeated. 'I had got the idea that every one here spent their lives in making little sacrifices for objects they didn't care for, to please people they didn't love; that they never learnt to be sincere—and, what's as bad, never learnt how to enjoy themselves. That's what I thought—what I thought at Monteriano.'

'Why, Miss Abbott,' he cried, 'you should have told me this before! Think it still! I agree with lots of it. Magnificent!'

But, despite his agreement, there is already a clue that they are really in disagreement, and this shows in their apparently trifling difference about 'selfishness'–'unselfishness'. If one dislikes a circle of people, it is convenient to detect a vice in them, and then to rationalise one's dislike on the basis of it, and this is what Philip is doing. To dislike people for a virtue—even a 'petty' one—is inconvenient, because it requires analysis, and this is what Caroline undertakes. She has detected that the Sawston virtue is insincere because it does not proceed from authentic feeling. Monteriano kindness, on the other hand, is selfish because it enhances the happiness of the givers, but for that reason it also issues from their living selves.

Caroline goes on to explain the bearing of her feelings about Sawston on her instigation of Lilia's marriage:

'Now Lilia,' she went on, 'though there were things about her I didn't like, had somehow the power of enjoying herself with sincerity. And Gino, I thought, was splendid, and young, and strong not only in body, and sincere as the day. If they wanted to marry, why shouldn't they do so? Why shouldn't she break with the deadening life where she had got into a groove, and would go on in it, getting more and more—worse than unhappy—apathetic till she died? Of course I was wrong. She only changed one groove for another—a worse groove. And as for him—well, you know more about him than I do. I can never trust myself to judge characters again. But I still feel he cannot have been quite bad when we first met him. Lilia—that I should dare to say it!—must have been cowardly. He was only a boy—just going to turn into something fine, I thought—and she must have mismanaged him. So that is the one time I have gone against what is proper, and there are the results. You have an explanation now.'

'And much of it has been most interesting, though I don't understand everything. Did you never think of the disparity of their social position?'

'We were mad—drunk with rebellion. We had no common sense. As soon as you came, you saw and foresaw everything.'

'Oh, I don't think that.' He was vaguely displeased at being credited with common sense. For a moment Miss Abbott had seemed to him more unconventional than himself.

(*chapter 5*)

In this exchange four qualities offer themselves for inspection: 'sincerity', 'cowardice', 'propriety', 'common sense'. Hitherto Lilia has been credited with no virtues by anyone; she has been distinguishable only by her foolishness. But Caroline has discovered her sincerity, at least in her capacity to enjoy herself, and suddenly she is set in opposition to Sawston by a mark of superiority. Has she also been cowardly? Her first and fatal breach with Gino has occurred in chapter 4, when she threatened to withdraw her income from him, and produced in him a manifestation of silent rage which entirely subdued her. To have resisted him at that moment would have required the kind of courage which depends on other capacities which she does not possess—insights into the character of Sawston from which she has fled and of Monteriano of which she is now a part, and a consequent sense of Gino's limitations and of her own rights. Courage of this sort is a manifestation of that native intelligence which Lilia is without. But when Caroline admits to going against 'what is proper', she is acknowledging an ambiguous restraint. The phrase brings to mind ridiculous conformity to what is unthinkingly accepted as 'right', and we think of trespassers over such a frontier as deserving credit. On the other hand, proprieties have originally taken rise from a collective wisdom and require reasoned confrontation, not the impulsive transgression of which she acknowledges guilt. Even Sawston proprieties have some justification, and it is 'common sense' not to be reckless about them. She pays Philip the just tribute that he possesses it. But, interestingly, he does not like the tribute: in theory, he is the heretic of Sawston. In practice, however—thereby showing his 'common sense'—he plays along with Sawston proprieties, because they are inbred in him and they work to his advantage. He has not yet faced this inconsistency in himself, and consequently lives with an internal moral disorder.

The conclusion of their conversation brings to light this moral discrepancy in their outlooks. Caroline acknowledges her illusions. She had wanted to accomplish a revolution against society with her own individual resources:

'... I wanted to fight against all the things I hated—mediocrity and dullness and spitefulness and society. I actually hated society for a day or two at Monteriano. I didn't see that all these things are invincible, and that if we go against them they will break us to pieces. Thank you for listening to so much nonsense.'

'Oh, I quite sympathise with what you say,' said Philip encouragingly; 'it isn't nonsense, and a year or two ago I should have been saying it too. But I feel differently now, and I hope that you also will change. Society *is* invincible—to a certain degree. But your real life is your own, and nothing can touch it. There is no power on earth that can prevent your criticising and despising mediocrity—nothing that can prevent you retreating into splendour and beauty—into the thoughts and beliefs that make the real life—the real you.'

'I have never had that experience yet. Surely I and my life must be where I live.'

Evidently she had the usual feminine incapacity for grasping philosophy. But she had developed quite a personality, and he must see more of her. 'There is another great consolation against invincible mediocrity,' he said—'the meeting a fellow victim. I hope that this is only the first of many discussions that we shall have together.'

She made a suitable reply. The train reached Charing Cross, and they parted—he to go to a matinee, she to buy petticoats for the corpulent poor. Her thoughts wandered as she bought them: the gulf between herself and Mr Herriton, which she had always known to be great, now seemed to her immeasurable.

Forster's handling of discussions between his characters seldom allows one to be right entirely at the expense of the other. Both are right, and to some extent wrong, but the rightness of one is seen to be superior in kind to that of the other. Just as Philip and his mother have been right in foreseeing that Lilia's marriage will be disastrous, so his common sense is still superior to Caroline's when he asserts the possibility of separating one's personal values from the life imposed by society, and to find contentment in doing so; he is wrong only in not recognising the moral mediocrity of such a course. Caroline is wrong in assuming that society must inevitably swallow her against her will, but she is right in a way superior to Philip's in refusing to recognise that the individual life can ever be vitally separated from the society in which the individual lives. It follows that Philip is wrong in assuming that he is in a position to 'educate' Caroline as a person; she, on the contrary, will educate him. She is thus wrong in supposing that the gulf between them is immeasurable. The education will, however, not come primarily through discussion—the only means that Philip can envisage—but through painful, squalid, and at the same time glorious, physical experience.

The first indication of this is that it becomes known in Sawston that Lilia has died in giving birth to a son. The news disconcerts the Herritons, but would not have done so seriously—the baby can, after all, conveniently be left with Gino—if it were not for a second interference by Caroline Abbott. She has come round to the Herriton view that Gino must be 'a cad', but she deduces that since she has been responsible for the marriage it is her responsibility—as it is that of the Herritons as Lilia's self-proclaimed protectors—to rescue the baby from him. Mrs Herriton, however, had 'protected' Lilia only in Herriton interests, to prevent her disgracing the family. Caroline's insistence that the baby must be rescued angers her greatly, but it forces her hand; if she does nothing, washing her hands of the responsibility as she wishes, then Caroline will act independently, and by doing so will bring disgrace upon her. Accordingly she changes tactics, professes concern for the baby, and sends Philip and her daughter Harriet to bribe Gino into surrendering it. It is Philip's first serious disillusionment with his mother, since he is much too intelligent not to perceive her disingenuousness. Caroline, who has seen through it long before, distrusts the Herriton disingenuousness so much that, unknown to them, she goes independently to Monteriano to ensure that the task will really be accomplished.

This second visit reverses the attitudes of both Caroline and Philip, changing their characters fundamentally. She makes herself known to him and to Harriet, but nonetheless visits Gino without their knowledge, and discovers what she has never suspected—the depth and reality of Gino's love for his child: to deprive him of it would not only be impracticable, but morally wrong.

> It was too late to go. She could not tell why, but it was too late. She turned away her head when Gino lifted his son to his lips. This was

San Gimignano, the basis for Monteriano

something too remote from the prettiness of the nursery. The man was majestic: he was a part of Nature; in no ordinary love scene could he ever be so great. For a wonderful physical tie binds the parents to the children; and—by some sad, strange irony—it does not bind us children to our parents. For if it did, if we could answer love not with gratitude but with equal love, life would lose much of its pathos and much of its squalor, and we might be wonderfully happy. Gino passionately embracing, Miss Abbott reverently averting her eyes—both of them had parents whom they did not love so very much.

'May I help you to wash him?' she asked humbly.

(*chapter 7*)

Caroline is undergoing the second stage of a conversion which had begun on her previous visit to Monteriano. Then, Monteriano had taught her hatred of Sawston society, but the narrowness of her experience had prevented her from seeing that Monteriano, too, had its serious faults; faced with these and with Lilia's unhappiness consequent on them, she had swung back to the Herriton view of Gino, without hating Sawston any the less. Now she sees that while Gino is indeed disreputable by one of the better Sawston tenets—he had barefacedly married Lilia for her money, and then assumed that both were entirely at his disposal—he nonetheless shares with his birthplace its deeper virtues of rich beauty and generous feeling. Gino's transfiguration is altogether unexpected by her, but she has been unconsciously prepared for it in the previous twenty-four hours by sharing the city and its life with Philip. On his side, the friendship with which Gino has received him when they met at the opera on the previous night makes him quite ready to accept Caroline's conversion to the belief that their mission has been mistaken.

They are, however, defeated by his sister Harriet. Harriet admirably balances Lilia in the novel: the latter is foolish, and the former is stupid. We tend to think of the words as practically synonymous but Forster shows us that foolishness can relax—Lilia can enjoy herself—but stupidity is rigid. Harriet does not bear the Sawston stereotype plastically as her mother does, adapting it to her purposes, and she is certainly not capable of detachment from it like her brother. For her it is dogma, and she is an excellent caricature of English insularity at its crudest—'Foreigners are a dirty nation' she remarks, as she cleans up a railway compartment. Consequently she refuses to accept what she regards as Philip's and Caroline's defeat; she kidnaps the baby, conceals it until she and Philip are in the cab on the way to the station, and loses it in an accident caused by their reckless driver.

For the first time Philip has to face responsibility for his helplessness: he returns to face Gino, who, but for Caroline's intervention, would have killed him. Just as she has been fundamentally altered by her vision of Gino and his son, so now he is changed by her trans-figuration as she rescues him, and receives the outburst of Gino's grief which succeeds his initial rage:

> All through the day Miss Abbott had seemed to Philip like a goddess, and more than ever did she seem so now. Many people look younger and more intimate during great emotion. But some there are who look older, and remote, and he could not think that there was little difference in years, and none in composition, between her and the man whose head was laid upon her breast. Her eyes were open, full of pity and full of majesty, as if they discerned the boundaries of sorrow, and saw unimaginable tracts beyond. Such eyes he had seen in great pictures but never in a mortal. Her hands were folded round the sufferer, stroking him lightly, for even a goddess can do no more than that. And it seemed fitting, too, that she should bend her head and touch his forehead with her lips.
>
> (*chapter 9*)

The revolution in the relationship between Philip and Caroline is epitomised in a few sentences from their final conversation when, much later, they are returning in the train:

> '... Will you be in Italy next spring?'
> 'No.'
> 'I'm sorry. When will you come back do you think?'
> 'I think never.'
> 'For whatever reason?' He stared at her as if she were some monstrosity.
> 'Because I understand the place. There is no need.'
> 'Understand Italy!' he exclaimed.
> 'Perfectly.'
> 'Well, I don't. And I don't understand you,' he murmured to himself, as he paced away from her up the corridor.
>
> (*chapter 10*)

He is now in love with her, but they cannot marry because she is in love with Gino, and she cannot marry Gino because he has already engaged himself to marry another woman, originally to help him care for the child now dead. Thus is the conventional 'happy ending' avoided, but the ending is at least positive. Philip has learned something of himself, and Caroline passes back into Sawston released from her sense of nonentity. He decides to separate himself from his mother, and Caroline knows that she has in him one friend who understands her to her depths.

One of the values of *Where Angels Fear to Tread*, Forster's first novel, is that it exhibits features of his art which recur in his later novels, and help us to recognise his character as a novelist. Six of these are conspicuous, three relating to themes and three to his technique. The themes are matriarchy, culture barriers, and insularity; the technical features are his use of epiphanies, of the spirit of place, and of rhythm.

Themes of the novel

The theme of matriarchy seems to derive from the peculiarities of Forster's own life; when we remember that his father died when he was a baby, and that he spent his solitary childhood in the care of strongly maternal women, we need not be surprised that he should feel the maternal role of women as a powerful influence in the shaping of human experience. Such influence can be benign or malign, and both sorts are features of the novels. Mrs Herriton is plainly malign, but the image of Caroline Abbott receiving the grief of Gino, as a mother responds to that of her child, is of practically divine benignity—she 'seemed to Philip like a goddess'. What is interesting here is that the love is given not to Philip but to Gino—himself the benign father which neither Philip (as far as the novel tells us) nor Forster himself had ever known. It is as though only those who have given parental love can deserve to receive it, and parental love seems to be one of the great gaps in Sawston experience. Mrs Herriton manages her children skilfully, and they respect her (until Philip perceives her to be the artful contriver she is), but she shows no love for them. Lilia does not care much for her Sawston daughter Irma, and we diagnose that this is because she is not allowed to: Mrs Herriton has robbed her of her daughter in order to assimilate the child into the Sawston code of values. Caroline has perceived that Sawston murders feeling whereas Monteriano nourishes it, and her triumph is to acquire the capacity for love in spite of Sawston. But it is Gino who earns it, because he himself has given it to his son, thereby revealing it to and releasing it in Caroline herself.

The theme of matriarchy is not merely an idiosyncrasy of Forster's, arising from the eccentricity of his own experience. One of the qualities by which we recognise major artists is their capacity to universalise what is at first merely personal to them, and through the image of the matriarch he taps one of the deep themes of European culture, whether we think of the malign Clytemnestra or Mary the Mother of God. This is implicit in the way Caroline twice recalls to Philip great pictures—first when he comes upon Caroline with the baby and Gino beside her ('to all intents and purposes, the Virgin and Child, with Donor') and again, more intensely, when he watches her sympathy for Gino in his tragic grief: 'Such eyes he had seen in great pictures but never in a mortal.' Our civilisation in the last two hundred years has obscured the importance of the great mother figure of which no previous age was unaware. Feminism has diverted our attention from the maternal role by directing it to the rivalry of men and women in the same spheres of action, and the modern dilution of the nuclear family has further weakened the image. Forster is one of the few writers of this century to have given it close attention, and he strengthens it by almost eliminating the father figure from his fiction; Gino is one of the few exceptions.

Benign matriarchy unifies disparate elements into an order of relationship; malign matriarchy works for exclusiveness. In this way the matriarchal theme merges with the more complex one of the culture barrier. This takes several forms in the novels. Culture snobbery, for instance, such as Philip is addicted to until the end of his story, contributes to his mother's authority even though it is anti-Sawston. The malign mother is a politician, and just as the state is content with culture so long as it does not impel the intelligentsia against it, so Mrs Herriton is indifferent to Philip's passion for Italy so long as it sustains his own feelings of superiority and so contributes to Herriton arrogance. But culture is not merely public; it is also intimate, the life of the human heart. Caroline learns this as she learns Monteriano architecture while pondering the problem of Gino and the baby:

'And he never mentioned the baby once,' Miss Abbott repeated. But she had returned to the window, and again her finger pursued the delicate curves. He watched her in silence, and was more attracted to her than he had ever been before. She really was the strangest mixture.

(*chapter 6*)

The difference is between museum culture and culture in the blood-stream: the former requires intellectual understanding, but the latter requires imagination; the former is academic and useful, but may nonetheless stultify the individual and become a barrier against the latter, which, released, sets the individual moving and growing. Forster continues to explore the two sorts of culture, their conflict and the barriers against both, in his next three novels, but in the last it is the second and deeper sort of culture, and the human barriers against it, which are his main theme.

Insularity, the third of Forster's outstanding themes, is of course a culture barrier, but, as he uses it, insularity defines the human condition as well as limits human cultures. Deriving from 'insula', the Latin for 'island', the word expresses the sort of culture barrier which is particularly relevant to Britain, and especially to the arrogant self-sufficiency of England in the Victorian and Edwardian periods. The best Victorian writers, Arnold outstandingly, had seen the need to break such complacency, and to open the eyes of the nation to the deprivation it was causing itself. But as a description of the human condition, insularity has more symbolic echoes. 'No man is an island,' wrote John Donne in his *Devotions*, 'entire of itself'; but Arnold, in one of his poems, 'To Marguerite', wrote:

Yes! in the sea of life enisled,
With echoing straits between us thrown,
Dotting the shoreless watery wild,
We mortal millions live *alone*.

Donne is, of course, right in the sense that nothing important can happen to any individual without some resonance in other lives, but Arnold is also right in the sense that so much human experience most of the time is incommunicable; human sympathy must be partial, and complete empathy is impossible. Forster is much concerned with insularity as a culture barrier in the novels; both Sawston and Monteriano are insular culturally. He also treats it in Donne's sense, by demonstrating the inter-linking of apparently remote destinies: Mrs Herriton wished to ignore Gino's baby, but its death is indirectly caused not only by her machinations but by her whole scheme of existence as reflected in Harriet, and it will divide her from her son. But Arnold's sense of insularity, according to which individuals are fated to be 'enisled', is one of Forster's conspicuous themes, and he treats it both comically and tragically. Comically, he shows how individuals may feel that they are intelligible to each other although in reality they are in total misunderstanding, like Gino and Lilia in the early months of their marriage; or one may suppose that he has reached complete understanding with the other whereas the other has in fact reached despair of it, like Caroline and Philip in their first conversation in the train. His tragic treatment of the theme distinguishes the two novels with unresolved endings from the other three. It is true that Caroline and Philip do at last achieve understanding in the last chapter of *Where Angels Fear to Tread*, but each is doomed to understand the other apart. Each will live alone, Caroline not more so than she has always done, but Philip, by achieving his integrity, has lost his former illusory affinities with his class. The novels with resolved endings, on the other hand, imply promise of happy futures issuing from the final union of the selves, and raise a doubt in the reader's mind whether the promise is authentic or rather wished on the characters by the author.

Forster's techniques

In major novelists, the difference between 'theme' and 'technique' is often difficult to make: what we see and understand has too much to do with the ways we see and understand. So when we distinguish 'epiphany' as a characteristic technique of Forster's, we are also pointing to what he sees as a quality of human experience which we might almost describe as one of his themes. But it is more convenient to think of it as a technique, since he uses epiphanies to mark turning points in his narratives and in the development of his characters. The word has, of course, a biblical origin: the feast of Epiphany commemorates the manifestation of the child Christ to the Magi. As a literary term, it is chiefly associated with James Joyce, whose 'epiphanies' were early sketches in which truths are revealed by isolating incidents in such a way as to reveal from them more than their usual significance. There is no reason to use the term as a link between Forster and Joyce, but it is convenient to signify those moments in every novel when a character is changed by an experience which is visionary to him or her, though through other eyes it might seem nothing extraordinary. Such moments occur when Caroline's conception of Gino is transformed by witnessing Gino's love for his child, and when Philip witnesses her profound sympathy with Gino in his grief at its death. If we can divide novelists into 'explainers' and 'seers', we may say that most of the time Forster is an explainer, demonstrating the ways in which human relationships are misunderstood, and how they can be understood better, but in his epiphanies he becomes a seer, demonstrating that the experience of certain incidents in an appropriate state of mind may lead to the transfiguration of our habitual notions.

The spirit of place is often associated with epiphanies in Forster's novels, and of course the spirit of Monteriano has much to do with Caroline's and Philip's epiphanies. But Forster's use of environment is usually specific; we are not given panoramas so much as descriptions of particular localities at particular times. We do not learn very much about the appearance of Monteriano—though enough to recognise that it is based on the actual town of San Gimigniano—and its spirit is conveyed less through its historic architecture than through the opera house which the English characters visit on the evening before their intended departure:

> He had been to this theatre many years before, on the occasion of a performance of 'La Zia di Carlo'. Since then it had been thoroughly done up, in the tints of beetroot and tomato, and was in many other ways a credit to the little town. The orchestra had been enlarged, some of the boxes had terra-cotta draperies, and over each box was suspended an enormous tablet, neatly framed, bearing upon it the number of that box. There was also a drop-scene, representing a pink and purple landscape, wherein sported many a lady lightly clad, and two more ladies lay along the top of the proscenium to steady a large and pallid clock. So rich and so appalling was the effect, that Philip could scarcely suppress a cry. There is something majestic in the bad taste of Italy; it is not the bad taste of a country which knows no better; it has not the nervous vulgarity of England, or the blinded vulgarity of Germany. It observes beauty and chooses to pass it by. But it attains to beauty's confidence. This tiny theatre of Monteriano spraddled and swaggered with the best of them, and these ladies with their clock would have nodded to the young men on the ceiling of the Sistine.

> *(chapter 6)*

Forster is often at his best when he defeats his reader's expectations, and he does so here both in his choice of setting to bring out the Monteriano spirit, and in the detail by which he shows the very ugliness of the setting to be evidence of that spirit at its best. Good and bad taste are commonly reserved for private discrimination—'there's no accounting for taste'—or for museum culture. Forster breaks down such barriers, showing that good and bad taste may equally be the products of an exuberance which brushes away conventional discrimination. The description precedes that of the opera itself, and of its reception, which outrages Harriet, delights Caroline, and snatches up Philip, releasing him into its conviviality. In his descriptions of place, Forster is expert at educing the spirit of material surroundings, so that place and mind manifest themselves in each other, preparing and accounting for the epiphanies which accompany or succeed them.

Rhythm, the last of the distinguishing techniques, consists in the use of references to small detail, repeated at intervals and accenting underlying significance in the novel as a whole. It is a technique of more importance in the last two novels; in the first, there are two notable examples of it. One is the inlaid box which Harriet lends Lilia—'lent, not given'—on the latter's initial departure; she never forgets it, and Lilia never returns it; it remains as loot from Sawston, with a place of honour in a dreary room in Gino's house, commemorating Lilia's death. The phrase 'lent, not given' is a repeated reminder of Sawston's over-valuation of even the smallest property, surviving (in Harriet, Sawston's purest representative) even when serious issues should seem to have obliterated it. As loot, it links with the other refrain through the book: 'Poggibonizzi, fatti in là che Monteriano si fa città'. The jingle is never translated, but means: 'Poggibonsians, move over so that Monteriano can become a city' and commemorates Monteriano's fight for freedom against a neighbouring city in the thirteenth century; it first occurs when Mrs Herriton discovers it in Philip's Baedeker, and the Monterianese have apparently never forgotten it, for individuals recite it gleefully to the English visitors. In the novel, the rhyme originates, stilted and impersonal, in the cold print of Baedeker, takes life in the human voices, and reaches climax in the dream consciousness of Caroline Abbott at the end of chapter 6, torn as she is between her sense of obligation to Lilia's baby and her sympathy with the spirit of the place:

She was here to fight against this place, to rescue a little soul who was innocent as yet. She was here to champion morality and purity, and the holy life of an English home. In the spring she had sinned through ignorance; she was not ignorant now. 'Help me!' she cried, and shut the window as if there was magic in the encircling air. But the tunes would not go out of her head, and all night long she was troubled by torrents of music, and by applause and laughter and angry young men who shouted the distich out of Baedeker:

> Poggibonizzi fatti in là,
> Che Monteriano si fa città!

Poggibonsi was revealed to her as they sang—a joyless, straggling place, full of people who pretended. When she woke up she knew that it had been Sawston.

(chapter 6)

Thus the rhythmic repetition achieves analogy between the ancient war of cities and the modern war of spirit: by the end, the Sawstonians have been obliged to move over, releasing Philip and Caroline into a new bond of community.

The themes and techniques in *Where Angels Fear to Tread* which we have been discussing are of course not the only ones in Forster's novels. The techniques have been singled out because they are special to him and help us to distinguish his uniqueness; others, for instance his ear for dialogue, he shared with other novelists. This is also true of his themes. Two of his themes, however, not so far mentioned in this section, are not only special to him but embrace all the others.

The first of these has been discussed in the section on his stories; it is that of 'breaking the circle'. Both Caroline and Philip free themselves from the constraints and prejudices of Sawston assumptions, achieving lucid individuality based on the firm foundation of self-understanding. The self-understanding is itself realised through understanding the true nature of their quarrel with their Sawston environment, by discerning the true nature of its opponent—Monteriano. Caroline, however, goes further than Philip in this: Caroline 'knows' Italy, whereas Philip, who has supposed that he did, no longer supposes it; he realises that his former complacent assurance of doing so concealed a greater ignorance than his present humility does. Caroline decides that she will probably never re-visit the country because, precisely by learning it and loving it, she has learned that it can never be hers; as she remarks in the earlier conversation, she and her life must be where she lives. Philip, we may assume, will come back, but he will return in a different spirit; Italy will no longer be a mere holiday for his spirit by providing a refreshing contrast to the spectacle of Sawston, but a place of trial offering further lessons in self-learning. Both are destined to be lonely except for their mutual friendship; 'breaking the circle' may entail loneliness, but at least it is a loneliness freed from the muddle of bafflement, frustration and illusion entailed by living in an antagonistic society unsupported by the mystery of self-knowledge.

Muddle and mystery, and the difference between them, is the second of Forster's inclusive themes, and we must investigate it in the next two sections.

10 The personal and the social: explorations of mystery and muddle

In this section we shall consider the three novels that intervene between *Where Angels Fear to Tread* and *A Passage to India*. In order of publication these are *The Longest Journey* (1907), *A Room with a View* (1908), and *Howards End* (1910). The order of publication is, however, rather confusing if we try to discern in it Forster's development, for his biographer, P.N. Furbank, shows that Forster was pondering the material of his second and third novels together with that of his first (*Where Angels Fear to Tread*, 1905) as early as 1904. Those three, then, constitute the first phase of his development; *Howards End*, showing greater detachment and increased scope in the handling of social material, is the second phase, and *A Passage to India* the third.

The theme of mystery and muddle, as Forster expounds it in his first and second phases, can be outlined in the following way. Human beings live, for most of the time unconsciously, in a world of muddled personal relationships imposed on them by an illusion of order in the society into which they are born. Societies, more often implicitly than explicitly, dictate patterns of human relations which compound primitive instinct with sophisticated self-interest. The self-interest distorts the primitive impulses and complicates them, so that individuals cease to be individual with a sense of spontaneous community with other individuals; they become stereotypes, bound to others by a system of obligations which blind themselves to themselves—to their authentic feelings. Yet, beneath the muddle of the factitious system, the mystery of the individual and his personal fulfilment remains valid and potentially realisable. The difference between the muddle and the mystery is an ultimate one, although superficially they are often confused: a muddle can be exposed, explained, and cleared away; a mystery cannot be exposed, for that would mean that human beings can get outside it, which is impossible since they are themselves the mystery. It can only be revealed, and that partially. It cannot be explained, because it is itself the explanation, and it cannot be cleared away because it is itself reality. These are profundities which Forster fully attains only in his last novel.

The Longest Journey

The opposition between the individual and society is a theme which has been shared among major novelists since the beginnings of the

English novel, and its full exposition requires understanding of two factors; the novelist needs to show us the working of society as well as the working of the individual. Exploring the opposition as a young man from a sheltered background, Forster portrays the individual in disproportion to society in his first phase; we know how Sawston behaves through its embodiment, Mrs Herriton, but we are not shown what causes such behaviour. The social aspect of *A Room with a View* is also very domestic, but in *The Longest Journey* the individual and the social are more balanced, if not more deeply analysed. The hero, Rickie Elliot, is far from heroic for most of the novel, but in the end he achieves apotheosis in a hero's death, thereby transcending the social barriers. He moves away from Cambridge, where he has enjoyed freedom as an individual, into the stereotyped world of Sawston School, typified by Mr Pembroke and his sister Agnes whom Rickie marries. The social arena is further enlarged by the crucial character of Stephen Wonham. Stephen, who turns out to be the bastard son of Rickie's own mother, is a type unknown to Cambridge (though Rickie's friend, Steward Ansell, has sympathies and affinities with him) and he is abhorred by Sawston. His world is of working-class individualism, physical instead of intellectual, and he is constitutionally rebellious against the social prestige and authority to which the school aspires. Rickie's Agnes and her brother do not wish to recognise him as kin, and it is only by the malice of Rickie's aunt, Mrs Failing, who plays the role of 'malign matriarch' to Stephen and Rickie, that he comes to know of the kinship. The crisis of the novel concerns the conflict in Rickie whether to acknowledge Stephen; his eventual insistence on doing so breaks the bondage of Sawston and marriage, but Stephen's drunkenness causes Rickie's death when saving his brother from being run over by a train. The conclusion, however, is a 'happy ending'; in the last chapter Stephen takes responsibility for Rickie's literary works in open hostility to Mr Pembroke, acknowledging the enormous debt of his own life and fortune to the brother who had died for him. It is as though Rickie lives again in Stephen, freed from his physical crippling while losing none of his generosity of mind, and enlarged into fullness of humanity.

Thus *The Longest Journey* attempts a larger view of social character than the other novels of the first phase, but it is still centred on a character not far from Forster himself. 'Rickie' is so called not because it is his real name but because he was partly crippled by rickets in infancy—a disability corresponding to Forster's own homosexuality. His spirit is released by Cambridge, as Forster's was, but his culture and his secure income isolate him from those who lack such privileges and lead a more physical existence, represented by Stephen Wonham, and this also corresponds to Forster's own experience. All his life, he was drawn to men of this type; one of his few childhood friends of his own age was a gardening boy called Ansell, and in manhood he made

E.M. Forster, 1911, by Roger Fry

intimate friendships with others. His feeling for 'the spirit of place', especially English place, is also prominent in the novel, and is characteristically specific. Rickie and his Cambridge friends have a favourite resort in a spot they call 'the dell'—an abandoned, wooded chalkpit near the village of Madingley—and the moment of truth, when his aunt casually drops the information that Stephen Wonham is his brother, takes place in Cadbury Rings, an ancient encampment on Salisbury Plain. In contrast to the Madingley dell, the chalk Rings are open and exposed to all the surrounding landscape, reflecting exposure of the individual to social truth transcending both the cosiness of Cambridge friendships and the claustrophobic oppressiveness of Sawston and Rickie's married life.

Forster once described *The Longest Journey* as his 'nicest novel', and perhaps he thought so because, of the novels published in his lifetime, it is the image which is closest to what he felt to be his personal predicament, and the one which offers the kind of resolution which had the most emotional appeal for him. Stephen in relation to Rickie resembles Gino in *Where Angels Fear to Tread* in relation to Philip; like Gino he is conspicuous by his physical exuberance, and like Gino he becomes the benign father. He has, of course, the secondary difference that he is thoroughly English, just as Gino is an archetypal Italian, but he also has the major difference of uniting with Rickie's spirit without the loss of any of his own physicality: it is as though Philip were able to subsume in himself the best of Gino's nature, thus enabling himself to win the passion as well as the understanding friendship of Caroline Abbott. It is as though Forster were imagining for himself a poetic release from his own most obsessive bondages—those of class and of homosexual prohibition. Unfortunately, however, it is precisely the qualities of *The Longest Journey* that may have made it especially congenial to Forster himself that make it the least satisfactory of his novels considered as artistic achievements, barring *Maurice*. A novelist must derive his art in some way from his personal emotions, but the art can only become universal when he can sublimate these emotions into a state acceptable as experience that can be shared—when he can detach himself from his private wishfulness, anxieties and proclivities. Until that happens, the work will be therapy rather than art, perhaps sustained by some philosophy. In this case the philosophy seems to resemble Edward Carpenter's, but used as a supporting strut rather than as an assimilated component. Stephen Wonham seems to be an image compiled out of Carpenter's socialistic idealism and Forster's private desire to complement himself by an antithetic embodiment; the character is implausible as a creation and shows the irresponsibility of fantasy. His physicality (he is always ready for a fight and delights in getting drunk) is brutish, and yet we are expected to believe that he is not a brute but on the contrary the embodiment of childlike idealism. He is Rousseau's myth of the noble savage resurrected on the Wiltshire downs. He offers nothing to our understanding of the physical man at his richest; that required a writer rooted in a different environment and informed by it—the imagination of Forster's friend D.H. Lawrence.

A Room with a View

Whereas Philip Herriton and Rickie Elliot are evidently based on Forster's self-image, Lucy Honeychurch in *A Room with a View* seems at first remote from him: a girl, with no academic background and cultural aspirations rather than pretensions, unequipped to sustain herself against her environment even by illusion (except through music—in which she does resemble the author), her predicament does not appear to offer analogies with a young man of Forster's temperament in the period. However the young men of the novels share with her a quality which is central to the predicament of all three—the quality of *virginality*. Virginality is not virginity. The latter is generally associated with a female condition, but this physical state has always carried connotations of an equivalent psychological state; the virgin is thought of as innocent and ignorant—unaware of and unconcerned with intrusion by the world which involves the individual in its anxieties and responsibilities and the complexities and corruptions that attend on them. Psychological virginality, as distinct from physical virginity, is a condition of young men as well as of young women, but it is easier—or was when Forster wrote—to associate it with the virginal girl. The girl did not have to pretend to maturity as the boy did. Philip has an illusion of it, and Rickie, who is candidly innocent, is expected to assume maturity when he marries; Lucy does not pretend, nor is she expected to assume anything except conformity of the feelings with propriety. Nor is she faced with an identifiable opposition corresponding to Mrs Herriton, Sawston School or Mrs Failing; her mother is not a malign matriarch, and her opponents—Mr Beebe, Cecil Vyse, Eleanor Lavish—are overcome separately; Miss Bartlett even turns out to be her secret ally. Thus *A Room with a View* turns out to have a theme similar to those of the other two novels of the first phase, but the choice of a feminine protagonist makes for fresh treatment of the theme, and on the whole a less challenging one. It belongs to a tradition in nineteenth century novels in which a young woman has to fight for independence against a society dominated by male prejudice, resembling Meredith's *The Egoist* in particular. To this extent it is an antidote to *Where Angels Fear to Tread*, in which the male prejudice of Monteriano is not put to the test. However, it shares one weakness, though less conspicuously, with *The Longest Journey*: Lucy's lover, George Emerson, is not fully realised. Like Stephen Wonham, he is more a symbol than a living person; such reality as he has derives mainly from the more extensive portrayal of his father.

In his first three novels, then, Forster seems to have been exploring his youthful self, in each of them seeing himself in a different aspect. Philip Herriton shows his more confident side—sensitive, but at the same time inclined to the arrogance of the self-consciously cultured young man, who needs to learn the insufficiency of what he takes to be his self-sufficiency. Rickie Eliòt shows Forster's more vulnerable aspect, responsive to friendship and dependent on his friends, easily dominated by women, yearning for and yet fearful of relationship with the masculine opposite to his temperament. Lucy is not so much a portrait of himself as an image of the virginality which is the uniting characteristic of all three characters. After that, he became sufficiently free of himself to undertake his first fully objective novel.

Howards End

Howards End contains no self-image of the novelist, apart from Tibby Schlegel, who is a minor character. It is also much more of a social panorama than the first three novels. The world of culture is set against the world of 'telegrams and anger'—of action and business, the Schlegels and the Wilcoxes. In addition, there are two other social entities: Mrs Wilcox and Leonard Bast. Mrs Wilcox is separate from her family who do not understand her, in deep sympathy with Margaret Schlegel, and yet uninitiated into Schlegel culture. She is the aristocrat, not in social status, but in breeding and feeling. Leonard, on the other hand, is the social underdog, not one of the very poor but among those who must struggle to survive. A lowly city clerk, he is above those whose survival absorbs all their energies, and he has cultural aspirations, but he lacks both the means of aspiration and any understanding of the goals he aspires to. Thus the novel presents the four main aspects of English society at the time: the rich cultured class that sustained intellectual life, the commercial and administrative world that provided the investments by which the cultured classes lived, the genuine aristocracy who purveyed the traditional continuities of English society, and the deprived class—the proletariat—which immensely expanded in the later nineteenth century.

Economically, this society operates as a machine: human beings become objects, and objects are commodities; only money is real. Humanly, it is a muddle, in which encounters occur by accident and misunderstandings make them meaningless; there are no connections, and the novel's epigraph is 'Only connect . . .'. On the other hand, no human being can be so materialised as to be totally dehumanised. The humanity in Henry Wilcox responds to the maturity of Margaret Schlegel whose discernment crosses the barrier between them; the blundering sympathies of Helen Schlegel force him to acknowledge the human reality of Leonard Bast, and Leonard's own humanity rises above the cruelty of his own oppression to accomplish—however blindly—a human synthesis under the benign matriarchy of Margaret Schlegel, generated initially by the human instinct of Mrs Wilcox.

At the centre of the complex is her house, Howards End, and houses, or rather attitudes to houses, constitute a chain of images, a rhythm, throughout the novel. It opens with letters from Helen Schlegel who is staying at Howards End with the Wilcoxes. Animal heat generates an illusion of love between Helen and the younger son, Paul. The Schlegel aunt, Mrs Munt, decides that the supposed engagement is far too sudden, and decides to visit the Wilcoxes to interfere. Immediately after her departure, Helen's telegram arrives announcing that the engagement is off. The result is that Mrs Munt arrives only to instigate an episode of muddle. She is met at the station by the elder son, Charles, who has heard nothing of the engagement and whose mind is occupied with other things, especially his car; she supposes that it is he, not his brother, who is the premature fiancé. The misunderstanding generates exasperation, and they arrive at the house in a violent quarrel. It is then that Mrs Wilcox comes upon the scene:

> She seemed to belong not to the young people and their motor, but to the house, and to the tree that overshadowed it. One knew that she worshipped the past, and that the instinctive wisdom the past alone can bestow had descended upon her—that wisdom to which we give the clumsy name of aristocracy. High born she might not be. But assuredly she cared about her ancestors, and let them help her. When she saw Charles angry, Paul frightened, and Mrs Munt in tears, she heard her ancestors say, 'Separate those human beings who will hurt each other most. The rest can wait.' So she did not ask questions. Still less did she pretend that nothing had happened, as a competent social hostess would have done. She said, 'Miss Schlegel, would you take your aunt up to your room or to my room, whichever you think best. Paul, do find Evie, and tell her lunch for six, but I'm not sure we shall all be downstairs for it.'
>
> (*chapter 3*)

Howards End is no mansion but a substantial old farmhouse, the kind of house that it is a privilege to live in; inherited, as this paragraph shows, it constitutes a civilisation and shapes character. Other houses invite or receive very different responses. The two Schlegel sisters and their brother inhabit a substantial Victorian house in the west end of London, vulnerable to speculators. It is sold and pulled down in the middle of the novel by a millionaire who has bought the freehold and wishes to substitute a block of flats. The Schlegels have felt neutral about it—it has contained them comfortably—but the absurdity of the uprooting oppresses them:

> It was absurd when you came to think of it: Helen and Tibby came to think of it: Margaret was too busy with the house-agents. The

feudal ownership of land did bring dignity, whereas the modern ownership of movables is reducing us to a nomadic horde. We are reverting to the civilization of luggage, and historians of the future will note how the middle classes accreted possessions without taking root in the earth, and may find in this the secret of their imaginative poverty. The Schlegels were certainly the poorer for their loss of Wickham Place. It had helped to balance their lives, and almost to counsel them. Nor is their ground-landlord spiritually the richer. He has built flats on its site, his motor-cars grow swifter, his exposures of Socialism more trenchant. But he has spilt the precious distillation of the years, and no chemistry of his can give it back again.

(*chapter 17*)

It is to this class of speculators that the Wilcoxes belong, with the exception of Mrs Wilcox. They do not engage professionally in building speculation, but Henry Wilcox is a business man, and for him, as for his children, houses are essentially to be bought and sold at profit. He has lived in Howards End because it is his wife's inheritance, but he is aware chiefly of its inconveniences. After his engagement to Margaret Schlegel, he buys Oniton Grange in Shropshire in hope of entering county society, but without feeling for the place. Meanwhile Wickham Place is pulled down:

It stood for a week or two longer, open-eyed, as if astonished at its own emptiness. Then it fell. Navvies came, and spilt it back into the grey. With their muscles and their beery good temper, they were not the worst undertakers for a house which had always been human, and had not mistaken culture for an end.

(*chapter 31*)

Thus we are shown three different attitudes to houses considered as homes—that of Mrs Wilcox, for whom Howards End is the meaning of life; that of the Schlegels, for whom Wickham Place is a basis for stability and order, and that of the other Wilcoxes, for whom Howards End, Ducie Street and Oniton Grange are all mere commodities. But there is also a fourth attitude—that of the clerk, Leonard Bast, for whom his dwelling is a prison. He inhabits a basement flat (Block B):

... an amorous and not unpleasant little hole when the curtains were drawn, and the lights turned on, and the gas-stove unlit. But it struck that shallow, makeshift note that is so often heard in the modern dwelling-place. It had been too easily gained, and could be relinquished too easily.

(*chapter 6*)

He sits in it, and, to improve himself, studies Ruskin on architecture ('he understood him to be the greatest master of English prose'):

'Let us consider a little each of these characters in succession, and first (for of the shafts enough has been said already), what is very peculiar to this church—its luminousness.'

Was there anything to be learnt from this fine sentence? Could he adapt it to the needs of daily life? Could he introduce it, with modifications, when he next wrote to his brother, the lay-reader? For example—

'Let us consider a little each of these characters in succession, and first (for of the absence of ventilation enough has been said already) what is very peculiar to this flat—its obscurity.'

Something told him that the modifications would not do; and that something, had he known it, was the spirit of English Prose. 'My flat is dark as well as stuffy.' Those were the words for him.

(*chapter 6*)

One of the distinctions of this novel is its graphic demonstration of the differences between spheres of society, making communication between them all but impossible. Margaret Schlegel has difficulties with Mrs Wilcox; she finds the latter's rage at the fate of Wickham Place incomprehensible, attributing it to hysteria brought on by fatigue. Henry Wilcox never guesses at the meaning of her house to his wife, but he ends by submitting to it through Margaret, the second Mrs Wilcox, who acquires it. In fact Mrs Wilcox, in her final illness, writes a note bequeathing it to her, but this the Wilcoxes disregard, supposing it to be the aberration of a sick woman and suspecting Margaret's contrivance. Only the accidents of personal relationship eventually put her in possession—her marriage to Henry Wilcox, Helen bearing a bastard son to Leonard, and Charles Wilcox's imprisonment for Leonard's manslaughter. But though Helen and Leonard's son end in the shelter of Howards End, Leonard himself remains the outsider, and his confinement in his gloomy flat with the dreary mistress who becomes his wife is the symbol of his deprivation; the other characters have in common at least that they can choose their residences.

SYMBOLISM: THE SWORD AND THE UMBRELLA It is not only houses that bestow a connecting rhythm on the narrative, relating characters through their disconnections. Two other symbols recur with a different kind of resonance: the sword and the umbrella. The sword is the Schlegel symbol, or more precisely that of the Schlegel father who had died before the narrative begins, but whose character is reviewed briefly but pregnantly at the end of chapter 4. He was a German who had fought bravely against Denmark, Austria and France, and then, foreseeing the horrors of German militaristic materialism replacing the idealistic Germany of Kant and Hegel, he removed to England, bringing his sword with him. A sword is a symbol of honour, and suggests that the connection between the worlds of culture and of the warrior, once so close in the English tradition, survived longer in the more idealistic German one. It is another example of Forster's practice of exposing the limitations—the insularity—of English culture by contrasting it to a foreign one with different assumptions. More important, however, is that it is also a symbol of death: it inflicts death, and it is the emblem of the soldier whose function is not primarily to inflict it but to face it. The sword remains with the Schlegel family, and is an indication that their allegiances are deeper than the comfortably insulated allegiances of English culture snobbery.

The umbrella, on the other hand, is the symbol of 'respectability'—of the surface of society which extols (without openly acknowledging) money as the primary reality. As such, it is the emblem of Leonard Bast's barely sustained minimal status. As Forster puts it in the opening of chapter 6:

> His mind and his body had been alike underfed, because he was poor, and because he was modern they were always craving better food. Had he lived some centuries ago, in the brightly coloured civilizations of the past, he would have had a definite status, his rank and his income would have corresponded. But in his day the angel of Democracy had arisen, enshadowing the classes with leathern wings, and proclaiming, 'All men are equal all men, that is to say, who possess umbrellas,' and so he was obliged to assert gentility, lest he slipped into the abyss where nothing counts, and the statements of democracy are inaudible.

He carries one, therefore, as part of his genteel uniform, and feels that he cannot appear in public without it any more than a soldier can appear without his hat on parade. But there are those of more secure status whose respectability has no risk of being impugned, and for them an umbrella is an object of mere utility. If they lose one they buy another, and if they take one by mistake they do not suppose that they have deprived anyone of an object of significant value. Such is Helen Schlegel, who takes Leonard's by mistake when the Schlegels first meet him at a Beethoven concert. He calls on them to retrieve it, and so the acquaintanceship is continued. But later, when Leonard temporarily disappears and his silly wife calls (supposing him to have an assignation with Helen) to inquire about him, Helen cheerfully remarks 'she asked for a husband as if he was an umbrella'. She is quite unaware of the irony of her flippancy; Leonard is important to his helpless wife much in the same way as his umbrella is important to him. He shelters her and sustains her in the only security she can hope for.

The sword is kept at Howards End with other Schlegel belongings when Margaret has become engaged to Henry Wilcox and neither has yet settled on a home. Meanwhile Leonard has had his brief affair with Helen—instigated by hysterical pity and indignation on her part and lonely desperation on his—and she is pregnant. In chapter 41, sick and remorseful at his behaviour to the Schlegels who had been so kind to him, he comes to Howards End to confess his guilt and meets Charles Wilcox:

> He entered the garden, steadied himself against a motor-car that he found in it, found a door open and entered a house. Yes, it would be very easy. From a room to the left he heard voices, Margaret's among them. His own name was called aloud, and a man whom he had never seen before said, 'Oh, is he there? I am not surprised. I now thrash him within an inch of his life.'
>
> 'Mrs Wilcox,' said Leonard, 'I have done wrong.'
>
> The man took him by the collar and cried, 'Bring me a stick.' Women were screaming. A stick, very bright, descended. It hurt him, not where it descended, but in his heart. Books fell on him like a shower. Nothing had sense.
>
> 'Get some water,' commanded Charles, who had all through kept very calm. 'He's shamming. Of course I only used the blade. Here, carry him out into the air.'
>
> Thinking that he understood these things, Margaret obeyed him. They laid Leonard, who was dead, on the gravel. Helen poured water over him.
>
> 'That's enough,' said Charles.
>
> 'Yes, murder's enough,' said Miss Avery, coming out of the house with the sword.

The episode is the climax of the novel not only in its narrative, resulting in reconciliation and retribution wherever they are deserved, but also in its symbolic and epiphanic design. Books fall on Leonard as he dies; the culture to which he aspired, which for the Schlegel father had dignity complementing that of the sword and for his children means freedom, has for Leonard been an oppression instead of a release. The mysterious Miss Avery is almost the spirit of the house: now the housekeeper, she has been connected with it since it was worked as a farm; representative of the class from which Leonard himself has sprung, she has a rootedness in English tradition identical with that of the house itself; from it, Leonard has been uprooted and alienated by the Wilcox civilisation. Of that, Charles is the pure embodiment and resembles Harriet Herriton in the first novel: he is stupid and rigid, able to judge situations only by the stereotypes which his prejudices impose on them. Leonard, in his view, has seduced Helen and is therefore 'a cad'; a cad deserves to be 'thrashed within an inch of his life' in the hackneyed phrase he associates with the class of which he likes to suppose himself a member. But it is not for the blunt discernment of such as Charles to judge inches any more than to judge people; the sword in his hands is degraded and becomes the instrument of brutality.

In the context of the whole novel this climactic episode reveals the full significance of the sword and the umbrella—death and money. In the social pattern, money rules: the Schlegels can afford their culture because they possess it, but they derive it from such as the Wilcoxes who 'make' it; in practice, Schlegels live from Wilcoxes and Leonard is the wage-slave of both. And yet the book and the sword do not for that reason lose their validity. It is the Schlegel sisters who perceive that the social system is ephemeral compared to the human realities which it masks. This is made explicit in the dialogue between Helen and Leonard in chapter 27:

> 'I wish I was wrong, but—the clergyman—he has money of his own, or else he's paid; the poet or the musician—just the same; the tramp—he's no different. The tramp goes to the workhouse in the end, and is paid for with other people's money. Miss Schlegel, the real thing's money, and all the rest is a dream.'
>
> 'You're still wrong. You've forgotten Death.'
>
> Leonard could not understand.
>
> 'If we lived for ever, what you say would be true. But we have to die, we have to leave life presently. Injustice and greed would be the real thing if we lived for ever. As it is, we must hold to other things, because Death is coming. I love Death—not morbidly, but because He explains. He shows me the emptiness of Money. Death and Money are the eternal foes. Not Death and Life. Never mind what happens behind Death, Mr Bast, but be sure that the poet and the musician and the tramp will be happier in it than the man who has never learnt to say, "I am I".'

'Death destroys a man: the idea of death saves him': this for Helen becomes the deepest truth. At the time, Leonard cannot understand it, but as he makes his way to Howards End the truth bears in upon him. His illness and the sense that the approaching encounter will be decisive make him half-aware that he is moving towards his death. And indeed it destroys him, but it is the instrument of salvation for Margaret, Henry, Helen and his as yet unborn child. His death becomes the great connector, forcing Henry to face the deeper facts, and Howards End, that vehicle of the past, becomes vehicle for the future.

CONNECTIONS AND CONSEQUENCES 'Only connect . . .' recurs throughout the novel: 'Only connect the prose and the passion'—chapter 18. The world of what are called practical realities is shown to be that of accidental connections, muddled connections, coincidental ones, and, above all, habitual connections which make sense on a mundane level only to belie deeper meanings. In the face of all these, the epigraph is both a judgement and an appeal: a judgement on a society which knows no other ways to understand connections, and an appeal to human imagination and sensitivity to take responsibility for accident so as to transform it into meaning and shape coincidence into coherence. And a just verdict on the novel might be that Forster succeeds brilliantly with the judgement but very unevenly with the appeal.

Forster makes free use of lifelike coincidence. It has always been a debatable factor in the realistic narrative which characterises the form of the novel; until the last quarter of the nineteenth century, novelists felt licensed to use it for its convenience in the contrivance of plots, but later ones abandoned it because of its implausibility. Some later novelists, however, Hardy among the first, revived its use on the grounds that coincidences occur in every life, and sometimes have significant or even fateful consequences in most lives. It is acceptable, then, that, after the embarrassing debacle of the Paul Wilcox and Helen Schlegel romance, relationships between the two families should come to be renewed by the coincidence that the Wilcoxes should happen to take residence in the immediate neighbourhood of the Schlegels, giving Margaret and Mrs Wilcox the opportunity to initiate their deep friendship. It is even acceptable that Leonard's wife should turn out to have been Henry's mistress ten years before, leading him to suppose, when the Basts are presented to him for justice, that he is being blackmailed. Lives run on the routine of apparently orderly connections, and are interrupted, muddled, and forced to change direction by such coincidences. However, it requires the human resources of personal responsibility and imaginative sympathy to make creative use of coincidence and accident—to make significant connections—and it is a failure on the part of Henry Wilcox and, to a lesser extent, of the Schlegel sisters to relate their separated worlds which is responsible for Leonard's initial disaster, although Henry does not even know him. Learning incidentally that Leonard works for the Porphyrion Insurance Company, Henry remarks that he had better leave it, because it is financially unsound. Leonard does, and is reduced to penury, but the Porphyrion recovers; Henry, however, acknowledges no responsibility for Leonard's fate. It is a disaster resulting from accident and muddle: Henry's advice was given in the course of conversation, not responsibly as he would give it to a client. The Schlegel sisters are too unversed in money and too indifferent to its workings—since they have more than enough—to realise that the advice needs checking before being passed on. The consequences are an apt example of the disconnection between the world of the rich and that of the poor on whom they depend. The Schlegels are too theoretical and the Wilcoxes too practical; neither understands, and the latter do not see the need to understand, the tragic possibilities of the mental limitations that circumscribe them.

So far, Forster's judgement on human nature in his society is original, witty, subtle and discerning. The originality consists in his fresh approach to his material, an approach which can be described as anthropological. Just as an anthropologist will study the ordinary objects in use in a society, and by learning the purposes and values attached to them will deduce the habits and value systems which distinguish it from other societies, so objects in *Howards End* achieve significance parallel to and enlarging the significance of the characters. Houses, umbrellas, the sword, the Wilcox cars (which are their status symbols), the Schlegel books—these not only enlighten us about the value systems of their possessors, but enlighten us about the divergency of such systems. We are presented with a given society: British society in the Edwardian era; but then we are shown that it is one society only in the sense of being a single monetary mechanism. Considered as a value system, it is divided into spheres, each with its own value system estranged from the others. Culture, which anthropologically has meaning in so far as it signifies the way of life of a whole society, has in this one a meaning which must be anthropologically exceptional: it is a special activity for a privileged caste, and is consequently exclusive rather than inclusive. We can understand from the novel better than we do from the essays why Forster was unable to accept Matthew Arnold's religion of culture; when the word denotes only a department of human activity, it must be a barrier to total human understanding. The destruction of Wickham Place is deplored because it 'had always been human, and had not mistaken culture for an end'. The Schlegel sisters, indeed, because they are not entirely English, do not completely fall into the fallacy, though their brother does. They derive from their father the older German cultural vision which was also that of pre-industrial England.

However, Forster's motive for making the Schlegels to some extent exceptions to their class leads into those elements of the novel which raise some doubts about its total validity. The motive seems to have been that he wanted to make the novel positive in its message—what I have called the 'appeal' aspect of the epigraph 'Only connect . . .'. He wanted to show how the class restraints which were special if not peculiar to English society could be transcended so as to achieve an image of an order of wholeness replacing the segmentation. It was interesting and reasonable to lead towards this end by making the Schlegel girls part inheritors of a foreign tradition, but then he was forced to find plausible means of uniting them to the other three constituents of the social pattern—Mrs Wilcox, the Wilcoxes, Leonard. Margaret's friendship with the first is presented convincingly, but then she has to marry Henry so as to become the second Mrs Wilcox, uniting the values of the first with her own Schlegel ones, and thereby opening the eyes of her husband as the first had been unable to do. But would she have married him? It is not impossible. He is the most intelligent of his family, able to appreciate her maturity though he does not understand her; she, in her own family, is the only one to realise that the Wilcox world is not valueless, and that its practical sagacity is necessary to the fulfilment of her own wisdom. It is understandable, too, that both have reached a stage of life which requires solace for loneliness. Nevertheless, the barriers between the two are great, and we are expected to believe that the engagement is not one of mere emotional convenience but of love. In presenting this, Forster becomes vague: when Henry proposes in chapter 18 we are told that Margaret experiences a 'central radiance' of mutual sympathy, and then recognises the experience as love. He also becomes misleadingly theoretical:

> It did not seem so difficult. She need trouble him with no gift of her own. She would only point out the salvation that was latent in his own soul, and in the soul of every man. Only connect! That was the whole of her sermon. Only connect the prose and the passion, and both will be exalted, and human love will be at its height. Live in fragments no longer. Only connect, and the beast and the monk, robbed of the isolation that is life to the other, will die.
>
> (*chapter 22*)

It is one thing to expect Henry with his materialism to appreciate Schlegel sensitivity, but another to equate prose with the former and passion the latter, as though practicality were identical with lucidity and Margaret lacked both; in fact he is shown to be often in a muddle whereas she is generally clear-minded. It is fair to oppose the beast to the monk, but not to associate them with Schlegels and Wilcoxes, since neither resemble either. A similar but less acceptable vagueness obscures the love-making of Helen and Leonard, resulting in their child. It is again possible, but not plausible. We know that he is desperate in his misery and deeply grateful for her sympathy, and that her pity and indignation amount to a passion. On the other hand we are not shown that either is in the least attracted to the other, or that there is anything sexual in the feelings which they arouse in each other. Both relationships, then, are too patently contrived not to be blemishes, and there is a double irony in the novel being flawed in such a way: Forster is failing just where greatly inferior novelists feel most at home, and yet the failures occur in a novel which otherwise treats the theme of relationship with extraordinary subtlety. Readers will disagree about how much they matter, and many will no doubt consider it pedantic to labour them so much. But the implausibility of the love-relationships does call in doubt the plausibility of the happy household at Howards End with which the novel ends. The flaws—if they are real—seem to have occurred because Forster was determined that the novel should have such an ending by any means, but he was writing at a time when happy endings were less likely than ever before to coincide with convincing ones in a serious work of fiction.

Maurice

Forster seems to have had a predilection for happy endings at about this time; he was aware of the difficulty of justifying them, but, as he wrote to Lowes Dickinson in 1914, 'the temptation's overwhelming to grant one's creations a happiness actual life does not supply'. He was referring, however, not to *Howards End* but to his next novel, *Maurice*, completed in the summer of that year but not published until 1971. Rumours of its existence persisted till this posthumous publication. When directly asked about it, Forster was evasive, referring inquirers to the existence of his uncompleted narrative, *Arctic Summer*, but a few of his friends read the manuscript, and he continued to revise it from time to time as he reacted to their responses. It was thus a work of personal importance to him, but if we are interested in his artistic development it reads now as an interruption, not as evidence of growth.

The reason for this is very clear: *Maurice* is not a further experiment in the endless mission to achieve a comprehensive image of human reality; it is a particular case-history. The 'case' is homosexuality, and therefore one that arouses instantaneous prejudices on either side in most readers. However the weakness of the novel as art is not its theme, but the fact that any 'case' is by definition a restricted study, closing on a segment of experience rather than—as a novel should—opening itself to the range of it. As a case-history, Forster treats the theme with an objectivity which deserves respect: Maurice is in many ways a character remote from the novelist himself, a Wilcox with no element in him of Schlegel. The novel is thus in no way a work of self-indulgence. The hero is a commonplace boy from a commonplace middle class family, regarded as a success by his public school because he attracts no attention there, and then disregarded at Cambridge until he gets sent down for insolence to the authorities. Even this is only a temporary setback to his conformity; he enters his father's stockbroking firm, and is respected by his fellow commuters for his practicality and normality, even when he sometimes teases them with unorthodox ideas. But alongside this external existence, Forster shows the painful exceptionality of his inner growth, explicable to no one about him and for a long time unintelligible to himself. He cannot explain his misery when he comes home from school to find that his friend, the gardening boy, has gone; he cannot understand his failure with girls, and suffers incommunicable agonies of jealousy when his best friend at Cambridge falls in love with his sister. Eventually—and this is the 'happy ending' which Forster agreed was artistically debatable—he removes himself from society to live alone with a young gamekeeper, in whom, across the immense social gulf which is shown very explicitly, he finds a powerful physical attraction. Forster does not directly explain how Maurice comes to be homosexual, but his family circumstances go some way to accounting for it, as do Forster's own in explaining himself. The story is thus on the whole convincing, and by it the reader can learn to understand and sympathise with the homosexual's predicament. Only at the conclusion, when Maurice vanished into the greenwood with Alec, does the implausibility of this happy ending raise doubts. What have they in common, besides their mutual physical attraction which may well prove temporary, to give such a union permanence? Evidently Forster needed a myth to console him, and so he contrives one.

Forster left the manuscript with a note which read: 'Publishable—but worth it?' As a contribution to his reputation, *Maurice* was not worth publication. On the other hand, any reader must respect and understand his need to write it, and without it we would not understand his other works so well. His real achievements were the fruit of his abilities to defy the barriers of inhumanity in his time—to break the circles. But he could not publicly break the circle which surrounded homosexuality and kept it taboo. He had, therefore, to release it privately for his own good, and by doing so he has helped us the better to understand his successes and failures in the portrayal of human relationships elsewhere. Moreover, without that release he could probably not have achieved his masterpiece which was yet to come. We can respect his motives, appreciate the greater understanding which he affords us, and admire the case-history, even though a case-history can never be a very good novel.

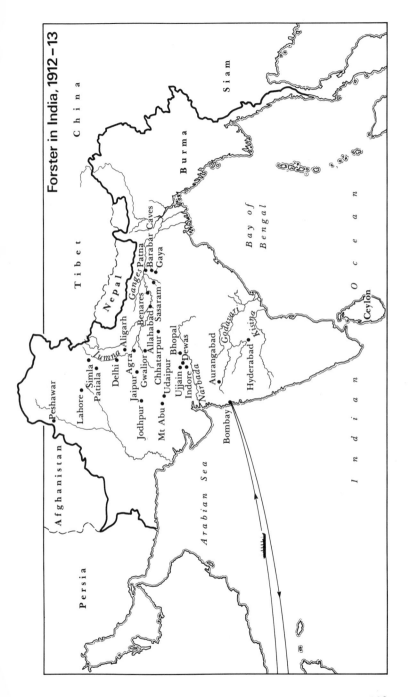

Forster in India, 1912–13

China

Siam

Tibet

Nepal

Burma

Afghanistan

Peshawar

Persia

Lahore

Simla

Patiala

Delhi

Aligarh

Jaipur

Agra

Jumna

Gwalior

Benares

Ganges

Patna

Allahabad

Barabar Caves

Gaya

Sasaram

Jodhpur

Chhatarpur

Bhopal

Mt Abu

Udaipur

Ujjain

Dewas

Indore

Narbada

Aurangabad

Godavari

Hyderabad

Krisna

Bombay

Arabian Sea

Bay of Bengal

Ceylon

Indian Ocean

129

11 A Passage to India

As we have seen, Forster made two visits to India. He began *A Passage to India* after the first; the war suspended it, but he took it back with him on his second visit, only to find that he could not complete it while he was immersed in the Indian scene. He continued it on his return to England but found such difficulty that he might never have completed it without the warning of Leonard Woolf, who told him that to leave it unfinished might be to afflict himself with permanent dissatisfaction. One difficulty was journalistic: the India of his pre-war visit had changed considerably by the time of his post-war return. Another was that he could no longer abide by his original conception of the novel, which was too light and gentle to accommodate the more sombre and complex experience provoked in him by the succeeding decade. Further, he was also dissatisfied with the scale of interest afforded by his characters. He wrote to a friend in 1922:

> the characters are not sufficiently interesting for the atmosphere. This tempts me to emphasise the atmosphere, and so to produce a meditation rather than a drama.

He implies that it is India that matters—not Indian politics merely, but India as a universe, a confusion of cultures and races, of religions and natural growth, such as defies the European instinct to find coherence and meaning in everything it contemplates. And yet a novel needs a setting accessible to normal experience, and so Forster invents one which is small and seems commonplace while exposed to all the muddle and mystery he wishes to convey. He describes it in his short first chapter, which is so characteristic of his style that it is worth fairly close study; it also indicates what he can have meant by describing the novel as 'a meditation', although we need not accept the description as adequate when we judge the novel as a whole.

> Except for the Marabar Caves—and they are twenty miles off—the city of Chandrapore presents nothing extraordinary. Edged rather than washed by the river Ganges, it trails for a couple of miles along the bank, scarcely distinguishable from the rubbish it deposits so freely.

So run the first two sentences, typical of the way in which Forster likes to begin the novel from the flat: the manner casual ('one may as well begin with Helen's letters to her sister'—*Howards End*), the tone pitched low as though deliberately to deny the reader any expectations. And yet, paradoxically, the style achieves the opposite of what it pretends. The first sentence mentions, as though casually, the

Marabar caves, which apparently are extraordinary; it is true that they are waved away from our attention at this moment, but a reader is likely to remember a name attached to the word 'extraordinary' in the very first sentence. And then the second sentence conveys movement, however sluggish, graphically by the precision of its verbs: 'edged rather than washed'—'trails'—'deposits so freely'. The place may be squalid but it lives, and we are already in it. As the description proceeds, we are led to a climax of inferiority, as though we are being made to feel that the very meanness of the town endows it with an essential importance:

> So abased, so monotonous is everything that meets the eye, that when the Ganges comes down it might be expected to wash the excrescence back into the soil. Houses do fall, people are drowned and left rotting, but the general outline of the town persists, swelling here, shrinking there, like some low but indestructible form of life.

Its importance seems to issue from the very fact that the place is, humanly, so unworthy of humanity. We are made aware that after all there is no frontier between human life and that of lower forms; where we might expect to find such a frontier, there we discover Chandrapore, an 'excrescence', splaying itself upwards and downwards.

The second paragraph opens: 'Inland, the prospect alters.' And indeed it does. We are on the heights, looking down on the native city, enjoying the privileged view of it from the British quarters. What we now see is not much of the human dwellings, but, instead, a forest of trees. Verbs and participles—Forster is sparse in his use of other adjectives—express energy and even exultation:

> They rise from the gardens where ancient tanks nourish them, they burst out of stifling purlieus and unconsidered temples. Seeking light and air, and endowed with more strength than man or his works, they soar above the lower deposit to greet one another with branches and beckoning leaves, and to build a city for the birds.

Again, the language purports more than it seems to. We may suppose that we are merely offered another view from a preferable viewpoint, but we are also being shown man and nature in an order that reverses the one to which the European is accustomed. Still beyond that is the sense of the European privilege in the point of vantage from which he surveys what we nowadays call the 'undeveloped world', and the implied illusions which this will produce. Nature is grand, but people (Indian people of course) are mean, and so the European receives unconscious nourishment of his sense of superiority. Then the paragraph ends with anti-climax: before the English can settle themselves in self-congratulation, what do they themselves produce to contrast with the Indian abasement, to match the splendour of nature released in the trees? The answer is a positive nothing:

> As for the civil station itself, it provokes no emotion. It has nothing hideous in it, and only the view is beautiful; it shares nothing with the city except the overarching sky.

So we pass from the river to the city, from the city to its vegetation, from the vegetation to the sky which unites all and is yet remote with its own existence. The third paragraph emphasises its separateness, its variety of colour and depth of mystery. The sky is not merely a dome as it is in Europe:

> Then the stars hang like lamps from the immense vault. The distance between the vault and them is as nothing to the distance behind them, and that farther distance, though beyond colour, last freed itself from blue.

But in the last paragraph we return to the earth, with the insistence that despite its remoteness the sky is the supreme power over India. The earth 'can do little—only feeble outbursts of flowers':

> But when the sky chooses glory can rain into the Chandrapore bazaars or a benediction pass from horizon to horizon. The sky can do this because it is so strong and so enormous. Strength comes from the sun, infused in it daily, size from the prostrate earth. No mountains infringe on the curve. League after league the earth lies flat, heaves a little, is flat again. Only in the south, where a group of fists and fingers are thrust up through the soil, is the endless expanse interrupted. These fists and fingers are the Marabar Hills, containing the extraordinary caves.

The almost mystical description of the sky concluding the chapter contributes to the panorama of place which is its subject, but its mysticism implies a dimension beyond the physically human; in the panorama of thought, religion is the equivalent of the dimension of the sky, and the chapter ending, as it began, hints at them as the spiritual vehicle of what is to come. People, so far, have been insignificant, and that differentiates this novel from all the previous ones, which have opened with abrupt introductions to individuals. Not just people, then, but the physical and metaphysical forces with which human beings have to contend, even when they are unaware of the contention, is to be the theme of this novel, and we may begin to understand what Forster meant when he told his friend that the atmosphere is more interesting than the characters, and that he has been tempted to produce 'a meditation rather than a drama'.

'A meditation', however, suggests absence of plot, and this novel has a plot which can be outlined as well as any other.

Mrs Moore comes out from England with Adela Quested to

Chandrapore, an Indian district capital. Adela is informally engaged to Ronny Heaslop, Mrs Moore's son by her first marriage, and Adela wishes to see him at work in the environment in which she will have to live before the engagement becomes final. The two women find the experience confusing; the English bureaucrats, including Ronny, are conscientious but complacently ignorant of the psychology of the Indians, whom they keep at a distance. Mrs Moore, however, makes friends with Aziz, a Moslem doctor in the bureaucratic service, and the friendship leads to acquaintance with Fielding, Aziz' friend; he is director of education and the only official in close touch with the Indians. He in turn introduces them to his assistant, the Hindu Professor Godbole (pronounced Godbolay). Flattered by the attention of the two English women, Aziz vaguely proposes to take them on a visit to the Marabar caves, mysteriously sacred to the Hindus. He is dismayed when they take his invitation seriously, but on reflection he sees it as an opportunity to enhance his prestige with the English officials, and so he makes elaborate preparations, which include Fielding and Godbole. The visit is, however, disastrous. The elderly Mrs Moore suffers a breakdown, and is dispatched back to England, dying on the voyage; Adela has the hallucination that she has been sexually assaulted by Aziz, and returns to Chandrapore in hysteria. Aziz is arrested, the town is in uproar, and Fielding is ostracised by his colleagues for maintaining his friend's innocence. However, when the trial occurs, Adela, who has made a religion of personal honesty, comes out of her hysteria and acknowledges under interrogation that she has no actual memory of Aziz following her into the cave where she supposed the assault to have happened. Aziz is acquitted, Fielding reinstated, and the English bureaucrats, who have been united in the conviction of his guilt, suffer a notable defeat. The disturbance is eventually quietened by senior officials from elsewhere.

The novel concludes with the aftermath of these events. Aziz is by now thoroughly hostile to the British, and he believes that even Fielding, who has dissuaded him from prosecuting Adela for damages, has been motivated by a desire to marry her. He moves in bitterness to a Hindu native state, and Fielding, two years later, visits him there with his wife (who is not Adela but Mrs Moore's daughter by her second marriage) and Ralph Moore, her brother. Aziz' suspicions are removed and his love for Mrs Moore is revived by Ralph's resemblance to her. Full reconciliation does not, however, occur, because Aziz has by now vested too much emotion in Moslem Indian nationalism, and Fielding has forsaken his former easy-going approach to Indians. However Godbole, who is now minister of education in the same state, achieves a kind of symbolic reconciliation in a religious ritual, though that is not his explicit intention.

Such is a bare synopsis, and like most synopses it indicates nothing of the novel's quality. To discover that, we have first to consider some salient questions. Is it fair to describe the book as 'about India'? Secondly, does it offer a central point of view through one character, or if Forster has disposed of this method, what kind of unity does he offer in its place? And thirdly, what did he mean when he said that he had been tempted to emphasise the atmosphere at the expense of the characters?

Whitman, Eliot and Forster's spiritual quest

To begin with the first question. The novel was much criticised on its publication for its unfairness in the portrayal of the British officials, and also for its inaccuracy in many details. Official policy had changed by the time of his second visit, having become less crudely authoritarian and more paternalist, but Forster preserved in his final version the impressions that he had received initially. As to inaccuracies, he himself, in his notes to the Everyman edition of 1942, acknowledged that they 'must be plentiful', especially in the trial scene in chapter 24. However, it is often difficult to decide how far a novelist should be judged by the standards of a journalist. If the latter makes errors of fact he is failing in his function, but a novelist is acknowledged to be more subjective. We are none of us entirely accurate about the times and environments in which we live, but we may nonetheless feel that we can be true to their reality. It is true that if a novelist departs too far from fact he will sacrifice the spirit as well, but it is hard to accept that Forster is guilty of that. He tried to solve the dilemma by setting the narrative 'out of time', conveying the spirit of British rule not according to the facts of any one period but in accordance with the assumptions and sympathies of the officials who, persisting from one phase of policy to another, continued to exert government.

An important clue to Forster's approach to his material lies in the source of the novel's title. He took it from that of a poem by the American, Walt Whitman: 'Passage to India', published in 1871, which appears here in full as an Appendix (p. 187). Whitman wrote it to celebrate the opening of the Suez Canal in 1869; he saw the canal, by its linking of Europe to Africa and Asia by the shortest route, as the culmination of world communications, and his poem, composed in nine sections, is in part a hymn to the triumph of nineteenth-century technology:

> Passage to India!
> Lo, soul, seest thou not God's purpose from the first?
> The earth to be spann'd, connected by network,
> The races, neighbors, to marry and be given in marriage,
> The oceans to be cross'd, the distant brought near,
> The lands to be welded together.

The technology that opened up America is now balanced, like a mirror image, by the technology that unites Europe and Asia. He imagines himself travelling westward across the American continent, glorying in the natural splendour and the splendour of technology alike—

> I hear the echoes reverberate through the grandest scenery of the
> world

—triumphant, affirmative echoes if ever there were.

But Whitman's purpose is not merely to hymn technology. Section 2 opens:

> Passage O soul to India!
> Eclaircise the myths of Asia, the primitive fables.

'Eclaircise', borrowed from the French 'éclairciser', seems to be an attempt to evade the more obvious words such as 'explain', 'elucidate', or 'clarify'. Such words might connote 'explain away' in the sense of removing mystery. This would mean that the myths of Asia were reduced to the terminology of western reason, but Whitman evidently considers them to be extensions of western experience, not merely reducible to it:

> Not you alone proud truths of the world,
> Nor you alone ye facts of modern science,
> But myths and fables of old . . .

For him, evolution is evidence of divine purpose; the meaning of it is ultimately spiritual, and its vehicle is poetry:

> After the noble inventors, after the scientists, the chemist, the
> geologist, the ethnologist,
> Finally shall come the poet worthy that name,
> The true son of God shall come singing his songs.

He is not claiming to be that poet himself. The scientific and technological triumphs had been achieved only after centuries of lonely struggle and many painful defeats; the spiritual triumph will likewise be attained only after lonely perilous striving. So the poem ends:

> Sail forth—steer for the deep waters only,
> Reckless O soul, exploring, I with thee, and thou with me,
> For we are bound where mariner has not yet dared to go,
> And we will risk the ship, ourselves and all.

But, of course, the twentieth century was to produce new culminations of western technology such as Whitman never anticipated, and the destructiveness of these inspired in another American poet a mood which Forster interpreted as the opposite of Whitman's. T.S. Eliot's *The Waste Land* appeared two years before *A Passage to India*; they do not express the same mood, but they are expressions of the same epochal spirit. In 1928, Forster stated his opinion of what *The Waste Land* is about:

> It is about the fertilizing waters that arrived too late. It is a poem of horror. The earth is barren, the sea salt, the fertilizing thunderstorm broke too late. And the horror is so intense that the poet has an inhibition and is unable to state it openly.

> (*Abinger Harvest*)

If we now consider *A Passage to India* in the light of the poems by Whitman and Eliot—the one the source of his title, and the other by a contemporary whom Forster found congenial and impressive—we shall see our way further into the novel than if we judge it as a fair or unfair account of Anglo-Indian relationships; they are a pretext rather than a purpose. The true theme of the novel is that of the poems: it is spiritual quest. It is true that none of the main characters is consciously a spiritual seeker; the mysteries which the novelist explores come upon them unsought, unwanted and unexplained, and are to them merely muddles. It is in this sense that there is no central character whose point of view unites the novel. Only one of them is aware of meanings, or of the need to seek meanings, beyond those in accord with their personal assumptions. This exception is Mrs Moore, and she is only a partial exception, since her breakdown is more a consequence of her spiritual unease than of conscious search. Nonetheless the spaciousness, confusion and alienness of India (even the Moslem Aziz is alien to the Hindus) enables the novelist to show how the assumptions by which the characters live can be seen as causing hiatus between consciousness and spiritual realities; it is thus that he emphasises the atmosphere at the expense of the characters, for it is the hiatus that is his purpose to explore. Nevertheless he uses one character as central to the mysteries and muddles which afflict the rest. This is the Hindu Professor Godbole. He is not a central character, since he is, in the plot, a minor one—almost part of the atmosphere more than a character in his own right—but he is a key, without which the theme of spiritual quest would lose all intelligibility. And just as he is a key to the theme though almost dispensable to the plot, so his importance is most clearly established in a chapter which the plot could dispense with altogether. This is chapter 19.

The circumstances of the episode are those which succeed Adela's hallucination in the Marabar cave and Aziz' consequent arrest. Fielding is in an anguish of uncertainty about his friend's possible guilt, and consequently exasperated when Godbole calls on him about a minor and seemingly ridiculous question affecting students at the college. Godbole then proposes to take his leave, but before doing so he makes a polite reference to the expedition to the caves, just as though nothing had occurred there. Impatiently, Fielding faces him with the question that is filling his mind: 'Is Aziz innocent or guilty?' In answer, Godbole seems to prevaricate: first he says that it is for the court to decide, but when the question is put to him in a different form—'Would he or would he not do such a thing?'—he replies that, 'in our philosophy', it is difficult to answer:

> 'because nothing can be performed in isolation. All perform a good action, when one is performed, and when an evil action is performed, all perform it. To illustrate my meaning, let me take the case in point as an example.'
>
> 'I am informed that an evil action was performed in the Marabar Hills, and that a highly esteemed English lady is now seriously ill in consequence. My answer to that is this: that action was performed by Dr Aziz.' He stopped and sucked in his thin cheeks. 'It was performed by the guide.' He stopped again. 'It was performed by you.' Now he had an air of daring and of coyness. 'It was performed by me.' He looked slyly down the sleeve of his coat. 'And by my students. It was even performed by the lady herself. When evil occurs, it expresses the whole of the universe. Similarly when good occurs.'

Fielding, understandably, waves away this account, supposing that Godbole is merely clouding an important factual issue with irrelevant philosophical mystification, and the reader may well feel the same. Only when we turn back to his account after we have seen the outcome of the events do we realise that Godbole—this unpractical Hindu professor who always detaches himself from what seem to be the actualities of any significant situation—has given the only true account of them. It is worth noting, first, that he is speaking only by theory; he knows nothing, first-hand, about the supposed 'evil action' and states only that he has been 'informed' of one, and yet each of his accusations makes sense. Aziz did not in fact assault Adela, but his organisation of the expedition (chapters 13 to 16) has been egotistically expensive and ostentatious, much concerned to display his talent as a host but very little concerned with the real comfort of his guests; whatever happened in the cave, the effects of exhaustion and discomfort on Adela and Mrs Moore had much to do with it. The guide employed by Aziz lost touch with Adela, so that his incompetence has also been a contribution. His inclusion of Fielding seems at first unfair: though invited, he had not been present, because he had been in the company of Godbole and both had missed the train owing to Godbole, characteristically, taking too long over his prayers. Yet if we think of the 'evil' as more a consequence of the moral climate of Chandrapore than of any particular event, he too has had responsibility. A great cultivator of friendship with Indians, he has been carelessly free in his conversation with them and has thus inadvertently heightened Indian misconceptions of British motives—for instance, by his remarks about religious belief in Britain in chapter 9. Godbole's own unpracticality has been the cause of their failure to join the expedition; if both had been present, the two women would have been more intelligently looked after and Adela's fatal delusion would certainly not have occurred. The students, too, have responsibility, by their propensity for using any disturbance as a pretext for political ferment. Finally, Godbole accuses Adela, and she has been herself the most immediate cause of the evil, since her crisis has almost certainly originated from her own conflicts with herself and her relationships. Godbole is therefore right in supposing—though he is speaking theoretically—that 'all have performed the evil action', himself included. But it is important for the truth of the analysis that, as we come to see, there was no 'evil action' in the cave. There is, on the other hand, evil in Chandrapore, and it is the nature of this evil, always latently present and made overt by whatever did occur in the cave, that Godbole is really discussing.

Fielding supposes that Godbole is characteristically removing himself from urgent personal issues by a scheme of thought so remote and comprehensive that all intelligible distinctions are obliterated, even that between good and evil. This Godbole denies, and in doing so he demonstrates the spiritual basis of what, so far, has been his system of moral insights:

> 'Oh no, excuse me once again. Good and evil are different, as their names imply. But, in my own humble opinion, they are both of them aspects of my Lord. He is present in the one, absent in the other, and the difference between presence and absence is great, as great as my feeble mind can grasp. Yet absence implies presence, absence is not non-existence, and we are therefore entitled to repeat, "Come, come, come, come."'

These remarks—which leave Fielding equally unimpressed—have many resonances backwards and forwards in the novel; many 'echoes' one might say, in a novel rife with symbolism, among which 'echo' is itself one of the most pregnant.

So far from being a major character, Godbole makes only two other conspicuous appearances (in chapters 7 and 33), and yet he is in an important respect a criterion for the others. He does not set a criterion in the sense of superiority as a person, for he is always presented with a degree of genial satire; when, for instance, he becomes Minister for Education in a native state, we see that he has allowed his college to be used temporarily as a granary (chapter 37), and that he is taking no steps to reconvert it. He is, however, a criterion in the sense that all the characters are differentiated, in a sense deeper than their other differences, by their attitudes to religion, with which only Godbole is totally imbued.

Ostensibly, the religious attitudes are classifiable under agnosticism and under the three religious systems. Adela and Fielding are agnostics, but the other British are at least nominally Christian. Aziz and his friends are Moslem, and Godbole is Brahman, more familiarly known as Hindu. The systems are, however, abstract whereas the attitudes of the characters—including Godbole, although he is also a theorist—are concrete; that is to say they are shaped more by historical tradition and immediate practical circumstances than by creeds. In this, Forster is surely being true to the facts of most societies: few individuals, even when they are strong believers or convinced unbelievers, would call themselves philosophers about religion, and yet religion remains one of the strongest influences over the minds of any society, shaping unconscious assumptions even in the minds of sceptics with all the accumulated force of a long history during much of which it was the established authority for moral conduct and even for the conduct of politics. Thus the officials in *A Passage to India* are Christians because they are British officials; they stand to attention during 'God save the King' for patriotic reasons, but the anthem—although the Indians, misled by Fielding, fail to see this—is nonetheless essential to their patriotism. Apart from such ritual, they consider it at best unnecessary and at worst bad taste to investigate religion further:

> Ronny approved of religion as long as it endorsed the National Anthem, but he objected when it attempted to influence his life. Thus he would say in respectful yet decided tones, 'I don't think it does to talk about these things, every fellow has to work out his own religion,' and any fellow who heard him muttered, 'Hear!'

This comment, at the end of chapter 5, comes after an earnest conversation with his mother, Mrs Moore, and she is another sort of Christian altogether. She has just done her best to convince him that the Christian ethic ought to dictate British conduct to the Indians. She fails, of course, because in western politics that ethic has been strongly qualified by pragmatism, though it still dictates, whether or not the British realise it, their political integrity, and she is herself embarrassed by her attempt. She is a practising Christian so far as the Christian ethic takes her in personal relationships, but the influence of India has made her for the first time aware of the constrictedness of the crude version of the Christian cosmos. It is like a circle, or a vault, and she is made to feel its limitation rather than its scope:

> Outside the arch there seemed always an arch, beyond the remotest echo a silence.

The same limitation has been demonstrated in chapter 4 in the discussion between the two missionaries 'who never came up to the club'. They argue about God's infinite mercy, and to what extent Heaven can be regarded as truly inclusive. The advanced Mr Sorley affirms that it may well show hospitality to mammals, even jackals:

> And the wasps? He became uneasy during the descent to the wasps,

and was apt to change the conversation. And oranges, cactuses, crystals and mud? and the bacteria inside Mr Sorley? No, no, this is going too far. We must exclude someone from our gathering, or we shall be left with nothing.

The easiest way to avoid the crudities of habitual Christianity (we do not, of course, have to suppose that Forster considered there to be no other sort) is by disbelief. This is why the two intellectuals among the British, Fielding and Adela, are agnostics, and they probably represent the viewpoint closest to that of Forster himself. And yet agnosticism, too, is a standpoint which undergoes severe trial. Fielding's attitude to life, until the last section of the novel, can be summarised by his belief in 'travelling light' (chapter 11), not merely in the sense of carrying few material belongings but in that of accumulating few attachments—religious, political or personal—beyond those which come to him spontaneously. The crisis over Aziz—one of the spontaneous attachments—breaks this freedom by giving him his first consciousness of serious responsibility, and in the last chapter we are told that 'he did not travel lightly as in the past': he has a family, and besides he has discovered that the mysteries of India are no longer mere muddles to him (chapter 7), but bafflements which afflict his spirit. More earnest than Fielding, Adela chooses honesty as her religion: 'if one isn't absolutely honest,' she asks Mrs Moore in chapter 8, 'what is the use of existing?' And yet it is the mysterious dishonesty induced by her hysteria in the cave which brings about the Aziz crisis, and nearly breaks her when she recognises it for what it is.

One of the consequences of religious superficiality among the British is that they fail to discriminate among the religious attitudes of the Indians. Indians are Indians, differentiated only by whether they comply with the British regime or not, and the distinction between Moslems and Hindus matters only when this is politically necessary or convenient. Yet the novel emphasises that this difference is profound: the Moslem Aziz finds Godbole's religion as unintelligible as do the Christians. However, they share at least, in contrast to most of the British, deep seriousness in their profession of belief. This mutual sympathy is shown in chapter 7 when Aziz, unable to explain the sacredness of the Marabar caves, refers the question to Godbole, and Godbole, while professing willingness, proves unwilling. Aziz is able to understand why; it is not that Godbole is himself ignorant, but that he cannot communicate the secret to a British audience (Mrs Moore, Adela and Fielding) who lack assumptions of the most intimate importance to himself. Nevertheless, Aziz not only professes a totally different creed; his attitude to his religion is also very different. Godbole is a mystic, whereas Aziz' devotion to Islam is essentially cultural. He is aware of himself as one of the Islamic race which once conquered India; in his speech, the names of its emperors interchange with those of its poets, and the mosque in Chandrapore is sacred to him not primarily for the doctrine it enshrines but for the culture it manifests, and this culture is his true home.

> A mosque by winning his approval let loose his imagination. The temple of another creed, Hindu, Christian, or Greek, would have bored him and failed to awaken his sense of beauty. Here was Islam, his own country, more than a Faith, more than a battle cry, more, much more ... Islam, an attitude towards life both exquisite and durable, where his body and his thoughts found their home.

This occurs in chapter 2, when Aziz meets Mrs Moore in the mosque at night and they become friends. Her Christianity and his Islam enable them to meet as individuals at a deeper level than that made possible by social codes and habits, initially because she, like him, takes her religion with full seriousness. Adela and Fielding likewise believe in the freedom of personal relationships from social constraints, and so, in a very different way, does Godbole. None of the three, however, would have visited the mosque in the spirit in which Mrs Moore visits it; for the first two, the visit would have entailed respect and been motivated by aesthetic interest, and Godbole, the Brahman, would not have visited it at all. She alone is able to win Aziz' respect with the sentence that rings sincerely from one who, as he does, seriously professes a monotheistic faith: 'God is here.' It is this that inspires him with a desire to know her personally, and his respect is deepened to warmth by the way in which she speaks of Mrs Callendar, the wife of his official superior. When her name comes up, he makes the sort of comment which he is accustomed to think the only safe one to make about a member of the British colony: 'Ah! a very charming lady.' Her response startles him: 'Possibly, when one knows her better.' This stimulates him into a diatribe of bitter resentment against the Callendars, and she listens.

> The flame that not even beauty can nourish was springing up, and though his words were querulous his heart began to glow secretly. Presently it burst into speech.
> 'You understand me, you know what others feel. Oh, if others resembled you!'
> Rather surprised, she replied: 'I don't think I understand people very well. I only know whether I like or dislike them.'
> 'Then you are an Oriental.'

He repeats the statement once more, in the penultimate chapter, to Ralph, her son by her second marriage, when the latter states that he always knows when a stranger is a friend. What does it mean? Ralph and his sister Stella, Fielding's wife, also feel sympathy with and openness to the Hindu rituals. It seems that personal relations as Aziz understands them must derive from a level of feeling deeper than the

Forster with his friend Syed Ross Masood upon whom he based the character of Aziz

hard soil of shrivelled religion and dry pragmatism such as he has found governing western minds, and that his level of feeling is also the stratum of eastern religions of whatever creed. It is also the soil which nourishes art. Mrs Moore has visited the mosque to escape a performance at the club of 'Cousin Kate', a trivial comedy which distracts the feelings instead of calling them to life. While Aziz lies sick in chapter 9, he and his friends recite Islamic poetry in a community of feeling.

We know, too, from his essays and especially 'What I Believe', that Forster shared this religion of personal relationships. And yet this novel is to show Mrs Moore abrogating the creed as well as Christianity, and Aziz turning away from it in bitterness into the circle of political loyalties. It is only Godbole, immersed in religion but apparently detached from any individual, who, in chapter 33, expands spiritually in an act of inclusive love. Thus the characters who vest most feeling in personal relations—Mrs Moore, Aziz, Fielding, Adela—are all severed from relationship into individuality, but the character who cares least for relationship on the plane of individual encounter ends by achieving it on another plane. Is this mystery or mystification—the worst form of muddle? 'A mystery is a muddle,' asserts Fielding to Mrs Moore in chapter 7 (replying to her remark that she likes the former but dislikes the latter)—'A mystery is only a high sounding term for a muddle.' Is the novel a refutation of his opinion, or merely a meditation on the statement?

A Passage to India has three parts, or, remembering Forster's interest in musical form, we may call them movements. They are 'Mosque' (chapters 1 to 11), 'Caves' (12 to 32), and 'Temples' (33 to 37).

'*Mosque*'

The first movement plainly derives its title from Mrs Moore's meeting with Aziz in the second chapter, but also from the architecture of the building itself—its simplicity, openness and graciousness. It seems to speak the language of personal encounter as it should be, and that between the Moslem doctor and the English lady offers a promising beginning. Nor is the promise totally belied: Aziz establishes a confident friendship with Fielding, and has a happy moment with a British subaltern playing polo; the club is blandly hospitable to Mrs Moore and Adela—the head of the district, Mr Turton, arranging for them a 'bridge party', so called because it is intended to bring the races together in amity; Adela and Ronny, after a breach, confirm their engagement; Fielding arranges a happy party for the visitors and includes Aziz and Godbole. However, the theme of cordiality is repeatedly encountered by contrary themes, and they tend to dominate: Ronny disapproves of his mother's meeting with Aziz, and misinterprets it; the 'bridge party' turns out only to confirm the gulf between the races; Fielding's tea-party is nearly ruined by Ronny's insensitive intrusion. Even Fielding's friendship with Aziz is smeared by the latter's contempt for his friend's indifference to calculating policy. Thus, although the movement is concerned above all with personal relations, it is the confusions, reservations and prejudices which dominate, permeating them as woodworm riddles even the best timber. It is not only the political alignment which is the cause of this corruption, but India itself, where nothing has distinct credibility and identity or is assuredly what it seems. And yet integrity and strong feeling can redeem a detail from the chaos and raise it into significance. As she retires to bed at the end of chapter 3, Mrs Moore takes an objective view of her son's disapproval of her meeting with Aziz and accepts that it is after all a plausible view. All the same, 'how false as a summary of the man; the essential life of him had been slain'. Then she finds that the peg on which she is about to hang her cloak is occupied by a sleeping wasp:

> Perhaps he mistook the peg for a branch—no Indian animal has any sense of interior. Bats, rats, birds, insects will as soon nest inside a house as out; it is to them a normal growth of the eternal jungle, which alternately produces houses trees, houses trees. There he clung, asleep, while jackals in the plain bayed their desires and mingled with the percussion of drums.
>
> 'Pretty dear,' said Mrs Moore to the wasp. He did not wake, but her voice floated out, to swell the night's uneasiness.

At the end of the next chapter, the missionary doubts a place in Heaven for wasps: he envisages God as an exalted version of himself, and if he does not like them, why should He? The western mind differentiates the world concentrically, defining the circles with geometric precision and centring them on its own egoism. But in India there are no circles, or else there are infinite circles beyond accountability. There is, for instance, the circle admittable to the Turton bridge party, and then the circle that waits for hearing outside the law court:

> And there were circles beyond these—people who wore nothing but a loin-cloth, people who wore not even that, and spent their lives in knocking two sticks together before a scarlet doll—humanity grading and drifting beyond the educated vision, until no earthly invitation can embrace it.

> (*chapter 4*)

And yet, just as it is a wasp that concentrates Mrs Moore's love when she has elucidated her feelings about Aziz, so it is the figure of a man from those unembraceable circles which restores lucidity to Adela when once she has been shocked out of her hysteria by the truth-speaking of Mrs Moore, who has been transformed into a rock of egoism. These transformations belong to the second movement—'Caves'.

'Caves'

As a structure, the mosque is an object of simple clarity and shapeliness; the caves are even simpler—circular, unadorned, with internal surfaces highly polished but not by man—and as sacred to the Hindus as the mosque is to Moslems. But the difference in their significance is extreme: the message of the mosque is explicit—'There is no God but God'; that of the caves defies human language. The contrast between the movements is parallel: 'Mosque' concerns human relationships which are in principle open and candid but in practice eroded by muddle and deceit; 'Caves' concerns misunderstanding and mystification, which are mysteriously transmuted into stark and dangerous clarity. The centre of the mystery is what happens to Mrs Moore and to Adela in the caves; their influence on the former is explained, though it remains very startling, but that on the latter is not, and it is in that episode that Forster takes the greatest risk in his use of imaginative licence.

Mrs Moore's breakdown is not as sudden as it may seem from a casual reading of the novel. She comes out to India a benign but far from complacent matriarch. She is anxious to do her best by the girl she brings with her and who may become her daughter-in-law, and she is open to and interested in the strangers of all races and persuasions whom she may meet. But after the promising opening with Aziz, the experience steadily exhausts her and strains her attachments and beliefs. Her hosts, the officials of Chandrapore, are conscientious and well-disposed, but she finds herself out of sympathy with their attitudes and policies, and this means that she is at cross purposes with her son. Indians prove elusive and exasperating, and she gets frustrated by the ups and downs of the relationship between Ronny and Adela. Worse still, she finds her basic convictions under stress; she is religious, but in India the Christian God, though constantly in her thoughts, has 'never satisfied her less' (chapter 5). Worse still, she has acquired new doubts about marriage in particular and about human relationships in general:

> She felt increasingly (vision or nightmare?) that, though people are important, the relations between them are not, and that in particular too much fuss has been made over marriage; centuries of carnal embracement, yet man is no nearer to understanding man. And to-day she felt this with such force that it seemed itself a relationship, itself a person who was trying to take hold of her hand.

This is in chapter 14 when she is in the train on the way to the caves, and we are clearly being given a lead. We put her state of mind together with the oppressiveness of the climate, Aziz' mismanagement of the occasion, and other forms of discomfort; and who, or what, is 'trying to take hold of her hand'?

But we are perhaps not prepared for the breakdown being so very complete. It is less physical than mental, and in being mental it is above all spiritual. The paragraph concluding chapter 14, describing how the panic of a visit to the first cave amid a crowd of natives sinks into her after she has escaped, makes her spiritual negation explicit:

> She tried to go on with her letter, reminding herself that she was only an elderly woman who had got up too early in the morning and journeyed too far, that the despair creeping over her was merely her despair, and that even if she got a sunstroke and went mad the rest of the world would go on. But suddenly, at the edge of her mind, Religion appeared, poor little talkative Christianity, and she knew that all its divine words from 'Let there be light' to 'It is finished' only amounted to 'boum'. Then she was terrified over an area larger than usual; the universe, never comprehensible to her intellect, offered no repose to her soul, the mood of the last two months took definite form at last, and she realized that she didn't want to communicate with anyone, not even with God.

This is the greatest of all Forster's 'epiphanies', or visionary moments, yet a negative epiphany, a vision of blackness and emptiness. But it is important to understand exactly what has happened to Mrs Moore. She begins by trying to secure her balance through the recognition that she is only an individual, suffering a despair which is hers alone, of no significance to others. This recalls words spoken by Godbole to Fielding in chapter 19:

> Suffering is merely a matter for the individual. If a young lady has sunstroke, that is a matter of no significance to the universe. Oh no, not at all. Oh no, not in the least. It is an isolated matter, it only concerns herself. If she thought her head did not ache, she would not be ill, and that would end it. But it is far otherwise in the case of good and evil. They are not what we think them, they are what they are, and each of us has contributed to both.

But Mrs Moore's religion is not Godbole's. The reflection of herself as a mere individual inevitably leads to her religion appearing 'at the edge of her mind', 'poor little talkative Christianity'. For this is the religion which places the individual at the centre of the universe: the very words 'Let there be light' were spoken by the divine Individual, and 'It is finished' are those of the divine Individual incarnated in a mortal individual at the end of suffering, and are interpreted as meaning that suffering is not merely of individual significance but—in opposition to Godbole—of significance to the universe. And yet that hollow echo 'boum', which annihilates the Christian vision in her, is itself the echo of the sacred syllable 'OM' signifying Brahma, the Creator. Mrs Moore does not know this (Godbole is not present to explain) nor does she know that for this reason, and because their polished interiors reflect perfect images of a living flame, the caves are sacred to Hindus as symbols in rock of their central beliefs.

The result of the experience is that this benign old lady is transformed into the spiritual equivalent of the astronomical 'black hole', which is said to be so dense with gravitational force that even light is unable to escape from it. She loses all concern for and interest in others, and in reply to her exasperated son she can only exclaim:

> 'My body, my miserable body . . . . Why isn't it strong? Oh, why can't I walk away and be gone? Why can't I finish my duties and be gone? Why do I get headaches and puff when I walk? And all the time this to do and that to do and this to do in your way and that to do in her way, and everything sympathy and confusion and bearing one another's burdens. Why can't this be done and that be done in my way and they be done and I at peace? Why has anything to be done, I cannot see. Why all this marriage, marriage? ... The human race would have become a single person centuries ago if marriage was any use. And all this rubbish about love, love in a church, love in a cave, as if there is the least difference, and I held up from my business over such trifles!'

> *(chapter 22)*

It is as negative, despairing, destructive a speech as could be. And yet two things are remarkable about it, and inconsistent with its negation. One is its eloquence: Mrs Moore has never spoken so eloquently before, and has never had the capacity to do so. The other is that it is the beginning of her influence as a positive force, first in temporarily removing the state of delusion from Adela's mind, and later, when she is dead, in her reaching a state of apotheosis as a Hindu goddess (Esmiss Esmoor) among the populace who never knew her. What, in the first place, is it about her utterance which, however temporarily, changes Adela's state of mind? And what can we suppose actually happened to Adela in the cave?

The two questions are related to the extent that if we can answer the second we shall be in a better position to answer the first. Ten years after the publication of *A Passage to India*, Forster wrote to William Plomer that:

> I tried to show that India is an unexplainable muddle by introducing an unexplained muddle—Miss Quested's experience in the cave. When asked what happened there, *I don't know.*

We may well ask, what is the use of the reader trying to guess where the novelist admits ignorance; however, that question is not so merely rhetorical as it must seem. A novelist's subject is human nature, and that is to say that he is concerned with a mystery of which he is himself a part. He does not therefore fail in his art if he is unable to explain all that is mysterious about one of his characters, nor if at a certain point in his narrative he feels impelled to introduce an event of which he cannot give a full explanatory account. He fails only if he introduces a mystery into his narrative without showing why it occurs there, and what relationship the mystery has to the rest of his text. Forster passes both these tests, and in doing so he makes it possible for us to infer the nature of the mysterious event, even though we cannot outdo him by discerning exactly what occurred.

To begin with we have those strange geological phenomena, the Marabar Hills and their caves. Strange as they are, they are by no means incredible, and they have been mentioned repeatedly in the novel, beginning with the first sentence of the first chapter: we know that they are geologically very ancient and that they are sacred to the Hindus, but that their sacredness is so mysterious that even Professor Godbole is unwilling to explain it to an audience ignorant of his religious idiom. Aziz, Mrs Moore and Adela undertake the expedition to them in the spirit of tourism—that is to say in the superficial state of mind of mere sightseers—but each of them is in a state of personal tension unsuitable to the relaxed condition which sightseeing requires if it is to be a pleasure. Adela, in particular, as she follows Aziz from cave to cave—each exactly similar to its predecessor—is bored, oppressed by the problem of her very mixed feelings for Ronny as well as by the heat. A slight awkwardness occurs just before she enters the cave in which she suffers her crisis. A chance association of ideas has made her suddenly conscious that she does not in the least love Ronny, although she has agreed to marry him. She then becomes fully aware of the physical attractiveness of Aziz as he hands her over the rocks, and asks him how many wives he has, vaguely supposing all Moslems to be polygamous. As an educated Moslem who has settled for monogamy, he is deeply shocked by the question and escapes into a cave to recover himself, while she vaguely wanders into another—'thinking with half her mind "sightseeing bores me," and wondering with the other half about marriage'.

We need to remember how Adela's character has been built up for us. Her religion of honesty depends on the assumption that personal issues can be seen with the absolute clarity of reason, and in this she belongs to the rationalistic western tradition which—stronger in the earlier part of our century—ignored the penumbra and the darkness of the consciousness, innocent of the sudden menaces that may arise out of them. As she enters the cave, her reasoning mind is stupefied by boredom and fatigue while it grapples feebly with a sudden emotional disturbance. She goes out of the hot sun into the chill dark: the transition is like an assault on her nervous system, and the physical contrast parallels the psychic conflict, uniting in shock. It is reasonable to assume that she rationalises the conjunction of physical with psychic shock by explaining it to herself as assault by the man whom a moment before she has recognised as physically attractive to her, especially in view of the inconvenience of this attractiveness, since she has almost simultaneously recognised that she is not attracted to the man she is to marry. Psychically, the image of Aziz has assaulted her; in a sudden hysteria, she translates this into a physical assault. Forster might have allayed our doubts with a more specific pretext—collision with a bat?—but he prefers to imply that Adela's disaster arises from the jungle of unexpected contrasts which constitutes India, and which he also sees as identifiable with the jungle of the human psyche when we are no longer able to square it with the elegant, rational proportions evolved by western culture.

How then does Mrs Moore's speech ('My body, my miserable body ....') reveal to Adela that she has made a mistake? We need to recall the extraordinary eloquence of that speech: it is the eloquence of deep spontaneous conviction, of Mrs Moore's despair at the futility of her own and other people's egos, which try to dictate meaning while they are themselves meaningless. The conflict of fears and desires in Adela's ego has ignited conflict in a whole community, although they have reality only for Adela herself. It is not through our egoistic desires that we individuals unite in community: 'Why all this marriage, marriage? ... And all this rubbish about love, love in a church, love in a cave, as if there is the least difference ...'. That has been the conflict in Adela's psyche, between the repression of appetite for one man and the fear of not desiring another to whom she has bound herself. Our egoism can only unite with other egoisms in antagonism to still others—Adela's with those of the British against those of the heterogeneous Indians—and the resulting conflagration has no more to do with reality than has that in the individual ego. Godbole is therefore perfectly right in supposing that the 'evil action' of which he 'has been informed' was 'even performed by the lady herself' and that 'when an evil action is performed, all perform it'.

Adela's recognition of her error is too inconvenient to her egoism to last, especially when that of the British community, except Fielding, sustains her hysterical delusion. For the British, her crisis is supremely valuable because it provides a suitable pretext for justifying their latent hostility to the Indians whom they govern. They know that they are in danger from the Indian rage at seeing one of their number used as a scapegoat for British prejudice, but they welcome that opportunity for united heroism; indeed Adela, as Forster puts it, 'brought out all that was fine in their character', characteristically expounding his paradox that people do not necessarily show themselves at their worst when they are wrong, just as now the Indians do not show themselves at their best although they are right. The British achieve solidarity in courage, control and reason, whereas the Indians, including Aziz but excepting Godbole who keeps his remoteness, lose all dignity and themselves give way to hysteria. And yet, when she faces her ultimate crisis at the trial, Adela manifests still greater courage and control through her western religion of honesty, and in doing so she achieves heroism, since she antagonises her compatriots while doing nothing to mitigate Indian hostility towards her. However, by a further twist to our expectations, she does not achieve this transcendence of her state by her own unaided effort, but under the influence of an individual who has no connection with herself or with the proceedings except that he pulls the fan that is supposed to cool the court—an image from the uttermost human circles of darkest India:

> The Court was crowded and of course very hot, and the first person Adela noticed in it was the humblest of all who were present, a person who had no bearing officially upon the trial: the man who pulled the punkah. Almost naked, and splendidly formed, he sat on a raised platform near the back, in the middle of the central gangway, and he caught her attention as she came in, and he seemed to control the proceedings.

Although he is of the lowest caste, of quite undeveloped mentality—'didn't even know he worked a fan, though he thought he pulled a rope'—in fact he does control them, because he controls Adela's state of mind.

> Something in his aloofness impressed the girl from middle-class England, and rebuked the narrowness of her sufferings. In virtue of what had she collected this roomful of people together? Her particular brand of opinions, and the suburban Jehovah who sanctified them—by what right did they claim so much importance in the world, and assume the title of civilization? Mrs Moore—she looked round, but Mrs Moore was far away on the sea; it was the kind of question they might have discussed on the passage out before the old lady had turned disagreeable and queer.

Mrs Moore crops up in the proceedings: the junior defence counsel accuses the British of having smuggled her away because she would have been his key witness; he makes a scene, and her name is caught up by the crowd in the street, 'travestied into Esmiss Esmoor, a Hindu goddess'. Eventually the issue is smoothed over by the Indian magistrate, and the prosecution is cynically relieved: 'There is no stay in your native. He blazes up over a minor point, and has nothing left for the crisis.' Legally this is true: Mrs Moore was not present when Adela and Aziz went into different caves, so her evidence would have been worthless. And yet for Adela's consciousness she is in her absence (and her death, for she dies at about this time) the key witness. It is the truthfulness of Mrs Moore and the remoteness of the punkah-wallah that dominate Adela's consciousness during her interrogation, transforming it into a perfect detachment and stillness:

> The fatal day recurred, in every detail, but now she was of it and not of it at the same time, and this double relation gave it an indescribable splendour. Why had she thought the expedition 'dull'? Now the sun rose again, the elephant waited, the pale masses

of the rock flowed round her and presented the first cave; she entered, and a match was reflected in the polished walls—all beautiful and significant, though she had been blind to it at the time.

In this state of mind, she becomes aware of the facts as she had not been aware of them at the time when she was undergoing them and was herself one of them. Asked the crucial question—'The prisoner followed you, didn't he?'—she asks for time, and then replies, 'in a flat, unattractive voice', in the negative. Amid an uproar, Aziz is acquitted. The court empties in tumult, but 'the beautiful naked god' remains:

> Unaware that anything unusual had occurred, he continued to pull the cord of his punkah, to gaze at the empty dais and the overturned chairs, and rhythmically to agitate the clouds of descending dust.

Good is reasserted, though the British see it as evil, and Godbole's dicta about good and evil have been justified. The trial has brought justice through Adela who has been the pretext for the evil; through the punkah-wallah, who has been absent in mind though present in the flesh, and by Mrs Moore, absent in the flesh though present in spirit.

'*Temples*'

The last movement of the novel—'Temples'—elucidates and allays the personal antagonisms—Aziz' misunderstanding of Fielding and his hostility to Adela, who is now in England. It also culminates the religious theme, and the two themes are of course closely related. The culmination, as we might expect, comes chiefly through Professor Godbole, in his performance in a religious festival which takes place in the palace of the rajah of the native state where both he and Aziz are now employed. The celebration is of the birth of God:

> God is not born yet—that will occur at midnight—but He has also been born centuries ago, nor can He ever be born, because He is the Lord of the Universe, who transcends human processes.

Paradox and inconsistency: muddle or mystery? There is certainly plenty of muddle, visible and audible; the beauty of the building is obscured by a dingy mess of ornament, and music issues simultaneously and cacophonously from several sources:

> they did not one thing which the non-Hindu would feel dramatically correct; the approaching triumph of India was a muddle (as we call it), a frustration of reason and form.

And yet at the heart of the muddle is mystery:

> When the villagers broke cordon for a glimpse of the silver image [of

the god], a most beautiful and radiant expression came into their faces, a beauty in which there was nothing personal, for it caused them all to resemble one another during the moment of its indwelling, and only when it was withdrawn did they revert to individual clods.

Moreover the muddle is not produced by ignorant misunderstandings, undisclosed prejudices, unacknowledged barriers, as it is in 'Mosque', in which the western and Islamic aspirations for order and coherence are complicated and defeated. The confusion in 'Temples' is of spontaneous joy which both accepts and ignores intervening inconsistencies and errors of both taste and reason for the sake of the unifying simplicity which is at the heart of them, although it is also their cause; one of the inscriptions pinned untidily about the walls

(composed in English to indicate His universality) consisted, by an unfortunate slip of the draughtsman, of the words, 'God si Love.'
God si Love. Is this the final message of India?

'God . . . is . . . Love' is what Mrs Moore had painfully impressed on her son in chapter 5, no longer herself fully convinced. But Forster seems to take the blunder in the inscription to imply that He is, although, in the infinite muddle that constitutes life, His ways are impossible to apprehend.

In the midst of the confusion Godbole, comical as usual, performs his dance. The musicians break into a new rhythm:

This was more exciting, the inner images it evoked more definite, and the singers' expressions became fatuous and languid. They loved all men, the whole universe, and scraps of their past, tiny splinters of detail, emerged for a moment to melt into the universal warmth. Thus Godbole, though she was not important to him, remembered an old woman he had met in Chandrapore days. Chance brought her into his mind while it was in this heated state, he did not select her, she happened to occur among the throng of soliciting images, a tiny splinter, and he impelled her by his spiritual force to that place where completeness can be found. Completeness, not reconstruction. His senses grew thinner, he remembered a wasp seen he forgot where, perhaps on a stone. He loved the wasp equally, he impelled it likewise, he was imitating God. And the stone where the wasp clung—could he . . . no, he could not, he had been wrong to attempt the stone, logic and conscious effort had seduced, he came back to the strip of red carpet, and discovered that he was dancing upon it.

Godbole and Mrs Moore are the poles of the novel's axis: Godbole the learned Brahman, immersed so deeply in the mysteries of his religion that relationships with individuals seem meaningless to him, and Mrs

Moore the earnest Christian, for whom the centre of life's meaning is personal relations; Godbole who nevertheless ends with this mystical expression of inclusive love, and Mrs Moore who ends up loving nobody, least of all herself. This seeming reversal of role is the deepest theme in the novel, underlying, but not distinct from, that of the relationships of the other three characters, and we need, if not an explanation of it, at least a key to one. If we look for such a key, we need to realise that a characteristic of the novel is what the novel shows to be characteristic of India: what is most important is often what is least in the foreground. We can take the wasp as an example: it focuses Mrs Moore's love in chapter 3 and Mr Sorley's distaste in chapter 4; it unites Godbole and Mrs Moore in chapter 33, and no doubt it is what distracts Aziz in chapter 37, causing him to add a sentence in his letter to Adela:

'For my own part, I shall henceforth connect you with the name that is very sacred in my mind, namely, Mrs Moore.'

But if we think of the wasp, we may go on to think of the stone on which, in Godbole's memory, the wasp had settled. The stone defeats him—he cannot love it, and stone in a more massive form has defeated Mrs Moore. Matter defeats humanity because it is dead and repels feeling with its annihilating echo; yet it is this echo that recalls the sacred syllable 'OM', the name of God. What is the meaning of this enigma? Perhaps that an echo is not its own original sound: there is an ultimate circle which human feeling cannot break, and if we try to break it, the futility of the endeavour rebounds on us, confusing our best efforts and impulses. Within that ultimate circle the mass of misunderstandings, ignorance, resentment and prejudice are more immediate constraints on the operation of human goodwill, and this is what Fielding comes to feel about India in chapter 31:

'In the old eighteenth-century, when cruelty and injustice raged, an invisible power repaired their ravages. Everything echoes now; there's no stopping the echo. The original sound may be harmless, but the echo is always evil.' This reflection about an echo lay at the verge of Fielding's mind. He could never develop it. It belonged to the universe that he had missed or rejected. And the mosque missed it too. Like himself, those shallow arcades provided but a limited asylum. 'There is no God but God' doesn't carry us far through the complexities of matter and spirit; it is only a game with words, really, a religious pun, not a religious truth.

Only Mrs Moore hears the ultimate echo, and although she is negated by it the subsequent beneficence of her spirit is not merely an ironical sequel. Her disillusionment is total (though it too has a sequel) but it is also a critical test of western values—those values from which Whitman foresaw an infinite spiritual progress. Her fallacy has been the western one of assuming that reality is humanity-centred (whereas, in chapter 19, 'Professor Godbole's conversation frequently centred on a cow'), to the extent of projecting itself upon its image of God. The consequence is a reduced universe, and how it is reduced Forster reveals in chapter 29, in which Adela and Fielding reach mutual understanding:

> A friendliness, as of dwarfs shaking hands, was in the air. Both man and woman were at the height of their powers—sensible, honest, even subtle. They spoke the same language, and held the same opinions, and the variety of age and sex did not divide them. Yet they were dissatisfied. When they agreed, 'I want to go on living a bit,' or, 'I don't believe in God,' the words were followed by a curious backwash as though the universe had displaced itself to fill up a tiny void, or as though they had seen their own gestures from an immense height—dwarfs talking, shaking hands and assuring each other that they stood on the same footing of insight. They did not think they were wrong, because as soon as honest people think they are wrong instability sets up. Not for them was an infinite goal behind the stars, and they never sought it. But wistfulness descended on them now, as on other occasions; the shadow of the shadow of a dream fell over their clear-cut interests, and objects never seen again seemed messages from another world.

That they are not professing Christians, as Mrs Moore had been, but agnostics, does not make much difference to the purport of this paragraph. They are unbelievers because Christianity has relaxed its hold on their imaginations until they have found themselves without it, but this—as Christianity has been presented in the novel—does not make their agnosticism a radically alternative position. On the other hand, it would not be true to say that Forster has been making a case against Christianity, though it probably is true to say that he has been making a case against conventional English Protestantism—'the suburban Jehovah'. This does not mean that he is anti-Christian, nor is he anti-Moslem and pro-Hindu. The religious theme concerns the affective power of religion: whether it is intrinsic to a culture in the sense of immediately affecting all ways of life, whether it retains a major influence on emotional values but not upon beliefs about the nature of existence, or whether it has become a mere shell, a pretext for some political and social forms but no longer a power to influence reason or feeling to any depth. In the novel, Hinduism is the all-pervading religion, Islam is a cultural force rather than a creed, and Christianity, except as Mrs Moore (and, in caricature, the missionaries in chapter 4) practise it, is a mere prescription for forms. We would be most unwise to infer from the novel any judgement on the three religions as universal and timeless creeds. Forster is merely presenting them as he found them, at a particular time and in a particular environmental context.

However, it is essential to *A Passage to India* that the environment has a much larger and deeper significance than is usual in a novel, and this is because it unites what are usually considered to be irreconcilable attributes. An environment, in a novel, may be a shapeless and meaningless state of nature, as it is in Conrad's *Heart of Darkness* about Africa; more usually it will be strongly moulded by a long entrenched civilisation, as it is in Europe and in most of the novels emanating therefrom. Civilisations usually exhibit themselves as circles which exclude what is inconvenient in nature, retaining and tailoring what remains, and shaping their religions in accordance with their own interests of coherence. But India, for Forster, is an environment which has never allowed itself to be so constricted, although it too has nourished an ancient civilisation. In India, the process has been the accommodation of civilisation and religion to nature instead of the reverse. Thus India is shown to be a condition of reality beyond the reach of Europe's shaping reason or Islam's emotional imperatives. Alien civilisations may construct and fortify their circles within it, but an earnest spirit such as Mrs Moore's, too serious to resign herself to such expediencies, must risk the annihilation of what has seemed to give her life its meaning. Is this, then, the final obliterating circle? Forster clearly does not wish us to suppose it, even for Mrs Moore.

Passages from India

We are not shown passages to India in the literal sense, but we are shown passages from India, and these help to elucidate the spiritual passage which is India itself, and its consequences for Fielding, Adela and Mrs Moore. In chapter 32, Fielding returns on leave, and as he passes through the Mediterranean he becomes newly aware of how India has after all baffled him but Europe has new meaning; it is 'the civilization which has escaped muddle, the spirit in a reasonable form, with flesh and blood subsisting'. In chapter 29, Adela has a more practical experience. On board ship, a trite play with words from an American missionary (Forster indicates meaningless verbal formulae as one of the contemptible outcrops of 'the spirit in reasonable form') reveals to her a personal mission to encounter Mrs Moore's children by her second marriage, Ralph and Stella. In chapter 23, Mrs Moore travels across the continent by train and embarks on the homeward voyage on which she is to die before entering the Mediterranean. Her passive cynicism in which 'the horror of the universe and its smallness are both visible at the same time' gives way to a new stirring of life as the variety of India unfolds itself to her—the splendour of Asirgah at sunset, appearing and reappearing as the train winds about it, and the thousands of coconut palms that seem to wave farewell when she is aboard:

'So you thought an echo was India; you took the Marabar caves as final?' they laughed. 'What have we in common with them, or they with Asirgah? Good-bye!'

The passage reduces her Marabar experience to one that is not, after all, universal in significance, but personal and temporary. Again we are reminded of Godbole in chapter 19: 'Suffering is merely a matter for the individual.'

Nevertheless it is the individual who matters. Mrs Moore still matters to herself when she has ceased to believe that marriage does, and it is as an individual that she continues to matter to others after her death, much more than as Esmiss Esmoor into which she is sublimated by the popular cult. Adela's mission to make friends with Ralph and Stella seems a slight task, but it leads to marriage with Fielding, and to the new 'passage to India' of Stella and Ralph, who inherit their mother's spirit. Younger and so more open to new experience, they pain Fielding because, as he complains to Aziz, he cannot understand why they like Hinduism:

'They won't talk to me about this. They know I think a certain side of their lives is a mistake, and are shy. That's why I wish you would talk to them, for at all events you're Oriental.'

But by now 'Oriental' has come to signify what is more than and different from eastern as opposed to western, and Fielding has become more sensitive to Hinduism than is Aziz. Geographically Aziz is oriental inasmuch as he is Indian, but his ancestral stock is more western, and his monotheistic religion shares its roots with those of Christianity. It is he who identifies Mrs Moore and Ralph as orientals because they respond to individuals spontaneously, not measuring emotions 'in proportion to their objects' as Fielding wants in chapter 27—which, in Aziz' opinion, is to treat them like a sack of potatoes. All the same, although his emotional response to individuals may be 'oriental', his religious emotion is restricted to his Islamic circle. It is Fielding who perceives, in chapter 31, that:

'There is something in religion that may not be true, but has not yet been sung.'
'Explain in detail.'
'Something that the Hindus have perhaps found.'
'Let them sing it.'
'Hindus are unable to sing.'

We recall that in Whitman's poem he foresees that it will be the poet, not the scientist or technologist, who will be the spiritual voyager to India. Fielding himself is too confined to his rationalistic circle to discern the 'something that ought to be sung', but Ralph and Stella, slightly sketched though they are, can travel further, and this shows them to be orientals in a deeper sense than Aziz. To respond to the individual spontaneously is already a beginning, for the individual is as such immeasurable, and any attempt to take his measure socially or politically is to falsify him. But the spontaneous response is superficial if it does not deepen into awareness of the spiritual space from which he emanates; to do that is to accept individuality in a deeper and more burdensome sense. The friendship of Fielding and Aziz is central in the novel, but in the first movement, when it is easiest, it is also shallowest, because neither sees what he is undertaking in the other. The last movement shows them reconciled after misunderstanding, and yet they end in separation because they cannot now bridge their differences. Nonetheless their relationship in separation is more real than their supposed union had been, because their mutual understanding of it is truer. Only Godbole understands the cost and arduousness of love, and he does so because his religion takes in the all as well as the each.

What Forster was 'after' in *A Passage to India* is communicated by a letter to a friend shortly after its publication. He begins by recalling his experience as a student at King's:

> King's stands for personal relationships, and these still seem to me the most real things on the surface of the earth, but I have acquired a feeling that people must go away from each other (spiritually) every now and then, and improve themselves if the relationship is to develop or even endure. *A Passage to India* describes such a going away—preparatory to the next advance, which I am not capable of describing. It seems to me that individuals progress alternately by loneliness and intimacy, and that legend of the multiplied Krishna ... serves as a symbol of a state where the two might be combined. The 'King's' view over-simplified people: that I think was its defect. We are more complicated, also richer, than it knew, and affection grows more difficult than it used to be, and also more glorious.

In Hindu religion, Brahma is the creator, Vishnu the preserver, Shiva the destroyer. Brahma is infinitely remote—the 'OM' of the caves, but Krishna unites Brahma and Vishnu, and he is the Lord whose presence and absence is expounded by Godbole in chapter 19. Godbole himself operates almost as a human manifestation of Krishna in the novel. He is only a character in it; as a priest of a religion to which Forster does not subscribe, he is presented with detachment and irony, but as a voice which articulates the novel's message, he is the central exponent of the novelist's own vision. And that vision is finally a religious one, although Forster is also too close to Fielding to proclaim any dogma.

A major literary form, such as the novel, resembles a botanical species, and outstanding practitioners of the form are like variants in the species. Just as a plant needs suitable climate, soil, and the neighbourhood of congenial species, so the novel throve in the eighteenth and nineteenth centuries because social values, philosophy and structure, as well as other literary forms such as journalism, encouraged its vigour. From time to time variants of novelist arose showing distinctive features which altered readers' conceptions of what a novelist could achieve, but the effect was to amplify the form until its scope seemed to have no definable limits. However, climate, soil and environment may alter, compelling a plant species to alter its character until it becomes unrecognisable, or else to dwindle and give place to new species better suited to the new conditions. By the beginning of this century, the novel was on the brink of just such a crisis. Its prosperity had coincided with that of the middle class and middle-class certainties: the individual and his or her society had been the solid realities, and social class a prerequisite for the rendering of character. But towards the end of the nineteenth century these certainties began to suffer erosion: the assumptions of political economy and of what Arnold called the philistine society were increasingly questioned from different directions by growing social conscience and aesthetic protest; the individual's sense of identity began to wither in the face of a society reinforced by larger and more anonymous organisations; the scientists, who had been shaking assumptions about the permanence of natural forms for two generations, began to invade the human mind, and philosophers as different as Marx and Nietzsche shook the foundations of middle-class assurance. Such influences permeated gradually and unevenly and at first affected only the few, but they purveyed a new scepticism among the intelligentsia; neither society nor the individual could be seen as the indisputable data of experience any longer. Just as the twentieth-century physicist has found matter dissolving and multiplying into unforeseeable quantities and particles, so the novelists began to see human identity dissolving at the centre and opening itself to unexpected forces.

Forster and D.H. Lawrence

'Am reading *Passage to India*', wrote D.H. Lawrence to a friend in 1924; 'It's good, but makes one wish a bomb would fall and end everything. Life is more interesting in its undercurrents than in its obvious; and E.M. does see people, people and nothing but people *ad nauseam*.' But in writing to Forster himself at the same time, Lawrence made a different criticism:

> ... I don't care about Bou-oum—Nor all the universe. Only the dark ahead & the silence into which we haven't yet spoken our impertinent echoes.—You saying human relationships don't matter, then after all hingeing your book on a very unsatisfactory friendship between two men! ... After one's primary relation to the X—I don't know what to call it, but not god or the universe—only human relations matter.
>
> (*Letters*, ed. A. Huxley)

We recall that Forster also thought that human relations were the most 'real things on the surface of the earth', but that he had come to think that there are times when people must separate themselves so that their relationships can be renewed and enriched. So far he and Lawrence are in agreement, but Lawrence implies a deeper relationship than the human one, whereas Forster retreats from that 'X' which, for his character Godbole, is the inescapable mystery of the universe. The difference is the plainer from a reading of Lawrence's short novel *St Mawr*, published a year after *A Passage to India*, and perhaps written under its stimulus. *St Mawr* begins in England and ends in New Mexico; the English setting is crowded with characters, varied in relationships, but the relationships all dissolve and the characters are shed one by one until, in New Mexico, the heroine is left to seek survival alone on a ranch which barely subsists in its environment of wild nature. It is this nature which is Lawrence's 'X' in his story; he gives pages to the vivid manifestation of it, and the characters lose their merely social reality against its overwhelming background. *St Mawr* is an example of Lawrence's departure from the familiar novel tradition—the tradition from which he considered Forster ought to have departed—and a comparison of the two novelists can help us to identify Forster's own place in it.

That tradition had seen the human being as rooted in his society; for good or ill, liking it or otherwise, the individual was what Lawrence called, in writing about Galsworthy, a 'social ego' or he had no identity. To an extent, this must of course always be true: every individual is a member of a social grouping; even if, like Crusoe, he is on a desert island, he has been excluded from one and brings his socially identifiable character along with him. Nevertheless, it is also true that humanity itself is greater than any given society, and true as well that some societies in some phases of their history restrict individuals to the extent that they are much less than fully human. Both Lawrence and Forster saw British society in their time as humanly constraining, and they further agreed that no society has yet been developed in which the individual has been deprived of all those resources which enable him to achieve human fulfilment beyond his social limits; both distinguish between those of their characters who neither can nor wish to escape their social constraints, and those who discover the means as well as the need to do so. Moreover both were in agreement that the individual can ultimately find himself or herself only in relationship with another, but that this fruition can only come to pass when, together or separately, they have overcome the entanglements in which the social environment has constricted them. Their divergence shows in the ways in which their minds focus on the problem of human identity beyond these agreements: Lawrence's central concern is those 'undercurrents' which make the human being continuous with nature and by which he or she can be released from the condition of a social ego; for Forster we all remain social egos even when experience has taught us the limitations of that condition. Yet Forster acknowledged and admired Lawrence's vision despite his unwillingness or inability to emulate it.

In his lecture 'Prophecy' in *Aspects of the Novel*, Forster describes Lawrence as 'the only prophetic novelist writing today', thereby implicitly excluding himself:

> It is the prophet back where he started from, back where the rest of us are waiting by the edge of the pool, but with a power of re-creation and evocation we shall never possess.

The pool to which Forster is referring is the one in chapter 19 of Lawrence's novel *Women in Love*, into which Rupert Birkin throws stones to fracture the reflection of the moon. 'Why he throws,' Forster remarks, 'what the scene symbolizes, is unimportant.' What is important is the visionary quality of the scene: 'the writer could not get such a moon and water otherwise; he reaches them by the special path which stamps them as more wonderful than any we can imagine.' 'We' are the ordinary readers and the usual novelist; 'we' live by a sense of humour, and by an absence of humility inasmuch as 'we' assume a world where behaviour and phenomena can be explained. The prophetic novelist—as Forster sees him—demands humility in the reader and suspension of his sense of humour; without those conditions the reader will not be able to listen to the prophet, whose function is not to explain the universe but to sing. But, whatever his respect amounting to reverence for the prophetic novelists, Forster leaves no doubt that he disclaims emulation of them. He makes clear that what he calls the sense of humour can be suspended but not dispensed with, and he admits that, in general, he hasn't much respect for the virtue of humility. He himself is not a prophet.

And yet, despite his own remarks and Lawrence's comments, critics have seen him attaining that stature in *A Passage to India*. We remember that Forster said that he didn't know what happened to Adela in the cave—a refusal to explain which is exactly the licence he

D.H. Lawrence (1885–1930) in 1923

allows to Lawrence as prophet. We also remember that Fielding tells Aziz in chapter 31 that Hinduism has a vision which 'may not be true, but has not yet been sung', and on a reasonable interpretation of the novel Forster's purpose has been precisely to give voice to that vision. However, it is true that Adela's experience, though accounted for, is not only unexplained but omitted; Forster, perhaps, would say that a prophetic novelist would not have shirked the task of directly presenting it. As to the Hindu vision, we have noticed that he displays it with ambivalence: Godbole is always rendered in two dimensions; as a sage his doings and sayings reach into absolute meaning, giving coherence to events and experiences as do nothing and nobody else, but as a character he is always quaint and comical, impossible to take seriously. It is as though Forster wants to concede everything as possibly valid in the prophetic vision, but at the same time admits that he lives without it, and even does not want it. This, however, seems the maintenance of a self-contradictory position. How can a novelist demonstrate the truth of a prophetic vision and not himself be a prophet? How can any individual acknowledge the validity of any view of experience and yet refuse adherence to it? The answer may be that what is logically impossible may be intelligible psychologically, and a psychological explanation of Forster's position can be developed from his habit of seeing human experience in terms of circles.

Much attention has been given in this study to that image. We have seen how Forster, in all his work, presents again and again the notion that each of us lives in his or her own horizon, and that we are much inclined to mistake our individual horizons for reality itself. He demonstrates that each of us has to learn that a horizon is an illusion, and that the illusion has to be broken if the individual is to grow, so that Sawston can understand Monteriano, the sensitivity of Rickie Elliot can blend with the physicality of Stephen Wonham, the conventional Lucy Honeychurch can live her music with George Emerson, and Wilcoxes can marry Schlegels. But Forster shows an equal belief that circles are indispensable to the human condition: horizons, however illusory, can be replaced but refuse to disappear, for without them individuals lack the principle of form which gives shape and order to their thoughts and feelings.

From one point of view, *A Passage to India* presents a world in which all circles are broken. Godbole declares that all perform a good or evil action when either is performed; an untouchable Indian, who is not even aware of the nature of the occasion, is instrumental in the acquittal of Aziz; at the climax of the ritual, the boats containing Aziz and Ralph, Fielding and Stella—all of them outsiders—collide with the raft bearing the image of God in an epitomal confusion:

> Looking back at the great blur of the last twenty-four hours, no man could say where was the emotional centre of it, any more than he could locate the heart of a cloud.

Such great breaking of all the circles looks at first like a final release. But then we need to remember that Forster gives us an alternative view of the nature of circles in each of his novels. In *A Room with a View*, *The Longest Journey*, *Howards End* and *Maurice*, the stories end with images of close relationship and enduring bonds; in *Where Angels Fear to Tread* and *A Passage to India*, they close with separation, and yet, deeper than the separations, they leave the impression of a surviving kinship between Philip Herriton and Caroline Abbott, Cyril Fielding and Aziz, even if each pair never communicates with each other again. Such union in separation is preferred, because it is more lastingly actual, to Godbole's random union with all or any—an old lady and a wasp, though not a stone—especially as the inclusiveness of his religion does not save even him from the constriction of circles. On the contrary, Hinduism divides humanity into a vast range of circles from the Brahmans to the Untouchables in ways that frustrate all spontaneous relationship except on occasions of ritual worship. When, in chapter 32, Fielding rejoices in the forms and order of Europe, we are in one way witnessing the superficiality of the man who has confused mystery with muddle, but the language does not convey criticism; the short chapter is almost a hymn of praise to his and Forster's spiritual home. When the echo destroys in Mrs Moore all sense of form, leaving her with only that of her own grotesque physical ego, we know that she may have penetrated into the fringe of the mysteries of Brahma, but in doing so she has gone beyond the horizon of human apprehension, which is to experience annihilation.

Forster would have been the first to admit that he was not so deep a novelist, but in one respect he had an advantage over Lawrence. As a self-declared liberal, he belonged (as Lawrence did not) to a central tradition of western thought, and it is part of the excellence of that tradition that awareness of its own limits is not a weakness but intrinsic to its strength. On the one hand, liberalism must take the risk of scepticism even about itself—*Two Cheers* for it—but on the other hand such scepticism must not obviate the very reason for its own existence: that the individual must retain a final importance overriding all beliefs—'I do not believe in belief.' He meant that he did not accept the sacredness of any belief once it demanded the sacrifice of the individual, but equally he did not believe that the individual contained in himself all the truths required for his own fulfilment. The strength of the liberal position is that the liberal can see within other horizons and acknowledge their validity without severing connections within his own. 'People, people *ad nauseam*', lamented Lawrence, declaring in another letter that Forster did not understand his Hindu; he wanted to release those forces which would enlarge human relations beyond the restraints of the social ego, but Forster, acknowledging the reality of those forces, insists nonetheless that in the meantime we are all of us just people, unable to escape from our limitations before we are ready to do so. The individual is not static; he must grow or diminish, but the growth is more evident from generation to generation than in any one individual in a single generation. Ralph and Stella, it is hinted, have the capacity to assimilate the truths of Hinduism beyond Fielding and Mrs Moore.

Forster as twentieth-century novelist

Forster and Lawrence agreed at least that human experience could no longer be adequately rendered within the older framework of the individual in society. In the nineteenth century, society had implied the individual and the individual implied society; the newer novelists considered that this complementarity was no longer adequate, and they criticised those novelists who continued the nineteenth-century tradition for their failure to see the change. Lawrence criticised Galsworthy pungently for this failure, and a very different novelist, Virginia Woolf, concentrated a comparable case mainly against Arnold Bennett. In her essay 'Mr Bennett and Mrs Brown' she distinguishes the conservatives, as 'Edwardians', from the more advanced writers, including Lawrence and Forster, whom she called 'Georgians'. She imagines three Edwardians—Bennett, Galsworthy and Wells—each in the corner seat of a railway carriage, the fourth being occupied by the fictional Mrs Brown. She supposes that each of them would speculate about Mrs Brown as potential material for fiction, and she diagnoses that each would, in his own mode, construct a realistic environment for her existence; she concludes, however, that none of them would succeed in portraying her in her own essential self. The axis between the poles has gone; the novelist may establish Mrs Brown's environment, but this no longer implies the soul of Mrs Brown, and for Virginia Woolf it is the individual soul that matters. So, in an essay on Forster in 1927, she describes his problem as follows:

> It is the soul that matters, and the soul, as we have seen, is caged in a solid villa of red brick somewhere in the suburbs of London. It seems then, that if his books are to succeed in their mission his reality must at certain points become irradiated; his brick must be lit up; we must see the whole building saturated with light. We have at once to believe in the complete reality of the suburb and the complete reality of the soul.

> (*The Death of the Moth*)

Her verdict is that Forster's success is only partial; all his novels have episodes which are in her sense 'irradiated', but he depends too much on symbolism which arouses the reader's distrust so that the miraculous fusion she desires is never complete. The essay is a discerning one, especially in view of its date, which is early for any critic to assimilate Forster's complexity. Nonetheless it is surely true that her diagnosis of what she sees as Forster's problem betrays more about her own shortcomings as a novelist than it discloses his. The red-brick suburb, after all, is what it is; it does not become irradiated except momentarily, and the solidity of the villa remains the most permanent fact about it. She had a case against Arnold Bennett, who makes the solidity prevail over the individual soul, but it is still true that the soul must accept the finality of the villa, as Caroline Abbott returns to Sawston because 'I and my life must be where I live', even though she has learnt to understand Italy.

Forster's position among twentieth-century novelists is therefore a peculiar one, but its peculiarity consists in its centrality. It is fair to maintain that he held a balance between the continuators of the great Victorian tradition, when the bond between reader and novelist had been so strong, and the 'Georgian' advance guard, who sacrificed that bond in the interests of their further exploration of the twentieth-century human predicament. So much may be said of his contemporaries, both readers and writers, but what of ourselves, over half a century after his last novel? Forster's centrality has achieved for us a different and more important significance, especially when we include with his fiction his essays and biographical work. He was not the greatest novelist of his generation, but no other links our historical epoch so well not only with his but with that which preceded him. He could see the virtues of the Victorian tradition as well as its obstructiveness, and he could affirm the essentiality of the individual as well as the looming forces that threaten it. Other novelists, for instance Lawrence and Joyce, strove to go deeper into human experience, and their achievements were more wonderful, but in doing so they could be accused of contracting out of the immediacies of the individual predicament; Forster never did.

Certainly, however, his reputation would not stand nearly so high if it were not for that one book, *A Passage to India*. And yet Virginia Woolf records in her diary that he finished it with the reflection—'This is a failure'. She on the other hand concludes her essay on him with the question: 'above all it makes us wonder, What will he do next?' As we know, he was to write much, but never another novel. Much speculation has been given to the reason for his cessation as a novelist, and he himself seems to have been uncertain of it. It is possible that the achievement so far excelled his previous work that he himself could not recognise it; he only knew that he could not carry his novelistic imagination any further.

However, there may be another reason for Forster's abandonment of prose fiction. In his essay 'English Prose between 1918 and 1939' (*Two Cheers*) he makes these remarks:

Can literary men understand Einstein? Of course they cannot—even less than they can understand Freud. But the idea of relativity

Virginia Woolf (1882–1941) by her sister Vanessa Bell

has got into the air and has favoured certain tendencies in novels. Absolute good and evil, as in Dickens, are seldom presented. A character becomes good or evil in relation to some other character or to a situation which may itself change. You can't measure people up, because the yard-measure itself keeps altering its length.

He goes on to pay another of his tributes to Proust, who, in his opinion, coped with the new relativity better than most. Like other critical passages by Forster, this one opens difficult questions while presenting itself as a simple answer in unassuming language. The questions are not whether 'literary men' can understand Einstein or Freud, nor whether Proust is as good as Forster thinks he is, though even these may be more important than seems likely by his airy references to them. The central question is whether the novel, as an imaginative vehicle, may not have lost the centrality which it has kept in the western mind for two hundred years. The telling sentence is the last in the quotation—'You can't measure people up . . .'. It is not difficult to maintain that the novel form arose in England with the social importance of the middle classes, and that the middle-class type of man and woman—the commercial type—felt the need to 'measure up' humanity, its environment, its commodities and its means of obtaining them, to an extent that no other class had felt in recorded history. So long as the middle classes retained social dominance this habit of mind made the novel its appropriate vehicle. The relativism Forster refers to emerged in this century when this middle-class stability was shaken, and one of its most conspicuous effects was to stimulate novelists into experimentation. Forster, as we have seen, retained an equivocal attitude to such experiments. The greater the uncertainty of the moral and the psychological compasses, the more he sustained an outward appearance of conformance to straightforward traditions of narrative directness. Even in the 1930s some novelists with contemporary consciousness subscribed to his influence. The most notable was Christopher Isherwood in *Mr Norris Changes Trains* (1935) and *Goodbye to Berlin* (1939). In his autobiography *Lions and Shadows* (1938), Isherwood quotes his friend Edward Upward (a novelist presented under the name of 'Chalmers') as remarking:

> Forster's the only one who understands what the modern novel ought to be . . . . Our frightful mistake was that we believed in tragedy . . . tragedy is quite impossible nowadays . . . . We ought to aim at being essentially comic writers . . . . The whole of Forster's technique is based on the tea-table . . . .

During and since the war it has been observable that the salient novelists have abandoned the experimentation of such writers as Lawrence, Woolf and Joyce and have followed Forster's example, even if, like Angus Wilson, they have gone on record as believing him to be overrated. Wilson, in *Anglo-Saxon Attitudes* (1956) and *The Middle Age of Mrs Eliot* (1958), and L.P. Hartley, in *The Shrimp and the Anemone* (1944) and *The Go-Between* (1953), both exemplify the practice of retaining surface lucidity and extensive reliance on dialogue which we remark in Forster's novels, while also exemplifying his use of surprise, comedy and irony to break the surface simplicity by compelling the reader to accept unexpected judgements. Anthony Powell, in his linked novels under the general title of *The Music of Time* begun in the 1950s and completed in the 1970s, seems to have combined Forster's techniques with those of Proust. However, for the first time since the seventeenth century, it has not been the novelists who have held most public attention, but rather the dramatists. It seems possible that Forster, though he may not have anticipated this return of the drama, was able to foresee that the scope of the novel had reached its limits in the atmosphere of mid-twentieth-century uncertainty and questioning.

Finally, in contemplating Forster's place among the twentieth-century English novelists, it is worth remarking the series of novels on Indian themes to which he was only one of the distinguished contributors. *A Passage to India* was preceded by Kipling's *Kim* (1901), and followed by L.H. Myers' *The Near and the Far* (1943), and then by Paul Scott's tetralogy *The Raj Quartet* (1976) and *Staying On* (1977). The fascination of India for English twentieth-century novelists, the distinction and variety of its inspiration of them, may one day be seen as one of the interesting features of the century's literature.

Forster in old age in his bedroom at King's College, Cambridge

Part Four

Reference Section

Short biographies

ACKERLEY, J.R. (1896–1967) The son of a director of Fyffes, banana importers. He was wounded in the war and taken prisoner. After the war he settled for a writing career, living in London on an allowance from his father. His first encounter with Forster was when the latter wrote to him in 1922 in appreciation of a poem of Ackerley's published in the *London Mercury*. In 1923 Forster suggested that he should apply for the post of companion-secretary to the Maharajah of Chhaturpur. He followed this advice, and Forster acknowledged that his letters from India greatly stimulated his own writing of *A Passage to India*. This mutual contribution to each other's work and welfare characterised their relationship. Ackerley was usually hard-up and Forster helped him with money; when Ackerley became literary editor of the *Listener*, he was eager to secure Forster's contributions as reviewer, and he was instrumental in Forster's career as broadcaster. P.N. Furbank says that Forster was also a kind of father-figure to him, sympathising with Ackerley's tangled and frustrated homosexual relationships. Ackerley was literary editor of *The Listener* from 1935 to 1959; his two most famous books are *Hindoo Holiday* (1931) about his Indian experiences, and *My Dog Tulip* (1954) about his unique relationship with Queenie, an Alsatian which he acquired almost accidentally. He also wrote a study of Forster, *E.M. Forster: a Portrait* (1970); an autobiographical study, *My Father and Myself* (1967); poems, *Micheldever* (1972); a play, *Prisoners of War* (1925), and a novel, *We Think the World of You* (1959).

BUCKINGHAM, BOB and MAY Bob Buckingham was a policeman to whom Forster was introduced in 1930, when the former was twenty-eight. He later became a probation officer. He came from a large, poor family in Somerstown; his father had been an unreliable earner of money, and before he entered the police Buckingham had been their main support in a variety of jobs—docker, mechanic, salesman. He was a warm-hearted man with a strong sense of responsibility, and a loyal friend. He responded strongly to Forster's easy, cordial approach, and remained perhaps Forster's closest friend in the later part of his life. When Buckingham married May Hockey in 1932 she at first resented Forster's importance in her husband's life, but later she accepted it and became one of the few women with whom Forster was entirely at ease. He died in the Buckinghams' house in Coventry, and his ashes were scattered over their garden.

CARPENTER, EDWARD (1844–1929) Son of a retired naval officer with a strong taste for philosophy, he entered Cambridge in 1864 with the intention of becoming a clergyman. He was ordained in 1869, and became a curate under F.D. Maurice, the famous Christian Socialist. By 1874 he had lost his faith; he resigned his orders and became an extra-mural lecturer. Thereafter he became first a disciple and then a leader of the agnostic, simple-life socialism whose most famous exponent was William Morris. Two strong influences upon him were the American poet Walt Whitman and Hindu mysticism; in pursuit of both he travelled in America and visited Ceylon. His books, especially a long poem *Towards Democracy* (1883) and *Civilisation, its Cause and Cure* (1889), gave him a following. In 1883 a legacy from his father enabled him to set up a market-gardening commune, abjuring meat and alcohol, cultivating open-air labour, sandal-making and writing. Later he became an exponent of the homosexual cause (*The Intermediate Sex*, 1908), living openly with a male lover. Forster knew of him through his works and through their common friendship with Goldsworthy Lowes Dickinson, and paid him a visit in 1913. The visit was an important event in Forster's career: Carpenter's quiet and strong personality was an antidote to the restless, over-talkative Bloomsbury circle, and it also released Forster from the isolation and repression he felt in consequence of his own homosexuality. The immediate consequence was the writing of *Maurice*, the only novel he wrote without forethought and extensive planning. He continued the relationship with Carpenter by correspondence.

DICKINSON, G.L.(1862–1932) Educated at Charterhouse and King's, where he obtained a permanent fellowship in classics in 1896, having renounced medicine after obtaining his second M.B. His circle in King's was a centre for political and religious discussion, and he was a leading member of the Apostles. He wrote prolifically on political, philosophical and historical themes (e.g. *The Greek View of Life*, 1896; *Letters from John Chinaman*, 1901; *A Modern Symposium*, 1905) always from a liberal-humanistic point of view, and was one of the founders of the *Independent Review* (1903), a periodical with a strong liberal standpoint to which Forster contributed, but his most important work was his influence on the establishment of the League of Nations for which he began projects in 1914. His friendship with Forster grew slowly; when they first met in 1899 at King's they parted, as Forster felt, 'unprepossessing and unprepossessed', but during his under-graduate years Forster was drawn increasingly into the Dickinson circle, especially after he became a member of the Apostles in his fourth year. The friendship continued and became slowly closer after Forster left Cambridge, and they were in India together in 1912–13, when Forster first became strongly impressed by the strength and independence of Dickinson's personality. Dickinson made him his literary executor, and his sisters invited him to write his biography, published in 1933.

'ELIZABETH' (1866–1941) The pen-name of the novelist Mary Annette Russell, Countess von Arnim by her first marriage in 1901. A cousin of Katherine Mansfield, she was herself a very popular writer of fiction. Her best known work was *Elizabeth and her German Garden* (1898). She liked to employ English tutors for her children on her husband's estate in Pomerania; Forster was one of these in 1905. She enjoyed treating them with a mischievous sense of humour, but Forster won her respect, though his feelings about her were more ambivalent. He shared a caravanning holiday with her family in England in 1907, but they never developed a close friendship. One of his successors as family tutor was the novelist Hugh Walpole. Other works by 'Elizabeth': *Princess Priscilla's Fortnight* (1905); *Vera* (1921); *Enchanted April* (1922).

FORSTER, ALICE CLARA ('LILY') (1855–1945) E.M. Forster's mother. Her family name was Whichelo, thought to be a corruption of the French 'Richelieu'. Her father had been a drawing master; he died long before Forster's birth, but her mother survived into his childhood and he was strongly devoted to her. Lily was an attractive and independent-minded child; Marianne Thornton, Forster's future great-aunt, happening to be living in the same neighbourhood, was strongly attracted to her and virtually adopted her at the age of twelve. Lily became a governess and was employed at Abinger Hall when she met Forster's father, a nephew of Marianne's. They married in 1877, and Forster was their second child, the first having died at birth. When he was not yet two his father died, leaving him and his mother in a close bond of love, though Lily had to compete with Marianne for attention to her son. Except when he was abroad for long periods in Egypt or India, Forster kept house with his mother until she died, when he was sixty-six. In later life he found this close association a severe constraint, but the bond remained so that her death was a severe loss to him. Forster's public reticence about his homosexuality was to a great extent due to his fear of disturbing her with the scandal.

FRY, ROGER (1866–1934) He grew up in a scientific atmosphere, and in 1884 gained an Exhibition in Science at King's. There he underwent the liberal, humanistic influence of his friend Lowes Dickinson (himself under the influence of Edward Carpenter) and of the Slade Professor of Art, J.H. Middleton. He became a member of the Apostles in 1887, and achieved a first class degree in Natural Science. After Cambridge he made a number of visits to Italy and acquired a reputation as a lecturer and writer on the history of art. From 1905 to 1910 he was Director of the Metropolitan Museum of Art in New York, and at the same time developed a strong interest in Cézanne and other post-impressionist painters. In 1910 he organised the first Post-Impressionist exhibition at the Grafton Galleries in London. It was fiercely attacked, and the attacks stimulated him to more positive and aggressive art criticism. Himself a painter, he associated himself with the new school of English painters, including Duncan Grant and Vanessa Bell, the sister of Virginia Woolf. He was now firmly in the aesthetic tradition of John Ruskin and William Morris, propagating ideas about the importance of art in the life of society, and in 1913 he established in Bloomsbury the Omega Workshops, the aim of which was to cultivate good design in useful objects. Forster's first encounter with Fry was in 1897, when he attended Fry's lectures which made a permanent impression on him. However, it was later, in the Bloomsbury circle, that they really got to know each other. Fry introduced him to the new aesthetics of modern art; he was enthusiastic about Forster's stories in *The Celestial Omnibus* (1911) and designed the cover for the book. He also had an influence on Forster's unfinished novel *Arctic Summer*, written just after *Howards End*. Forster's appreciation of Fry in *Abinger Harvest* shows him to have had the kind of mind that Forster most admired.

LAWRENCE, D.H. (1885–1930) His father was a coal-miner and his mother had a middle-class background. He studied at Nottingham University and for a time taught at the Davidson Road School, Croydon. In 1914 he married Frieda, a German, formerly the wife of a Nottingham professor, Ernest Weekley. By this time he had published *The White Peacock* (1911), *The Trespasser* (1912) and his important autobiographical novel *Sons and Lovers* (1913). The last is partly an attempt to analyse the dangerously intense relationship which he had had with his mother—a factor in his life which he shared with Forster. They also shared the experience of having undergone the influence of Edward Carpenter, though this was less strong on Lawrence. In 1915, when he and Forster had their brief personal encounters, he issued one of his greatest novels, *The Rainbow*. His war years were unhappy; he was twice rejected for military service owing to his tubercular condition, but his German wife and his own heterodoxy caused them to be victims of suspicion by the authorities; in consequence he left England for good (apart from brief visits) after the war. Lawrence seems to have been one of the few people whom Forster respected to subject his character to candid criticism—Carpenter perhaps being another. This made for a stormy relationship, but for Forster a healthy antidote to his Bloomsbury ones, and their mutual sympathy and respect survives in their post-war correspondence. In 1924, acknowledging *A Passage to India*, Lawrence wrote: 'there's not a soul in England says a word to me—save your whisper through the willow-boughs'. The disparaging obituaries of Lawrence roused Forster to indignant defence. Among Lawrence's novels, he eventually preferred *The Plumed Serpent* (1926).

MAHARAJAH OF DEWAS STATE SENIOR See TUKOJI RAO III.

MASOOD, SIR SYED ROSS (1889–1937) Grandson of Sir Syed Ahmed Khan, founder of the Muslim Anglo-Oriental College at Aligarh. Masood was educated at Aligarh and New College, Oxford. He later taught in India, becoming Director of Public Instruction in Hyderabad from 1916 to 1928, and Vice-Chancellor of Aligarh in 1929, doing much to restore the college's fallen fortunes. Forster's first encounter with him was as his Latin coach in 1906. They quickly became friends. Masood attached supreme value to friendship, and Forster said of him that he awakened him from his narrow middle-class and academic English view of life into the horizons of quite a different civilization; Masood in turn praised Forster's understanding of 'the Indian soul' in 1911, and urged him to write a book about India. They went on a holiday in Italy, and Forster spent much time in Masood's company during his first and second Indian visits. Masood was the basis of the character of Aziz in *A Passage to India*, but did nothing practical in response to Forster's request to correct the factual inaccuracies in that novel.

MEREDITH, H.O.M. (1878–1964) Known to his friends by the nickname 'Hom', he came from a large lower middle-class family, and had a troubled childhood, but went on to a brilliant school career, academically and athletically, at Shrewsbury. He and Forster were at the same preparatory school and entered King's in the same year. He was a fellow of the college from 1903 to 1908, and became Professor of Economics at Belfast in 1911. Besides works on economics, he published *Poems* in 1911 and *Four Dramas of Euripides* in 1937. At King's his friendship with Forster was very close, and released Forster from some of his inhibitions and repressions. He sponsored Forster's election to the Apostles. He seems to have been the main model for the character of Ansell in *The Longest Journey*.

MOORE, G.E. (1873–1958) In 1898 a fellow of Trinity College, later a lecturer in Moral Science, and from 1925 to 1939 Professor of Philosophy at Cambridge, Moore was one of the most brilliant and influential philosophers of his day. He was at first closely associated with Bertrand Russell, also at Cambridge, and his most famous book, *Principia Ethica*, came out in the same year as Russell's *Principia Mathematica* (1903). The character of his philosophy was to counteract the mystification associated with the Hegelian school; he maintained that philosophical thought is available to anyone capable of consistently strenuous and honest reasoning. The questions posed by his *Principia* have been summarised as follows: (1) what has intrinsic value? (2) what actions ought we to perform? (3) what are the relevant arguments for proving statements in answer to questions (1) and (2)? He maintained that 'the Good' is itself indefinable, but that it can be recognised subjectively by 'good states of mind' and that these are achieved in part by right personal relationships. Forster was himself not interested by abstract thought and did not read Moore, but Moore's influence dominated the Apostles when Forster was a member of 'the Society'; Forster valued the blend of intellectuality and friendship which characterised it, and the concept of 'the good state of mind' was a permanent touchstone for him.

PLOMER, WILLIAM (1903–1973) Born in South Africa, he was educated in England, eventually settling here, and became a novelist and poet. In 1926 he published his novel *Turbot Wolfe* about race relations in South Africa, and aroused controversy. He also travelled in the far east; his novel *Sado* is centred in Japan. He was a strongly emotional man under a cool, ironic surface, and Forster relates that they became friends in 1932 when he caught Plomer 'at an unguarded moment'. Like Forster he became a librettist for Benjamin Britten: *Gloriana* (1953); *Curlew River* (1965); *The Burning Fiery Furnace* (1966); *The Prodigal Son* (1968). He and Forster corresponded frequently and the latter invited him to write his life, but he neglected to consult Forster about the facts because he did not want to remind him of his death, and the task was transferred to Furbank. He was one of the first of the younger generation of writers whom Forster got to know personally, and introduced him to Christopher Isherwood. His *Collected Poems* came out in 1960, and he edited Kilvert's *Diary* from 1938.

SHEPPARD, J.T. (1881–1968) Provost of King's, 1933–54. He had been an undergraduate friend of Forster's, and was instrumental in securing for him honorary fellowship of the college with residence there. His paper to the Apostles on the 'King's versus Trinity' attitudes to human nature may have influenced *The Longest Journey*. He was a classical scholar, and wrote on Greek tragedy, especially Sophocles, whose *Antigone* was of special significance to Forster.

STRACHEY, LYTTON (1880–1932) As an undergraduate he was a contemporary at Trinity of Forster at King's; after Cambridge he made a career in literary journalism and history (*Landmarks in French Literature*, 1912) and later a most distinguished one in biography: *Eminent Victorians* (1918); *Queen Victoria* (1921); *Elizabeth and Essex* (1928); *Portraits in Miniature* (1931). He transformed the art of biography by the informality and irreverence with which he treated his subjects, making them much more accessible to readers but without condescending to them by vulgar popularisation. He was a leading member of the Apostles at Cambridge, adopting the arrogant attitude to human relationship which Forster rejected, and later he became one of the most prominent figures of the Bloomsbury circle. His friendship with Forster developed slowly: he was quizzical about Forster's shyness and elusiveness, and in turn Forster was intimidated by Strachey's incessant talk in his high-pitched voice. After Cambridge they became gradually closer; Strachey did not admire *The Longest Journey* though he found the Cambridge parts amusing, but he greatly admired *Maurice* while making constructive criticisms of it.

THORNTON, HENRY (1760–1815) Forster's great-grandfather. He was the son of one of the leaders of the first generation of the evangelical movement: a director of the Bank of England, he gave away a large part of his income annually, and had been a patron of the evangelical poet William Cowper. Henry lived in the same tradition of a life of finance and philanthropy. In 1782 he became MP for Southwark, and retained the position for the rest of his life. He joined no party but was Whig in sympathy, supporting a motion for parliamentary reform in 1797 and legislation for income tax in 1798, raising his own contribution when he thought it appropriate even when it was not demanded. In 1802, when he had himself become a director of the Bank of England, he wrote a classic financial pamphlet: *The Nature and Effects of the Paper Credit of Great Britain*. In 1792 he bought the house Clapham Rise on Clapham Common, and took into it William Wilberforce, the leader of the anti-slavery movement. The library in the house became the headquarters of the movement of evangelical reformers which became known as the Clapham Sect. It included Zachary Macaulay, father of the historian, and James Stephen, ancestor of Virginia Woolf. He supported the establishment of Sierra Leone as a state for freed slaves, with Zachary Macaulay as its first governor. In 1804 he became the first treasurer of The British and Foreign Bible Society. Like his father (and Forster, his descendant) he was extremely generous with his money: until he married in 1796 he gave away six-sevenths of his annual income.

THORNTON, MARIANNE (1797–1887) Forster's great-aunt, and the eldest of Henry Thornton's nine children. She continued to live in Clapham but, owing to a family quarrel, no longer at Battersea Rise. She regarded herself as the last of the Clapham Sect since her relatives had become high church Conservatives, but she did not exhibit the Sect's low church evangelical piety. She never married, and as she had a strong, autocratic personality she tended to dominate her protegées (such as Forster's mother) and those of her relatives in whom she felt interest. Her tendency to possessiveness made Forster the main focus of her attentions in his early childhood, and she left him the private income which enabled him to devote himself to a literary career. Late in life he became very interested in her personality and relationships, seeing her life-story as the history of a tradition of which he was himself the unlikely product, for though he continued the Thornton liberal faith he was antipathetic to the philistinism of the Thorntons, as he knew they would be to his homosexuality. He published *Marianne Thornton* in 1956.

TREVELYAN, G.M. (1876–1962) A fellow of Trinity when Forster was at King's, he became the most famous English historian of his day. As well as being a fine scholar, he wrote historical works for the intelligent general reader in the tradition of his great-uncle, Lord Macaulay. His best-known works included *History of England* (1926), *England under Queen Anne* (1930–34), and *English Social History* (1944). Intellectually he belonged to the agnostic, liberal Victorian tradition, and he took the lead in establishing the *Independent Review* in 1903. He was one of the more austere members of the Apostles, in opposition to the libertarianism of Lytton Strachey. Family history connected him with Forster: the father of his famous great-uncle, Zachary Macaulay, had been a member of the Clapham Sect. His relationship with Forster seems to have been paternalistic, consisting of practical advice about the conduct of his career and about his war service. Forster had a closer relationship with his elder brother, R.C. Trevelyan, who gave him helpful criticism of his literary work and with whom he travelled in India on his first visit.

TUKOJI RAO III, MAHARAJAH OF DEWAS STATE SENIOR Ruler of a small state in Central India. Forster visited him in 1913, and in 1916 he invited Forster to become his private secretary, a function he fulfilled as well as he could in the confusion of the Maharajah's court in 1921. Tukoji's career culminated in ruin in 1928; the causes were partly his own financial incompetence and partly the intrigues of neighbouring princes, driving his son into open hostility with his father. The British supported his abdication and the substitution of his son; their treatment of Tukoji was summarised by Forster as 'impeccably correct' and 'absolutely wrong'. Their correctness was a consequence of his incompetence as a ruler, but they were wrong because they were coldly unsympathetic to his personal predicament insofar as he was guiltless of it. Forster not only found Tukoji a very endearing friend but a man of great spiritual distinction, a view shared by their mutual friend Malcolm Darling, of the Indian Civil Service, and his wife Josie.

WEBB, SIDNEY (1859–1947) and BEATRICE (1858–1943) Leaders of politically radical thought, they believed in the progressive establishment of socialist society by means of a spearhead of intellectual elite. They launched the Fabian Society in 1885, the London School of Economics in 1894, and the socialist periodical *New Statesman* in 1913. Among their most influential works was their 'Minority Report of the Royal Commission on the Poor Laws', and among their most controversial, *Soviet Communism: a New Civilization?* The Webb standpoint was one that Forster greatly respected while dissociating himself from it. He was deeply sceptical of their belief that the right social structure would bring about the good society, believing that right human relationships depended on what is more than and different from good institutions. Forster's alternative view is best shown in his essay 'Two Cheers for Democracy' and in his essay 'Webb and Webb' in the same volume.

WOOLF, LEONARD (1880–1969) A contemporary of Forster's at Cambridge and an Apostle, he served in the Ceylon Civil Service from 1904 to 1911 but thereafter gave himself to literary, publishing and editorial work. He wrote a few novels (e.g. *The Village in the Jungle*, 1913) but thereafter concentrated on political affairs; he was a prominent member of the Fabian Society and associated with Lowes Dickinson in propaganda for the League of Nations. He married Virginia Stephen (later the famous novelist, Virginia Woolf) in 1912, and founded the Hogarth Press in 1917. Their house in Gordon Square was the centre for the Bloomsbury Group. Among his services to Forster was to persuade him to finish *A Passage to India* at a point when Forster was ready to abandon it. At the end of his life he produced an autobiography in successive volumes; Forster's review of the second of these (*Growing*, 1961), was the last that he wrote.

WOOLF, VIRGINIA (1882–1941) Daughter of the distinguished critic Leslie Stephen, she was mainly educated by him, receiving from him a rich literary culture. She suffered a mental breakdown when he died in 1904, and was to suffer recurrences of this throughout her life. It threatened her again in 1906, on the death of her favourite brother Thoby. She, her sister Vanessa and her brother Adrian kept house in Gordon Square; this became the centre of what was to be known as the Bloomsbury Group, initially made up of Thoby's Cambridge friends, most of them members of the Society of Apostles: Roger Fry, Maynard Keynes, Lytton Strachey, Forster, Leonard Woolf, Clive Bell. She reviewed for the *Times Literary Supplement* and studied the art of writing. In 1912 she married Leonard Woolf, and his protectiveness enabled her to produce her succession of novels and literary essays. The first two novels—*Voyage Out* (1915) and *Night and Day* (1919) were comparatively conventional. Thereafter her fiction developed in her original style: *Jacob's Room* (1922), *Mrs Dalloway* (1925), *To the Lighthouse* (1927), *The Waves* (1931). *The Years* (1937) showed reversion to a more conventional method, but *Between the Acts* (1941) was again experimental. She also wrote biographies (*Orlando*, 1928; *Flush*, 1933; *Roger Fry*, 1940) and feminist pamphlets—*A Room of One's Own* (1929) and *Three Guineas* (1938). Her principal literary criticism is collected in the two volumes of *The Common Reader* (1925 and 1932). Forster was usually shy of women and she found him at first either uneasy and withdrawn or composed but aloof, but she greatly valued his criticism, especially his appreciation of *To the Lighthouse*. He consulted her when composing his lectures *Aspects of the Novel* but disagreed with her in her conception of the manifestation of 'life' in fiction.

Gazetteer

BATTERSEA RISE, CLAPHAM, LONDON The home of Henry Thornton, Forster's great-grandfather, the centre of the anti-slavery movement known as the 'Clapham Sect', which met in the library. Forster's great-aunt, Marianne, was born and brought up there, but owing to a family quarrel she later moved to a house on the other side of Clapham Common known as 'East Side' or 'The Cockpond'. Battersea Rise was pulled down in the nineteenth century. Forster describes it and its surroundings in his biography of Marianne Thorntion.

6 MELCOMBE PLACE, DORSET SQUARE, LONDON N.W.1. Forster's birthplace, near Marylebone Station. Shortly after his birth, his father fell ill of consumption and the family moved to Bournemouth, where Edward Forster died in October 1880.

ROOKSNEST, STEVENAGE, HERTFORDSHIRE For many months after her husband's death Forster's mother lived in lodgings or stayed with friends, unable to find a suitable dwelling-place for herself and her child on her small income. When at last she found Rooksnest she described it to a relative as follows:

> It is a very old gabled house, & yet it is perfectly new. It has been rejuvenated, the inside scooped out—everything as pretty and nice as possible—good sanitary arrangements. The rent is £55 with 4 acres of land ... I should not have *chosen* to live in such a lonely place if I could have helped it but I can't find anything else & here is winter upon me again.

Forster was four when they came to Rooksnest, and they lived there until he was fourteen. He developed a deep and lasting affection for it, describing it later as 'my childhood and my safety', and using it as the basis of Howards End in the novel with that title. However, his unhappiness at his boarding-school—Kent House School, Eastbourne—led his mother to believe that at his next school he must be a dayboy. Accordingly when he was to enter Tonbridge School she moved to 'Dryhurst', Dry Hill Park Road, Tonbridge.

TONBRIDGE SCHOOL A public school which Forster used as the basis for Sawston School in *The Longest Journey*. Forster attended it from the age of fourteen to seventeen. He was very unhappy there; as late as 1933 (in *The Spectator*) he wrote: 'School was the unhappiest time of my life ...'. The public school tradition represented what he hated most about English life: its snobbery and philistinism, and its crude insistence on middle-class conformities. However, later in his career there he made a circle of friendships, some of which he was to continue at Cambridge. He also achieved some academic distinctions; prizes for a Latin poem and for an English essay on 'The influence of climate and physical conditions on national character.'

KING'S COLLEGE, CAMBRIDGE Forster spent four academic years there, from 1897 to 1901. For three centuries, until the 1850s, the college had been exclusive and moribund; as a joint foundation with Eton, it admitted only Etonians as Scholars, and had the privilege of claiming degrees without examination. Then came university reform, and in the 1880s King's acquired an entirely new character dominated by such independent and idiosyncratic minds as those of Oscar Browning and Nathaniel Wedd. Forster's career there—especially the fourth year—was crucially formative, thanks to the influence of such personalities and the friendships he formed with fellow undergraduates. He returned to King's in 1947 when the college offered him an Honorary Fellowship for life, and he spent the rest of his days there.

11 DRAYTON COURT, SOUTH KENSINGTON, LONDON For several years after leaving King's Forster either travelled or worked in London or taught extra-mural classes at the Working Men's College, Great Ormond Street in Bloomsbury. He was above all preparing himself for a literary career. Accordingly he needed a centre in London, and he and his mother took a flat at this address.

HARNHAM, MONUMENT GREEN, WEYBRIDGE, SURREY His mother's longing for a settled existence caused the Forsters to move here in 1904. The original name of the house had been 'Glendore', but they disliked it and changed it. They were to live here for twenty years, apart from Forster's sojourns abroad.

ALEXANDRIA Forster worked here for the Red Cross from November 1915 to January 1919, at the Red Cross Hospital. He made congenial friends, and the experience fortified his anti-imperialist convictions. His *Alexandria, A History and a Guide* was published in 1922.

INDIA Forster made three visits to India; in 1912–13, in 1921–22, and in 1945. The second of these was the most important, when he acted as private secretary to Tukoji Rao III, Maharajah of Dewas State Senior, and the crucial elements for *A Passage to India* entered his experience. During the first visit, when he travelled widely, he obtained a more panoramic view of India, but he spent most of his time with Moslems, whereas Dewas was a Hindu state. During his third visit he was feted as a celebrity, and took part in a PEN Conference at Jaipur. Indian friends remarked on his enthusiasm for mosques, where he behaved like a believer.

WEST HACKHURST, ABINGER HAMMER, NEAR DORKING, SURREY This house was designed by Forster's architect-father for his sister Laura, and was originally known as 'Laura Lodge'. Forster and his mother moved into it when Laura died in 1925, and they remained there until his mother's death in 1945. Forster had a *pied-à-terre* in London, first at 27 Brunswick Square and later (to be near his friends the Buckinghams) at 9 Arlington Park Mansions, Sutton Lane, Chiswick. After the death of his mother Forster had to leave West Hackhurst, since the ground-lease had expired. Fortunately King's College came to his rescue.

Bibliography

All Forster's writings are in process of publication by Edward Arnold in *The Abinger Edition of E.M. Forster,* ed. Oliver Stallybrass. Heavily annotated.

Novels

1905 *Where Angels Fear to Tread*
1907 *The Longest Journey*
    The World's Classics edition of 1960 includes an Introduction by Forster.
1908 *A Room with a View*
1910 *Howards End*
1924 *A Passage to India*
1971 *Maurice*
    Written after *Howards End* and published posthumously.

All the novels are available in the Arnold Pocket Edition and in Penguin paperback. USA: Vintage Books.

Stories

1911 *The Celestial Omnibus and Other Stories*
1928 *The Eternal Moment and Other Stories*
    These two collections are combined in *The Collected Tales of E.M. Forster* (Penguin).
1972 *The Life to Come and Other Stories*
    A posthumous collection of Forster's unpublished shorter fiction.
1980 *Arctic Summer and Other Fiction*

Non-fiction

1922 *Alexandria: A History and a Guide* (M. Haag)
1923 *Pharos and Pharillon*
    Essays
1927 *Aspects of the Novel* (Penguin) (Arnold Pocket Edition)
    Criticism
1934 *Goldsworthy Lowes Dickinson* (Pocket Edition)
1936 *Abinger Harvest* (Pocket Edition; Penguin)
    Essays
1951 *Two Cheers for Democracy* (Pocket Edition; Penguin)
1951 *Billy Budd*

Opera with music by Benjamin Britten and libretto by E.M. Forster and Edward Crozier.

1953 *The Hill of Devi, Being Letters from Dewas State Senior*
Reminiscences of Forster's second visit to India, 1921.

1956 *Marianne Thornton, 1797–1887, A Domestic Biography*

1981 *Only Connect: Forster's Letters to Indian Friends*, ed. Syed H. Husain (Heinemann)

Books on Forster

Biography

P.N. FURBANK, *E.M. Forster: a Life*, Secker & Warburg, 1979.
The only full length biography, not likely to be superseded as the standard life.

FRANCIS KING, *E.M. Forster and his World*, Thames & Hudson, 1978.
A short life, very well illustrated.

Criticism

ROSE MACAULAY, *The Writing of E.M. Forster*, Hogarth Press, 1938.
The first extended study; still in print.

LIONEL TRILLING, *E.M. Forster*, Hogarth Press, 1944.
Trilling was one of the most distinguished American critics of this century; the book has special interest as a study of Anglo-American liberal values.

J. McCONKEY, *The Novels of E.M. Forster*, OUP, 1958.
One of the best studies of the fiction, and one of the first to give preeminence to *A Passage to India*.

F.C. CREWS, *E.M. Forster: The Perils of Humanism*, OUP, 1962.
A study of Forster's humanistic values, suggesting that he had increasing difficulty in sustaining them.

K.W. GRANSDEN, *E.M. Forster*, Oliver & Boyd, 1962.
A concise and illuminating introduction.

J.W. BEER, *The Achievement of E.M. Forster*, Chatto & Windus, 1962.
Especially interesting for its relating of Forster to the Romantic tradition, and for discussion of his symbolism.

ALAN WILDE, *Art and Order: a Study of E.M. Forster*, Peter Owen, 1965.
Helpful attitudes to Forster's aesthetic beliefs.

MALCOLM BRADBURY, *Forster: A Collection of Critical Essays*, Spectrum Books, 1966.
A survey of Forster's literary reputation.

WILFRED STONE, *The Cave and the Mountain*, OUP, 1966.
A deep psychological analysis, of special importance for the study of *A Passage to India*.

GEORGE H. THOMSON, *The Fiction of E.M. Forster*, Detroit: Wayne State UP, 1967.

Central concern: the nature of Forster's symbolism.

J.P. LEVINE, *Creation and Criticism: 'A Passage to India'*, Chatto, 1972. Especially interesting for its comparison of Forster's view of India with other views.

PHILIP GARDNER, *E.M. Forster: The Critical Heritage*, Routledge, 1973. A collection of reviews and criticism current throughout Forster's career.

JOHN COLMER, *E.M. Forster: The Personal Voice*, Routledge, 1975. Makes use of biographical material not hitherto available.

G.K. DAS and JOHN BEER (eds.) *E.M. Forster: A Human Exploration*, Macmillan, 1979. Centenary essays by distinguished critics of Forster's work.

GLEN CAVALIERO, *A Reading of E.M. Forster*, Macmillan, 1979. A warm, lucid appreciation; an excellent introduction to Forster's work.

Bibliographies

B.J. KIRKPATRICK, *A Bibliography of E.M. Forster*, Rupert Hart-Davis, 1968.

F.P.W. McDOWELL, *E.M. Forster: an annotated bibliography of writings about him*, Illinois UP, 1976.

Some useful essays

VIRGINIA WOOLF, in *The Death of the Moth and Other Essays*, Hogarth Press, 1942.

F.R. LEAVIS, in *The Common Pursuit*, Chatto & Windus, 1952; Peregrine, 1962.

G.D. KLINGOPOULOS, in *The Modern Age* (ed. Boris Ford), Pelican, 1961.

STUART HAMPSHIRE, in *Modern Writers and Other Essays*, Chatto & Windus, 1969.

R. LANGBAUM, in *The Modern Spirit*, Chatto & Windus, 1970.

ELIZABETH BOWEN, in *Aspects of E.M. Forster*, Arnold, 1969.

WILFRED STONE, in *Aspects of E.M. Forster*, Arnold, 1969.

K. NATWAR-SINGH, in *Aspects of E.M. Forster*, Arnold, 1969.

DAVID GARNETT, in *Aspects of E.M. Forster*, Arnold, 1969.

MALCOLM BRADBURY, in *Aspects of E.M. Forster*, Arnold, 1969.

KENNETH BURKE, in *Language as Symbolic Action*, CUP, 1967.

Appendix

Passage to India

1

SINGING my days,
Singing the great achievements of the present,
Singing the strong light works of engineers,
Our modern wonders, (the antique ponderous Seven outvied,)
In the Old World the east the Suez canal,
The New by its mighty railroad spann'd,
The seas inlaid with eloquent gentle wires;
Yet first to sound, and ever sound, the cry with thee O soul,
The Past! the Past! the Past!

The Past—the dark unfathom'd retrospect!
The teeming gulf—the sleepers and the shadows!
The past—the infinite greatness of the past!
For what is the present after all but a growth out of the past?
(As a projectile form'd, impell'd, passing a certain line, still keeps on,
So the present, utterly form'd, impell'd by the past.)

2

Passage O soul to India!
Eclaircise the myths Asiatic, the primitive fables.

Not you alone proud truths of the world,
Nor you alone ye facts of modern science,
But myths and fables of eld, Asia's, Africa's fables,
The far-darting beams of the spirit, the unloos'd dreams,
The deep diving bibles and legends,
The daring plots of the poets, the elder religions;
O you temples fairer than lilies pour'd over by the rising sun!
O you fables spurning the known, eluding the hold of the known,
    mounting to heaven!
You lofty and dazzling towers, pinnacled, red as roses, burnish'd with
    gold!
Towers of fables immortal fashion'd from mortal dreams!
You too I welcome and fully the same as the rest!
You too with joy I sing.

Passage to India!
Lo, soul, seest thou not God's purpose from the first?
The earth to be spann'd, connected by network,
The races, neighbors, to marry and be given in marriage,
The oceans to be cross'd, the distant brought near,
The lands to be welded together.

A worship new I sing,
You captains, voyagers, explorers, yours,
You engineers, you architects, machinists, yours,
You, not for trade or transportation only,
But in God's name, and for thy sake O soul.

3

Passage to India!
Lo soul for thee of tableaus twain,
I see in one the Suez canal initiated, open'd,
I see the procession of steamships, the Empress Eugenie's leading the
     van,
I mark from on deck the strange landscape, the pure sky, the level sand
     in the distance,
I pass swiftly the picturesque groups, the workmen gather'd,
The gigantic dredging machines.

In one again, different, (yet thine, all thine, O soul, the same,)
I see over my own continent the Pacific railroad surmounting every
     barrier,
I see continual trains of cars winding along the Platte carrying freight
     and passengers,
I hear the locomotives rushing and roaring, and the shrill steam-
     whistle,
I hear the echoes reverberate through the grandest scenery in the
     world,
I cross the Laramie plains, I note the rocks in grotesque shapes, the
     buttes,
I see the plentiful larkspur and wild onions, the barren, colorless, sage-
     deserts,
I see in glimpses afar or towering immediately above me the great
     mountains, I see the Wind river and the Wahsatch mountains,
I see the Monument mountain and the Eagle's Nest, I pass the
     Promontory, I ascend the Nevadas,
I scan the noble Elk mountain and wind around its base,
I see the Humboldt range, I thread the valley and cross the river,
I see the clear waters of lake Tahoe, I see forests of majestic pines,
Or crossing the great desert, the alkaline plains, I behold enchanting
     mirages of waters and meadows,

Marking through these and after all, in duplicate slender lines,
Bridging the three or four thousand miles of land tavel,
Tying the Eastern to the Western sea,
The road between Europe and Asia.

(Ah Genoese thy dream! thy dream!
Centuries after thou art laid in thy grave,
The shore thou foundest verifies thy dream.)

4

Passage to India!
Struggles of many a captain, tales of many a sailor dead,
Over my mood stealing and spreading they come,
Like clouds and cloudlets in the unreach'd sky.

Along all history, down the slopes,
As a rivulet running, sinking now, and now again to the surface rising,
A ceaseless thought, a varied train—lo, soul, to thee, thy sight, they
    rise,
The plans, the voyages again, the expeditions;
Again Vasco de Gama sails forth,
Again the knowledge gain'd, the mariner's compass,
Lands found and nations born, thou born America,
For purpose vast, man's long probation fill'd,
Thou rondure of the world at last accomplish'd.

5

O vast Rondure, swimming in space,
Cover'd all over with visible power and beauty,
Alternate light and day and the teeming spiritual darkness,
Unspeakable high processions of sun and moon and countless stars
    above,
Below, the manifold grass and waters, animals, mountains, trees,
With inscrutable purpose, some hidden prophetic intention,
Now first it seems my thought begins to span thee.

Down from the gardens of Asia descending radiating,
Adam and Eve appear, then their myriad progeny after them,
Wandering, yearning, curious, with restless explorations,
With questionings, baffled, formless, feverish, with never-happy
    hearts,
With that sad incessant refrain, *Wherefore unsatisfied soul?* and *Whither O
    mocking life?*

Ah who shall soothe these feverish children?
Who justify these restless explorations?

Who speak the secret of impassive earth?
Who bind it to us? what is this separate Nature so unnatural?

What is this earth to our affections? (unloving earth, without a throb
   to answer ours,
Cold earth, the place of graves.)

Yet soul be sure the first intent remains, and shall be carried out,
Perhaps even now the time has arrived.

After the seas are all cross'd, (as they seem already cross'd,)
After the great captains and engineers have accomplish'd their work,
After the noble inventors, after the scientists, the chemist, the geologist,
   ethnologist,
Finally shall come the poet worthy that name,
The true son of God shall come singing his songs.

Then not your deeds only O voyagers, O scientists and inventors, shall
   be justified,
All these hearts as of fretted children shall be sooth'd,
All affection shall be fully responded to, the secret shall be told,
All these separations and gaps shall be taken up and hook'd and link'd
   together,
The whole earth, this cold, impassive, voiceless earth, shall be
   completely justified,
Trinitas divine shall be gloriously accomplish'd and compacted by the
   true son of God, the poet,
(He shall indeed pass the straits and conquer the mountains,
He shall double the cape of Good Hope to some purpose,)
Nature and Man shall be disjoin'd and diffused no more,
The true son of God shall absolutely fuse them.

6

Year at whose wide-flung door I sing!
Year of the purpose accomplish'd!
Year of the marriage of continents, climates and oceans!
(No mere doge of Venice now wedding the Adriatic,)
I see O year in you the vast terraqueous globe given and giving all,
Europe to Asia, Africa join'd, and they to the New World,
The lands, geographies, dancing before you, holding a festival garland,
As brides and bridegrooms hand in hand.

Passage to India!
Cooling airs from Caucasus far, soothing cradle of man,
The river Euphrates flowing, the past lit up again.

Lo soul, the retrospect brought forward,
The old, most populous, wealthiest of earth's lands,

The streams of the Indus and the Ganges and their many affluents,
(I my shores of America walking to-day behold, resuming all,)
The tale of Alexander on his warlike marches suddenly dying
On one side China and on the other side Persia and Arabia,
To the south the great seas and the bay of Bengal,
The flowing literatures, tremendous epics, religions, castes,
Old occult Brahma interminably far back, the tender and junior
    Buddha,
Central and southern empires and all their belongings, possessors
The wars of Tamerlane, the reign of Aurungzebe,
The traders, rulers, explorers, Moslems, Venetians, Byzantium, the
    Arabs, Portuguese,
The first travelers famous yet, Marco Polo, Batouta the Moor,
Doubts to be solv'd, the map incognita, blanks to be fill'd,
The foot of man unstay'd, the hands never at rest,
Thyself O soul that will not brook a challenge.

The mediæval navigators rise before me,
The world of 1492, with its awaken'd enterprise,
Something swelling in humanity now like the sap of the earth in
    spring,
The sunset splendor of chivalry declining.

And who art thou sad shade?
Gigantic, visionary, thyself a visionary,
With majestic limbs and pious beaming eyes,
Spreading around with every look of thine a golden world,
Enhuing it with gorgeous hues.

As the chief histrion,
Down to the footlights walks in some great scena,
Dominating the rest I see the Admiral himself,
(History's type of courage, action, faith,)
Behold him sail from Palos leading his little fleet,
His voyage behold, his return, his great fame,
His misfortunes, calumniators, behold him a prisoner, chain'd
Behold his dejection, poverty, death.

(Curious in time I stand, noting the efforts of heroes,
Is the deferment long? bitter the slander, poverty, death?
Lies the seed unreck'd for centuries in the ground? lo, to God's due
    occasion,
Uprising in the night, it sprouts, blooms,
And fills the earth with use and beauty.)

7

Passage indeed O soul to primal thought,
Not lands and seas alone, thy own clear freshness,
The young maturity of brood and bloom,
To realms of budding bibles.

O soul, repressless, I with thee and thou with me,
Thy circumnavigation of the world begin,
Of man, the voyage of his mind's return,
To reason's early paradise,
Back, back to wisdom's birth, to innocent intuitions,
Again with fair creation.

8

O we can wait no longer,
We too take ship O soul,
Joyous we too launch out on trackless seas,
Fearless for unknown shores on waves of ecstasy to sail,
Amid the wafting winds, (thou pressing me to thee, I thee to me, O
    soul,)
Caroling free, singing our song of God,
Chanting our chant of pleasant exploration.

With laugh and many a kiss,
(Let others deprecate, let others weep for sin, remorse, humiliation,)
O soul thou pleases me, I thee.

Ah more than any priest O soul we too believe in God,
But with the mystery of God we dare not dally.

O soul thou pleasest me, I thee,
Sailing these seas or on the hills, or waking in the night,

Thoughts, silent thoughts, of Time and Space and Death, waters
    flowing,
Bear me indeed as through the regions infinite,
Whose air I breathe, whose ripples hear, lave me all over,
Bathe me O God in thee, mounting to thee,
I and my soul to range in range of thee.

O Thou transcendent,
Nameless, the fibre and the breath,
Light of the light, shedding forth universes, thou centre of them
Thou mightier centre of the true, the good, the loving,
Thou moral, spiritual fountain—affection's source—thou reservoir,
(O pensive soul of me—O thirst unsatisfied—waitest not there?
Waitest not haply for us somewhere there the Comrade perfect?)
Thou pulse—thou motive of the stars, suns, systems,

That, circling, move in order, safe, harmonious,
Athwart the shapeless vastnesses of space,
How should I think, how breathe a single breath, how speak, if out of
    myself,
I could not launch, to those, superior universes?

Swiftly I shrivel at the thought of God,
At Nature and its wonders, Time and Space and Death,
But that I, turning, call to thee O soul, thou actual Me,
And lo, thou gently masterest the orbs,
Thou matest Time, smilest content at Death,
And fillest, swellest full the vastnesses of Space.

Greater than stars or suns,
Bounding O soul thou journeyest forth;
What love than thine and ours could wider amplify?
What aspirations, wishes, outvie thine and ours O soul?
What dreams of the ideal? what plans of purity, perfection, strength?
What cheerful willingness for others' sake to give up all?
For others' sake to suffer all?

Reckoning ahead O soul, when thou, the time achiev'd,
The seas all cross'd, weather'd the capes, the voyage done,
Surrounded, copest, frontest God, yieldest, the aim attain'd,
As fill'd with friendship, love complete, the Elder Brother found,
The Younger melts in fondness in his arms.

9

Passage to more than India!
Are thy wings plumed indeed for such far flights?
O soul, voyagest thou indeed on voyages like those?
Disportest thou on waters such as those?
Soundest below the Sanscrit and the Vedas?
Then have thy bent unleash'd.

Passage to you, your shores, ye aged fierce enigmas!
Passage to you, to mastership of you, ye strangling problems!
You, strew'd with the wrecks of skeletons, that, living, never reach'd
    you.

Passage to more than India!
O secret of the earth and sky!
Of you O waters of the sea! O winding creeks and rivers!
Of you O woods and fields! of you strong mountains of my land!
Of you O prairies! of you gray rocks!
O morning red! O clouds! O rain and snows!
O day and night, passage to you!

O sun and moon and all you stars! Sirius and Jupiter!
Passage to you!

Passage, immediate passage! the blood burns in my veins!
Away O soul! hoist instantly the anchor!
Cut the hawsers—haul out—shake out every sail!
Have we not stood here like trees in the ground long enough?
Have we not grovel'd here long enough, eating and drinking like mere
    brutes?
Have we not darken'd and dazed ourselves with books long enough?

Sail forth—steer for the deep waters only,
Reckless O soul, exploring, I with thee, and thou with me,
For we are bound where mariner has not yet dared to go,
And we will risk the ship, ourselves and all.

O my brave soul!
O farther farther sail!
O daring joy, but safe! are they not all the seas of God?
O farther, farther, farther sail!

Walt Whitman

Index

General Index

Ackerley, J.R., xi, 16, 38, 172
'Apostles', 20, 21–24, 25, 26, 173, 177, 179, 180
Arnold, Mathew, 12, 55, 57, 58, 59, 61, 62, 82, 107–108, 125, 158
Arnold, Thomas, 12
Auden, W.H., 39, 82–83, 84–85
Augustine, St., 75
Austen, Jane, 10, 67–71, 73

Battersea Rise, 9, 12, 13, 18, 88, 181
Bell, Clive, 26, 27, 180
Bell, Vanessa, 26, 175
Bennett, Arnold, 66, 164, 165
Bentham, Jeremy, 50, 54, 55, 62
Billy Budd, 32, 38
Blake, William, 75
Bloomsbury Group, 26–29, 30, 33, 39, 59, 83, 175, 177, 180
Britten, Benjamin, 32
Buckingham, Bob, 33, 172
Butler, Samuel, 73–75

Carlyle, Thomas, 62, 75, 82
Carpenter, Edward, 62–64, 115, 172–173, 175
Chesterton, G.K., 33, 66
Clapham Sect, 9, 10, 12, 13, 51, 178, 179
Coleridge, 62
Conrad, Joseph, 40, 66, 76, 90, 155

Dante, 74, 75
Dewas Senior, *see* Tukoji Rao
Dickens, Charles, 76, 78, 167
Dickinson, Lowes, 25, 35, 126, 173
Donne, John, 107–108

Eliot, George, 76
Eliot, T.S., 26, 39, 83, 89, 91, 135–136
Elizabeth, Countess von Arnim, 25, 34, 174
Fry, Roger, 21, 26, 27, 85, 174–175, 180

Galsworthy, John, 66, 159, 164
Gibbon, Edward, 67, 74, 75

Hardy, Thomas, 76, 79
Hartley, L.P., 168

Independent Review, 25, 51
Isherwood, Christopher, 39, 82, 167, 177

James, Henry, 40, 66, 67, 72, 76, 94
Joyce, James, 40, 66, 108, 165, 167

Keynes, Maynard, 21, 26, 29, 180
King's College, 20, 22, 24, 39, 157, 173, 182, 183
Kipling, Rudyard, 60

Lawrence, D.H., 27, 29–33, 40, 83, 89, 116, 158–159, 160, 163, 164, 165, 167, 175
Leavis, F.R., 27, 89
Lewis, Wyndham, 27, 39, 83

Macchiavelli, 75
Masood, 33, 35, 36, 37, 38, 176
Melville, Herman, 32, 33, 79
Meredith, George, 73, 75–79, 116
Meredith, H.O.M., 24, 176
Mill, John Stuart, 50, 51, 54, 55, 57, 62, 82
Moore, G.E., 21, 176
More, Hannah, 9, 88
Morrell, Ottoline, 30
Morris, William, 62, 173, 175
Myers, L.H., 27

Orwell, George, 83, 87

Plomer, William, xi, 147, 177
Powell, Anthony, 168
Proust, Marcel, 72–73, 167, 168

'Rooksnest', 16, 18, 19, 79, 181
Rousseau, 115
Ruskin, John, 12, 62, 82, 119, 175
Russell, Bertrand, 21, 32, 176

Shakespeare, 67, 81
Shaw, Bernard, 39, 79, 83
Shelley, 22, 94
Sheppard, J.T., 22, 24, 177
Sophocles, 44, 75
Stephen, Leslie, 26
Strachey, Lytton, xi, 21, 24, 26, 88–89, 177–178, 179, 180
Swift, Jonathan, 75

Thornton, Henry, 9, 12, 178
Thornton, Marianne, 9, 12, 14, 25, 174, 178
Tonbridge School, 16, 19, 20, 181–182
Tolstoy, 74, 75
Trevelyan, G.M., 25, 179
Trilling, Lionel, 50, 64
Tukoji Rao, Maharajah of Dewas Senior, 35, 36, 37, 179, 182

Voltaire, 75, 81

Webb, Beatrice, 27, 64, 179–180
Wells, H.G., 30, 39, 40, 46, 48, 66, 94, 164
West Hackhurst, 183
Whichelo, Laura (Forster's aunt), 14, 18
Whichelo, Lily (Forster's mother), 9, 174
Whitman, Walt, 64, 134–135, 154, 156
Wilberforce, William, 9
Wilson, Angus, 167–168
Woolf, Leonard, 21, 26, 27, 130, 180
Woolf, Virginia, xi, 10, 21, 26, 27–29, 66, 90, 92, 164–165, 167, 178, 180

Index to Forster's Works

Abinger Harvest, 18, 58, 85, 87–88, 90, 91, 92, 175
'Adrift in India', 92
Alexandria: a History and a Guide, 34, 182
'Anonymity: an Enquiry', 91
Ansell, 24
Arctic Summer, 127, 175
'Art for Art's Sake', 58, 94
Aspects of the Novel, 32, 72, 76, 79, 91–92, 180

'Book that Influenced Me, A', 74, 75

'C Minor of that Life, The', 72
Celestial Omnibus, The, 40, 44, 175
'Challenge of of Our Time, The', 50, 58, 61, 75

'Does Culture Matter?', 59

'English Prose betwen 1918 and 1939', 165–167

Eternal Moment, The, 40, 44–46

Goldsworthy Lowes Dickinson, 20, 51

Hill of Devi, The, 34
Howards End, 16, 18, 20, 27, 29, 30, 34, 48, 58, 67, 71, 73, 83, 96, 112, 117–126, 130, 162, 163, 175

'Ibsen the Romantic', 90

'Last of Abinger, The', 92
Life to Come, The, 24, 49
'London is a Muddle', 93
Longest Journey, The, 19, 22, 24, 25, 32, 33, 112, 113–116, 162, 176, 177

'Machine Stops, The', 40, 44, 46–49
Marianne Thornton, 9–13, 178–179
Maurice, xii, 29, 49, 115, 126–128, 163, 173
'Me, Them and You', 85–87

'Not Listening to Music', 72
'Note on the Way, A', 58

'Notes on the English Character', 13, 19

Passage to India, A, xii, 30, 33, 35, 37, 38, 46, 58, 67, 73, 91, 96, 112, 130–157, 158–159, 164, 172, 176, 182
Pharos and Pharillon, 34
'Point of It, The', 44

'Raison d'Etre of Criticism, The', 71, 85, 89
'Road from Colonus, The', 34, 40, 43–44, 46
Room with a View, A, 34, 67, 68–71, 78–79, 112, 113, 116–117, 162, 163

'Story of a Panic, The', 25, 40–43, 46

Two Cheers for Democracy, 18, 29, 58, 64, 79, 83, 87, 89–91, 92, 94, 165

'What I Believe', 27, 32, 58, 75, 83–84
Where Angels Fear to Tread, 25, 34, 71, 96–111, 112, 115, 116